# Creative Economies of Culture in South Asia

This book explores the crafts and performing arts of South Asia through a focus on labour and livelihood. It brings to light little-researched angles of social and political economies of culture and the ways in which they have shifted and changed in different historical eras and different political, economic, and social formations up to the present. In particular, through this focus on labour and livelihood, the contributors analyse the extensive parallels and similarities of arts and crafts on the one hand and music and performing arts on the other, ranging from questions of lineage, transmission, class/caste/community, professional versus amateur performers and artisans, to the impact of globalisation, neoliberal reforms, and mediatisation. Given the role of gender inequalities and differences within caste/community-based cultural production in South Asia across visual, material, and performing arts and crafts, this interdisciplinary perspective is particularly salient and links together broader sociological and historical trends in South Asian cultural or creative economies.

*Creative economies of culture* explores labour and livelihood through a gamut of crafts and performing arts ranging from courtly and classical to commissioned to mass-produced, and in epochs ranging from colonial or feudal to globalised and neoliberal. In the process, it revisits, refines, or revises notions of social and cultural capital; socio-economic mobility; the value, role, and agency of crafts and performing arts; and the status of their artisans and performers. Original chapters written by contributors with an interdisciplinary background look at the survival and adaption of traditional artisanal communities; traditional forms of practice; historical shifts such as colonialism, industrialisation, and nationalism; as well as modern industries and institutions, including technologies of mass production and creative entrepreneurship.

This book contextualises current debates within art, craft, music, and dance in South Asia. It develops new theoretical understandings of creative culture through a focus on labour and contributes to a range of social sciences, arts, and humanities disciplines, including South Asian studies, Ethnomusicology, Crafts and Design, Economic Anthropology, (Historical) Sociology and (Historical) Economics, Cultural History, Human Geography, and Creative Industries and Economies.

**Anna Morcom** is the Mohindar Brar Sambhi Chair of Indian Music in the Department of Ethnomusicology at UCLA. She studies the performing arts of India and

Tibet from diverse perspectives analysing shifting configurations of social power and has published on courtesans, bar girls, queer performers, and classical musicians in India.

**Neelam Raina** is an Associate Professor of International Development and Design at Middlesex University London. Her grant-funded research focusses on conflict and post-conflict economic reconstruction, material cultures, indigenous knowledge, displacement, and gender. Her interest lies in intersectional inequalities and inequities in fragile settings.

## Routledge Contemporary South Asia Series

157 **Fifty Years of Bangladesh**
Economy, politics, society, and culture
*Edited by Rounaq Jahan and Rehman Sobhan*

158 **Urban Mobility Development in Northeast India**
Sustainable city with green and inclusive transportation
*Tumbenthung Humtsoe*

159 **Vulnerable Communities in Neoliberal India**
Perspectives from a feminist ethnographic approach
*Edited by Deepanshu Mohan, Sakshi Chindaliya, and Ashika Thomas*

160 **Foreign Aid and Bangladesh**
Donor relations and realpolitik
*Mohammad Mizanur Rahman*

161 **Empowering Marginalised Women in Remote Indian Villages**
An impact study
*Udoy Saikia, Jim Chalmers, Dency Michael, and Janice Orrell*

162 **Marginalised Groups in India**
Historiography, politics, and policies
*Edited by Kunal Debnath and Souvik Chatterjee*

163 **Creative Economies of Culture in South Asia**
Craftspeople and performers
*Edited by Anna Morcom and Neelam Raina*

For the full list of titles in the series please visit: https://www.routledge.com/Routledge-Contemporary-South-Asia-Series/book-series/RCSA

# Creative Economies of Culture in South Asia

## Craftspeople and Performers

**Edited by**
**Anna Morcom and Neelam Raina**

Routledge
Taylor & Francis Group
LONDON AND NEW YORK

First published 2025
by Routledge
4 Park Square, Milton Park, Abingdon, Oxon OX14 4RN

and by Routledge
605 Third Avenue, New York, NY 10158

*Routledge is an imprint of the Taylor & Francis Group, an informa business*



Chapter 12 of this book was supported by the United Kingdom Research and Innovation's grant to the UKRI GCRF Gender, Justice and Security Hub [grant number AH/S004025/1] 2019-2024.



*British Library Cataloguing-in-Publication Data*
A catalogue record for this book is available from the British Library

*Library of Congress Cataloging-in-Publication Data*
Names: Morcom, Anna, editor. | Raina, Neelam, editor.
Title: Creative economies of culture in South Asia : craftspeople and performers / edited by Anna Morcom, Neelam Raina.
Description: Abingdon, Oxon ; New York : Routledge, 2025. |
Series: Routledge contemporary South Asia series ; 163 | Includes bibliographical references and index.
Identifiers: LCCN 2024035899 (print) | LCCN 2024035900 (ebook) | ISBN 9781138492172 (hardback) | ISBN 9781032887982 (paperback) | ISBN 9781351031028 (ebook)
Subjects: LCSH: Cultural industries—South Asia. | Handicraft industries—South Asia. | Performing arts—South Asia.
Classification: LCC HD9999.C9473 S64 2025 (print) | LCC HD9999.C9473 (ebook) | DDC 338.4/77095—dc23/eng/20241029
LC record available at https://lccn.loc.gov/2024035899
LC ebook record available at https://lccn.loc.gov/2024035900

ISBN: 978-1-138-49217-2 (hbk)
ISBN: 978-1-032-88798-2 (pbk)
ISBN: 978-1-351-03102-8 (ebk)

DOI: 10.4324/9781351031028

Typeset in Times New Roman
by codeMantra

# Contents

# Illustrations

# Table

# Contributors

**Priyanka Basu** is a Lecturer in Performing Arts at the Department of Culture, Media and Creative Industries, King's College London. Her research interests include cultural histories, folklore, and intermediality of print and performance. Her first monograph, *The Poet's Song: 'Folk' and its Cultural Politics in South Asia,* is published by Routledge (2023).

**Thomas Chambers** is a Senior Lecturer in Social Anthropology at Oxford Brookes University. He has published widely on labour, migration, gender, domestic care work, and the state in India. He has a monograph, *Networks, Labour and Migration among Indian Muslim Artisans* (2020), and numerous articles in leading journals.

**Hanne M. de Bruin** holds a PhD in Indology from the University of Leiden. She has published widely on Kattaikkuttu and the role of women performers. Her book *Kattaikkuttu: A Rural Theater Tradition in South India* was published in 2023.

**Alicia Ory DeNicola** is an Associate Professor of Anthropology at Oxford College of Emory University with research interests in craft, labour, and authenticity. She is the author of a number of articles on textile craft in India. She is co-editor, with Clair Wilkinson, of *Critical Craft: Technology, Globalization, and Capitalism* (Routledge, 2016).

**Stefan Fiol** is a Professor of Ethnomusicology at the University of Cincinnati. He is the author of *Recasting Folk in the Himalayas: Indian Music, Media and Social Mobility* (2017). He conducts interdisciplinary research on music's role in stimulating memory and cognitive function and investigates Himalayan drumming as a mode of historiographic enquiry.

**Zahra Hussain** is an Architect and Cultural Geographer working primarily with mountain communities on documenting and preserving their material and immaterial heritage through participatory and interdisciplinary methods and forms of representation.

**Nikita Kaul** is a Craft Anthropologist. Her ethnographic research with walnut wood carvers in Kashmir explores the cultural and symbolic making of craft in Kashmir. Her previous research with the wood carving artisans and traders explored the impact of raw material crisis on the wood carving industry in Saharanpur, Uttar Pradesh.

**Nitasha Kaul** is a multidisciplinary academic, novelist, economist, poet, and public intellectual. She holds a Chair in Politics, International Relations, and Critical Interdisciplinary Studies and is the Director of Centre for the Study of Democracy (CSD), University of Westminster, London.

**Aarti Kawlra** is an Anthropologist interested in the methods of oral history, geography, and cultural studies to discursively interrogate colonial, postcolonial, and global discourses of culture, heritage, education, and development. She is the author of the monograph *We Who Wove with Lotus Thread: Summoning Community in South India* (2018).

**Amanda Lanzillo** is an Assistant Professor in the Department of South Asian Languages and Civilizations, University of Chicago. She is the author of *Pious Labor: Islam, Artisanship, and Technology in Colonial India* (University of California Press, 2024). She holds a PhD in History from Indiana University and was previously a Cotsen postdoctoral fellow at Princeton University's Society of Fellows and Lecturer in South Asian History at Brunel University, London.

**Tiziana Leucci** is Dance Historian and Anthropologist at the *Centre d'Etudes de l'Inde et de l'Asie du Sud* of the French *Centre National de la Recherche Scientifique* (CNRS, Paris-Aubervilliers). Her research includes Indian courtesan culture. She coordinates research projects and seminars and has authored and co-edited several volumes and articles.

**Seher Mirza** is a Design Practitioner, Facilitator, and Post-doctoral Research Fellow at the Centre for Sustainable Fashion, University of the Arts London, UK. She has a PhD in textiles from the Royal College of Art (2020). She founded and runs, S jo, a craft initiative with women artisans in Pakistan.

**Anna Morcom** is the Mohindar Brar Sambhi Chair of Indian Music in the Department of Ethnomusicology at UCLA. She studies the performing arts of India and Tibet from diverse perspectives analysing shifting configurations of social power and has published on courtesans, bar girls, queer performers, and classical musicians in India.

**Daniel M. Neuman** is the author of *The Life of Music in North India* and *Studying India's Musicians: Four Decades of Selected Articles* as well as co-author of *Bards, Ballads and Boundaries: An Ethnographic Atlas of Music Traditions in West Rajasthan*. He is now Professor and Provost emeritus at UCLA.

**Dard Neuman** is the Hasan Endowed Chair in Classical Indian Music and Associate Professor of Music at the University of California, Santa Cruz, where he was also the co-founder and co-director of the Center for South Asian Studies. His research interests concern the pedagogical and performance practices of Hindustani music.

**Brahma Prakash** is an Assistant Professor of Theatre and Performance Studies at Jawaharlal Nehru University, New Delhi. He is the author of *Cultural Labour: Conceptualizing the 'Folk Performance' in India* (2019). His research focusses on cultural performance in relation to questions of marginality, aesthetics, and cultural justice.

**Neelam Raina** is an Associate Professor of International Development and Design at Middlesex University London. Her grant-funded research focusses on conflict and post-conflict economic reconstruction, material cultures, indigenous knowledge, displacement, and gender. Her interest lies in intersectional inequalities and inequities in fragile settings.

**Kristen Rudisill** is a Professor of Popular Culture and Director of the Asian Studies Program at Bowling Green State University. Her research focuses on Tamil theatre and dance. Her book *Honeymoon Couples and Jurassic Babies: Identity and Play in Chennai's Post-Independence Sabha Theater* was published in 2022.

**Shweta Sachdeva Jha** teaches English at Miranda House, University of Delhi. She researches women's history and gender studies, including the history of *tawa'if*, forgotten women writers of Urdu romances and gothic fiction, and digital archiving projects on women's higher education institutions. She has published in various journals and edited books.

**Clare M. Wilkinson** is an Associate Professor of Anthropology at Washington State University, with research interests in craft and media production. Since 2002 she has been studying the culture of film production in Mumbai, India. She is the author of *Fashioning Bollywood: The Making and Meaning of Hindi Film Costume.*

**Richard David Williams** is a Senior Lecturer in Music and South Asian Studies at SOAS University of London. His research brings music and sound studies into conversation with the study of religion and Indian cultural history, especially in the early modern and colonial periods.

# Creative Vocabularies of Work and Value in South Asia

## A Foreword

*Nitasha Kaul*

Critical interdisciplinary work illuminates marginalised knowledge and perspectives and also fertilises new directions of enquiry, since it equips us with an understanding of important questions that can only be sensibly addressed by traversing across narrow disciplinary divides. An enduring division in social sciences and humanities has been one of viewing culture and economy as separate spheres, often with presumed nonoverlapping endogenous logics. This collection edited by Anna Morcom and Neelam Raina brings together a wide body of work that shows us precisely how and why the separation of culture and economy is neither tenable nor helpful.

Indeed, how could it ever have been possible to think in terms of binaries that separate art and craft from music and performance, or to view these practices and professions outside of the socio-political materialities of preindustrial, colonial, or nationalist historical structures? And how can one refuse to acknowledge the many ways in which gender, caste, religion, and class together determine perceptions of worth, pervasiveness of stigma, and possibilities of transforming practice? Yet, the entrenched and conventional accounts of arts versus performance have often been slow to include the role of wider histories, social structures, and individual identities upon the many ways in which culture and economy are always already interwoven and often indistinguishable.

The editors of this volume are committed and accomplished South Asia scholars whose work resonates both regionally and internationally, and who have brilliantly forged a distinct body of work in this area. It would perhaps be interesting to mention that I met Anna at the foremost international convention on Himalayan Studies and Neelam at a similar conference on International Studies. In these wide-ranging conversations, we spoke of the Hindi voice-typing keyboard on modern phones and depictions of the female dancer's dilemma and struggle against social stigma in the 1965 Hindi movie *Guide* (adapted from an R.K. Narayan novel), as well as of the lives and narratives in conflicted Kashmir and war-torn Afghanistan. Morcom and Raina have created a most impressive body of work in their engagements with lived South Asian art cultures, and whether it is music or craft, they are mindful of the socio-political and economic links to identities and histories, as well as trajectories of development or impoverishment. When they reached out to me to ask if

I would write the foreword to their new volume, I was delighted. It has been most pleasurable and enlightening to read this book.

As a heterodox economist who, over the last two and a half decades, journeyed into becoming a recognised multidisciplinary academic and writer, my scholarly endeavours have been motivated by the need to foreground and critically analyse the institutionalisations and systematisations of knowledge trajectories and their link to systems of oppression, discourses of legitimisation, and narratives of dispossession. As I articulated in my first book *Imagining economics otherwise: encounters with identity/difference* (Kaul 2007), an important strand in my work was to emphasise the link between Value and values and to question the separation of economy and culture. In my later work on 'postcolonial neoliberal nationalism' (Kaul 2019), I have argued for challenging the oppositional understanding of neoliberalism and nationalism and seeing the domains of the economy and nation as co-constructed. By viewing the political and economic as separate categories, we only serve to embed a binary that further maps onto national/international, material/symbolic, and regressive/progressive. The simplistic distinction between political economy and cultural politics is one we must challenge.

Creative practice does not, and cannot, exist apart from an understanding of time periods, socio-economic and global forces, and the intersectionality of identities. The authors in this volume enlighten us about the locations and shifts of creative practices. This is both an intellectual enquiry and one that has continuous and urgent implications for the craftspeople and performers themselves and their livelihoods, dignity, circumstances of work, and accumulations of skill. These are all at stake in relation to how institutional and national policymakers perceive their profession, its history, and its lived practice as they ascertain its value to ideas of the nation and the economy. This value is seemingly reflected in such assessments, but it is also simultaneously constructed in the very knowledge through which we approach an understanding of creative practices. It is for this reason that a volume such as this one is important and timely.

Reading the chapters of this book, I was struck by how the authors combine the emplaced and contextual granularity of specific creative practices and performances with significant crosswinds of larger feudal, colonial, or post-colonial nationalist histories. This is a collection not only about craft or performance but also, upon careful reading, turns out to be an anthology about the contextual ways in which the social, political, and economic are interwoven, what I have elsewhere called 'contextual social political economy.' The chapters in this collection historicise creative practices, drawing attention both to how performers retain historical concepts of the meaning of their labour and the pride they take in it, and to how feudal structures, colonial legislations, or post-colonial nationalist projects have impacted creative cultural practices and economies. The resulting multidimensional shifts and adaptations were never linear processes. Hereditary and hierarchical social structures played an important role here, as did newer technological artefacts and the social ideals of an incipient modernity with its particular brand of sanitising morality that meant female performers or rural non-Brahmanical art forms became stigmatised and viewed with contempt. With the wider global economic transformations, the gentrification of certain art forms, and the rise of the middle classes as avid consumers of now sacralised high art, came other transformations, such as the valorisation of certain kinds of arts as deserving of national celebrity, and specific crafts that were re-signified as authentic and traditional.

The examples in the volume are many and I would like to offer a few comments across the various chapters to illustrate the complex socio-economic and political transitions covered by the contributions. One of these, which we see in Williams' chapter, is how the fall of the Mughal Empire, and the crumbling of imperial and noble centres of power in Delhi and Lucknow, led to the decline of traditional patronage and shifting cultural and economic landscapes for musicians in a differentiated manner for hereditary and non-hereditary performers. Another example, in Sachdeva's chapter, concerns how these changing patterns affected the social role and status of women performers (*tawaifs*) skilled in poetry, music, and dance; and in Leucci's, the impact of the modernising morality of missionary and reformist anti-*nautch* (anti-dance) campaigns in the colonial period on patronage and performance opportunities for *devadasis* (female dancers, courtesans, performers for temple deities, royalty and nobility, and for social religious occasions). In addition, Lanzillo's chapter considers the impact of nineteenth-century British colonial legislation and licensing laws that forbade Indians from manufacturing or owning weapons, creating a crisis for regional centres of artisan weapon smithing in North India and Northeast Pakistan.

In the later colonial and post-colonial nationalist period, still other transformations shape the creative and cultural economies. It is significant, as Neuman's chapter explores, that newer technologies of mechanical reproduction, such as the gramophone, have reshaped the role and place of Hindustani musicians who emerge by contrast as a celebrity and a national protagonist who performs in public. As we see from Kawlra's chapter, it is also important to consider how Kanchipuram handloom saris from south-eastern India have been re-signified as authentic and traditional in the neoliberal economy. In addition, as Morcom describes, widespread practices of spontaneous payment to performers during a performance have been tied to ideas of corresponding obligations and the nature of the audience themselves. As classical music transitioned out of the aristocracy and into the middle classes, it became sacralised and set off against popular art, making such payments incongruent, and they were replaced with symbolic and sensory appreciation in return for the value provided.

The lived marginalities of the artists, craftspeople, and performers are vividly depicted throughout the volume, and these also force accommodations of creative practice. In Basu's chapter, we encounter women performers who are doubly marginal, as Muslim scroll painters, and the Chitrakar community in West Bengal that shifted to different kinds of mediums and depictions to align with issues and social campaigns run by government. We also see in Mirza's essay how textile craft in Sindh in Pakistan links to social value and articulation of experience. In addition, as Chambers explores, temporal negotiations of work and value feature in a non-unionised wood craftwork labour in a North Indian city in a ghetto that is socially marked by class divisions while imperfectly sutured by appeals to a shared religious (Islamic) identity.

The stigmatisation of non-elite creative labour is central to the landscape of cultural production, and it is also resisted through re-appropriations of meaning by those affected. As de Bruin describes, the popular non-Brahmanical rural Tamil theatre was not seen as legitimate, typifying an attitude of contempt towards folk cultures. In the chapters by Prakash and Fiol, we also learn of how singers and musicians function in a caste society where their music is both special and also an obligation that can be demanded, and how attempts are made to reframe this, such as via contemporary drumming practices of Dalit Bahujans who re-claim this as a political articulation. In addition, we see in Rudisill's chapter how the consumerist gentrification trajectories of popular Tamil film dance or Kollywood in Chennai proliferate via reality TV to competitions for fitness and fun and thus offer dance as a viable middle-class profession with income and respect.

Creative labour is also manifestly relational and, on occasion, intersects with explicit political antagonisms or geopolitical changes. As Kaul's chapter examines, the walnut wood carving workers in the militarised conflict zone of Kashmir forge commercial and personal relations with the military men who are posted there through military *kaam*, or craft produced for the men in uniform, and objects that underscore shared masculinist ideas of expertise and skill through sustained training as undertaken by the craftsmen and the army men. The carpet weaving in the mountain landscapes of northern Pakistan described by Hussain is relational and central to community identity but poised to change in view of the road-building and changing infrastructural landscapes. Raina's chapter analyses the intersections between material culture, gender, and politics of the practices of making in Indian Kashmir.

This threat to creative and cultural labour forms and structures has always been present and, fortunately, never fully realised. An interesting paradox explored in Wilkinson and DeNicola's chapter is the constant contradiction of handicrafts in India as always dying, never really dead, and always able to be resuscitated with initiatives that suggest revivals alongside a forgetting of prior attempts at such revivals. The work in this volume is diverse but unified in staunchly challenging the culture and economy divide, as well as tracing the historic and current transformations through its concurrently material and symbolic, embodied, and abstract itineraries.

The chapters can thus be read for their accounts of the adaptations of the performers, artisans, and craftworker producers over time in India and Pakistan; for the livelihood challenges stemming from colonial policies, state regulations, globalisation, or societal and structural experiences of marginalisation; for the impacts of modern values, the growth of the middle class, and associated values in re-signification of certain cultural pursuits; for the attempts to wrestle against historical stigmatisation of certain forms of creative labour by re-appropriating those cultural forms in order to force their re-evaluation; for the specific ways in which female and non-Brahmanical performers became the targets both of the colonial state and the social reformers whose perceptions of their work and its value were informed by an idea of the moral modern moment; for an understanding of how the modernisation and the monetisation of creative labour has been marked by various continuities and discontinuities, by spaces of resistance and resilience within the broader transformations, and by contesting social imaginaries for the role of arts in society and the nation.

I have worked for a long time on Kashmir and Indian politics, and hence for me, the book also leads to thought-provoking reflections on the nature of cultural labour and its place in the nation juxtaposed against the backdrop of polarised political claims-making. It makes me think of the mobilisations of identities and incentives in creative and cultural economies through selective attempts at the revitalisation and promotion of specific art forms against the wholesale and intentional rewriting of cultural history and social memory as an intrinsic part of an economically powerful majoritarian political project that is ascendant in the region.

Anna and Neelam have given us an accomplished and path-breaking volume that tells us that when it comes to creative practices and professions, there are no clear historical breaks, only shifts with differentiated impacts. There is also no grand meta-narrative of linear and all-encompassing decline. The different kinds of cultural labour gain and lose value against the societal representations and their potential use to elite interests or as part of ascendant political or governmental projects. They are constantly reinvented, occasionally celebrated, and also continuously face particular social stigmatisations and vulnerabilities in line with individual performers' identities and their collective group value in any prevalent hierarchy. The work here alerts us to the role of larger political and historical forces and to the power of imaginaries. The transformations will continue through geopolitical and globalising commodity value chains, newer infrastructures, and enactments of legislations and policies. To understand this, we must note that the distinction between labour and capital is not straightforward in these creative economies, and neither are the material and the affective clearly delineated. A nuanced, historicised, relational, embodied, and socio-economically and politically embedded nature of creative practices, by both craftspeople and performers, in India and Pakistan, shines through this work. I hope that you will enjoy this excellent work that is informative, engaging, and generative of further enquiries, as much as I did!

## References

Kaul, N 2007, *Imagining economics otherwise: encounters with identity/difference*, Routledge, London.

Kaul, N 2019, 'The political project of postcolonial neoliberal nationalism,' *Indian Politics & Policy*, vol. 2, no. 1, pp. 3–30.

# Living, Adapting, and Creating
## Craftspeople and Performers in South Asia: A Foreword

*Daniel M. Neuman*

South Asia is known for many things, but unique to its society is the ubiquity of hereditary occupations covering an unparalleled array of work, and often embedded in caste status.[1] Indeed, in the performing arts essays – the ones I shall mostly address in this foreword – almost all involve, either presently or in the past, some kind of hereditary specialists. Of course, hereditary specialists are known the world over, and we have to only look at the case of J. S. Bach to see this as far from unique. But for sheer variety as we read in these pages, through space, from the Himalayas to South India, and persistence through time, from eleventh-century Tevaram singers, singing a form till today, or Kanchipuram silk production known at least from the fourteenth century, to, in contrast, the recent 1950s introduction of carpet weaving in the inaccessible Laspur region in Pakistan, South Asia as a civilisational space in this respect, I would aver, is unique.

My own interest in the performing arts generally, and music specifically, arose from the mystery of why and how societies afford the very major investment in years of training, to produce performing artists whose product – true before the era of recordings – disappeared in the immediacy of their creation and, in that sense, had no obvious utilitarian value. Accordingly, as I often correct others, I am not so much a specialist in Indian music, but rather my focus has been on Indian performers. It is they who typically spend years learning and developing their very special skills. But what was sometimes a weakness in my work and, to be candid, also in the work of many others was the insufficient attention paid to being paid.

In this collection of essays, the editors have assembled an outstanding group of scholars who do indeed pay close attention to being paid, to the political economy of creators, to performing, making things and labour. These papers cover South Asia, North to South, past to present, arts to crafts, professional to amateur, women, men, and transgender people, and finally performers and people who make things. This last points to a distinction between performers and craftspeople (or artisans as I have called them in the past), although in one paper we learn of the community of scroll painters with some who are also scroll painting singers. But with this exception noted, it might be useful to think of this collection as a *jugalbandi*, a duet, not between, as one sometimes hears between North and South Indian music, but a duet between the performing body of the executant and the body performing of the craftsperson. Among performers, these bodies range from those not seen, but only heard and imagined in early twentieth-century recordings, to the high exertion athleticism of dancing bodies in formal performances. For artisans, bodies can be bombarded by the senses of touch, smell, and sight while handling textiles or simply survive while 'pressing one's feet (on the loom)' (Kawlra, this volume).

Bodies, however, have to be nurtured and sustained, and in this collection, we read about the strategies that all such bodies invent in order to survive. Whether it is the performing body of the dancer or musician, or the body performing to create a carpet, sari, shawl, or sword, the challenges of the last two centuries are, if not identical, very much parallel. Matching the variety of actions gathered in this assemblage of creative economies is the variety of paying and getting paid, from showering bills in performances to bespoke orders for walnut wood carvings by military personnel in Kashmir.

For many of the essays, the facts of colonialism, either directly through legislation or indirectly by removing or changing the basis of patronage, have had profound effects. The emergence of new technologies – from railways and telegraph, through records and films and now to television – have had parallel deep consequences. Accordingly, the impact of colonialism is a common theme, ranging from the well-known ouster of Wajid Ali Khan from Oudh in 1856 and what it meant to Hindustani music to the little-known fact that in 1878, it became illegal to make weapons without a license. Women performers were stigmatised as prostitutes with the passage of the Contagious Diseases Act first in 1864, while in the south, various regulations regarding *devadasis* were enacted in the nineteenth century and became further instantiated after Independence.

Indeed, women specialists, both as performers and as producers, are central to many of the studies related here. In the performing arts area, professional women performers were a subject virtually ignored when I first started doing fieldwork in India more than half a century back. At the time, the stigma concerning professional women was so strong that Indian scholars, with very rare exceptions, and musicologists with no exceptions, did not engage the subject, and the subjects themselves were extremely reluctant to be interviewed and rarely allowed publication. We still know little of their practices as they had been increasingly suppressed throughout the twentieth century. And the stigma of association extends until today for their Hindustani accompanists on the *sarangi*. Fortunately, there are a number of papers in this collection that importantly enrich our knowledge of these women artists as workers.

Perhaps the central theme addressed in this important collection is remuneration; the shift from inherited patron-based work receiving in-kind remuneration to work based on monetary exchanges. And in this sense, the typical categories of urban, classical, 'art' contrasted with rural, folk, 'craft' invite much interpellation. As recently as 1990, I documented a hereditary Manganiar musician in Rajasthan, returning home from his patron with a large bundle of hay atop his horse that he had received as in-kind remuneration. Indeed, this collection makes the same point that feudal patronage extended well into the mid-twentieth century. But as all these essays demonstrate, cash, although far from unknown in the past, has now become the standard and universal.

For some, the traditional exchange of obligatory service for in-kind remuneration is highly exploitative, although this kind of exploitation can also become enhanced in a cash economy as well. This is not unrelated to another well-documented theme, namely, the paradox as some have called it in these essays, between the high value of the ritual or ritualised performance and the low or highly restricted social status of the performers. Caste, India's particular modality of social organisation, begins to get the attention it deserves in some of these essays.

It is perhaps surprising how much of both the performing and craft specialists in the North are Muslims although in at least one case religious identity is fluid, much as I found for hereditary performers in Haryana in the 1970s. We also learn of the depth of training that upper caste Bengalis engaged in as disciples of Muslim *ustads*. Speaking of *ustads*, many of us are familiar with the use of this term among musicians, but, as we read in these essays, it is also a term found among craftsmen including wood crafting and weaponsmiths. I remember first learning about the use of this term outside a musical context from a motorcycle mechanic who was addressed as *ustad*.

In 1985, India created and promoted its Festival of India programmes around the world, and Pupul Jayakar, the Doyenne of textile knowledge in India was a central figure in that Festival of India project.[2] This points to the centrality of textile manufacture and design not only as a well-known historical fact – or Gandhi's *Swadeshi* movement making it a central symbol of national self-reliance – but also at the highest government circles now and as we learn here, deep into the colonial and pre-colonial past.

I want to point out three additional themes that are important in this collection, not only in themselves but also because they have received insufficient attention in the past. One common, albeit sobering theme for both performers and craftspeople is precarity and its too often concomitant, suffering. With few exceptions, the subjects in these essays suffer from uncertainty in their income (which is often a pittance), low and often despised social rank, and little social or political attention to their plight unless it promotes a political agenda.

Another theme that emerges is the importance of identity formation and maintenance, particularly among craftspeople. Perhaps as a corrective to the common indignities that many suffer, the alliance of work with pride in their own creativity strengthens a social and individual structure of being that provides an important source of strength against the multiple challenges that face artists and artisans today.

Arguably, the most prominent theme in this collection is agency emerging as it does from identity formation. For all the challenges that individuals experience in contemporary South Asian society, victims of caste and class power systems that many of the subjects of this book continuously experience, negotiate, and, at times, fight against, the role of agency in performance and craft practices across multiple political economies reveal the meaning and dignity that accrue from the products of labour through the practice of performance and artisanship.

We are fortunate that this collection encompasses such a wide range of performative and crafts activities otherwise not available in any other work I know. If information is the currency with which we as scholars mainly deal, the reader of this volume will indeed become rich in knowledge and I believe, much wiser for it.

## Notes

1 Oddly, in Jan Lucassen's recent global survey (Lucassen, J 2021, *The story of work: a new history of mankind*, Yale University Press, Kindle Edition), the hereditary aspect of labour specialties is basically ignored, despite, at least for India, the importance of this as, historically, a typically determinant factor of occupation.

2 Jayakar, P 1980, *The earthen drum: an introduction to the ritual arts of rural India*, National Museum, New Delhi.

# Introduction

## Living, Adapting, and Creating: Craftspeople and Performers in South Asia

*Anna Morcom and Neelam Raina*

India is well known the world over for its stunning textiles and handicrafts, mesmerising classical performing arts, and, in recent decades, the rich aural and visual panoply of its popular culture, in the form of films, music, and fashion. These creative arts have both supplemented and substantiated the idea of an ancient culture and people that drives trade and tourism and are also increasingly seen as a unique Indian selling point in the plethora of culture from Asia as a whole. But how are these crafts and performing arts produced in terms of human livelihoods, labour, social structures, and social status? How have these creative economies sustained, transformed, or diminished because of historical factors, such as colonialism, industrialisation, the birth of new nation states, regionalism, economic development, neoliberalism, and digitalisation? How do ideas of identity, dignity, adaptation, agility, and resilience form and shift within this sector?

The chapters in this book address intersecting questions that are key to the understanding of creative practices in the context of South Asia. We explore craftspeople and performers in what can be termed traditional structures as well as new models of creative work that have emerged in more or less recent forms of modernised, middle-class, urban communities. The chapters are focused on the lives, livelihoods, multidimensional challenges, and paradoxes of craftspeople and performers, foregrounding inequality-based issues of caste, class, gender, religion, and creative labour. Core human values of joy, dignity, respect, security of income, and food repeatedly appear within these pages, providing insights into the everyday within large changes of history.

This volume encourages us to think critically and comparatively about how traditional performers and craftspeople have evolved in both similar and diverging ways over the last century. This marks a departure from the binary ways in which the creative sector separates art and craft from music and performance or distinguishes arts versus crafts or classical versus folk or popular performing arts, and national versus regional provenances. We explore the systems of evaluation, engagement, consumption, promotion, and value of handmade crafts and performing arts in the recent history of India. These have varied starkly in some ways in the worlds of crafts when compared with performing arts, but they also exhibit significant parallels. Our aim, therefore, is to look at culture and creative practices in a more cohesive manner. In this introduction we highlight the ways in which the different

DOI: 10.4324/9781351031028-1

materialities of crafts and performing arts have shaped the roles they play in national culture, identity, and economy from the late colonial period to the present. We explore the changing and enduring realities of creative labour and contextualise the chapters in the volume, introducing our interdisciplinary approach.

## Performers and Craftspeople and Pre-industrial Creative Economies

Craftspeople and performers in what can be termed traditional or pre-industrial economies in India share many commonalities regarding status, patronage, and questions of the dignity of creative labour, as explored, in different ways, by many chapters in the volume. Many such professionals are hereditary artisan craftspeople and performers from the lower social orders, some intensely stigmatised, and often embedded in patronage relationships with upper castes or elite groups. In numerous cases, craftspeople also perform, or vice versa, an example of which Basu explores in this volume. However, cultural economies have not remained static; shifts in power due to trade, disease, famine, wars, and the fall and rise of empires have affected the ability of elites to (re)allocate resources for performing arts and beautifully crafted textiles, objects, and paintings. It is also important to remember that many traditional craftspeople and performers are only seasonally employed, and some are not professionals (i.e., do not rely on the activity for their primary livelihood). Yet, as Kaul and others in this volume discuss, they embody the values of practice, strength, hard work, discipline, endurance, and sometimes sacrifice.

Within crafts, the Hindu system of caste order is a marker of hierarchy that spans makers of uncut cloth for ritual worship to those who work with polluting leather or animal products, with many variations in between. Other communities of craft makers remain embedded within socio-economic hierarchies that are driven by identity constructs. Similarly, performers range from Brahmin singers of devotional music to Dalits who play instruments made from leather, such as drums, as Fiol and Prakash both explore (this volume; see also Sherinian 2014). As de Bruin analyses in the context of the non-elite *Kattaikkuttu* Tamil theatre, hard physical labour itself implies a low or no caste status (this volume). Over the centuries, many musicians and craftspeople have converted to Islam or Christianity to enable employment or avoid untouchability, and some groups performing on instruments with polluting substances, such as the Kathaks, have shown remarkable social mobility (Walker 2014). However, regardless of caste status or religion, most pre-industrial craftspeople and performers were poor, as are the vast majority of those who operate in these arenas today.

The creative economies of many traditional professional craftspeople and performers have been bound in *jajmani* relationships of service provision; whether elite or lowly, they are almost always low in status and/or caste relative to those they served (Ayyagari 2022; Catlin-Jairazbhoy & Jairazbhoy 2008; Mason 2013; Neuman 1992; Qureshi 2002; Ramaswamy 2004; Wade & Pescatello 1977). These dynamics are explored by Basu, de Bruin, Fiol, Lanzillo, Leucci, Morcom, Prakash, and Williams in this volume. Payment is usually in kind. It, therefore, depends on the duty and generosity of patrons and other audiences or consumers to provide subsistence, support or make gifts, which have various terms in South Asia, including *nazrana, bagshish, iman,* and *dakshina*, and include land given to craftspeople and performers who settle near their patrons. However, performers and craftspeople did not always exclusively serve their own patrons. Craftspeople produced goods for trade locally, sometimes limited to a small catchment for a specific caste of clients as can be seen in the case of the *Khatris* in present-day India and Pakistan (Edwards 2005). Performers were also invited by aristocratic or mercantile patrons other than their own. This has been crucial for the adaptability and resilience of traditional craftspeople and performers, as we see in contexts of conflict (Kaul and Raina, exploring Kashmir, this volume), or the turbulence of social, economic, and technological change under colonialism (Chambers, Sachdeva, and Williams, this volume).

Certain distinctions emerge between craftspeople and performers due to the different materialities and intimacies of maker and consumer. Live performing arts cannot be separated from the body of the performer, leading to particularly powerful intersections with gender. Chapters by Leucci, Neuman, and Sachdeva illuminate these in different historical and technological contexts. Women, unless they performed only in the company of women or domestic contexts, were generally not able to combine performing with marriage until a new model of middle-class artist emerged in the 1930s, and only in the world of the classicised performing arts for upper castes (Morcom 2013; Soneji 2012). The widespread incidence of female impersonation or cross-dressed performance is also connected to the stigma of traditional performing women as well as to the appeal of female impersonators (Hansen 2002; Morcom 2013). Such performers could be low status, erotic, and transgender, such as *hijras*, *kothis*, and *zananas* (overlapping groups of female-identifying men, including those commonly termed 'third gender' or 'eunuch') (Morcom 2013). They could also be high status and hegemonic, as with the Brahmin men from Kuchipudi village who shaped femininity and came to define the classical dance form of that name (Soneji 2004; see also Hansen 2002).

While less stark, the contours of gender are still apparent in craft production. An example is India's national Shilp Guru award to recognise skills, where *guru* is a word that typically indicates men. Both men and women present themselves as specialists with a significant skill set in different kinds of crafts, but professionally recognised, awarded, and celebrated craftspeople are mostly men; women, where present, contribute to practices of making, but their labour is often categorised as a 'hobby' to pass time engaging in practices of cultural value alone, as Raina explores amidst the impact of conflict in present-day Kashmir. However, women also engage in the making and embodying of crafts in home-based forms, as Mirza shows in her chapter by exploring notions of memory, emotion, belonging, and identity in the making of the traditional *gajj* attire by women of Sindh. Many such craftswomen are not held within *jajmani* patron-client relationships, but rather make objects for domestic use, similar to household women who sing auspicious songs in the company of other women or family.

Hereditary craftspeople and performers have generally been of a low status, in contrast to modern middle class or elite artists and performers who do not serve a patron but instead devote themselves to art or God (Morcom, this volume).

Nevertheless, there are complexities regarding the ways in which status or dignity are gained, asserted, and used as currency. Craftspeople, and some performers, draw on a dignified and transcendent origin, tracing their lineage to Vishwakarma, the Maker of Everything, a Vedic deity who is depicted in many different forms across India (Narayan & George 2017). The low status is believed to have come about through a primordial act of pollution (Fiol, this volume). Not dissimilarly, many low-status courtesan and dancing girl groups trace Rajput origins (Dewan 2019).

The status of performers and craftspeople can also become intertwined with that of the art and craft they create for their patrons. The proximity of performers to their patrons itself creates the potential for intimacy, as Qureshi (2002) and Schofield (2007) have explored in the case of elite performing arts. However, as Prakash argues in his chapter on three different communities of Dalit and low-caste drummers, there is no such liminal intimacy with non-elite performers. With material arts, the art or craft is not immanent in the body of the maker, but there are intimate relationships between the maker, making, and made, and inanimate aspects of objects can be almost lifelike in the imagination of the maker. This is described in chapters by Hussain and Mirza in terms of landscapes and embodiment (this volume). This intimacy also allows the labour of making specific objects to be linked to professional status and not always the caste to which the maker belongs (Lanzillo, this volume). This perceived mobility between caste and class, and the role of the blessed maker who creates forms that reflect God, have allowed crafts to be flexible and adaptive in many cases, as explored by Chambers in the context of artisans and global production networks, and Raina and Kaul in the context of conflict and Kashmir (this volume). Performers, too, though the affect or the religious or ritual efficacy of their arts may straddle extremes of importance and prestige and of degradation, stigma, and low social status (Fiol and Prakash, this volume).

## Colonialism, Capitalism, and Nationalism, 1857–1947

India underwent tumultuous political and economic changes following the 1857 uprising, including an increasing connection with the global economy and trade led by colonial powers; the rise of mass production and mechanisation; the introduction of rapid transportation (railway) and communication (telegraph); colonial reform and the 'civilising' of Indian society; rising nationalism and the struggle for freedom; and the growth of certain hegemonic high-caste, middle-class groups. These changes affected craftspeople and performers in distinct ways due to the different materialities of their arts, and the consequent varying economic, social, and political potentials within the changing lines of power.

Colonialism had direct and drastic impacts on traditional craft production. The British East India Company extracted raw materials and handmade products for export. The *Swadeshi* movement created by Mahatma Gandhi directly challenged British imports, promoting instead the making and consuming of locally produced products, and this goal of self-reliance became central to the push for independence. The place of Indian handicrafts in the national imagination is such that, as Upadhyay states, to write about them is almost like writing about the country itself. This type of Indian folk art is often described as vast, complex, and colourful, while exhibiting a unique simplicity and charm (Upadhyay 1976). This made-by-self approach shaped the future of the village-based informal sector of crafts. However, as DeNicola and Wilkinson argue in their chapter on the survival and revival of crafts (this volume), Gandhi's charisma was responsible for promoting a utopic vision of the village economy. The romanticising of the craft maker and their relationship with their tools, their art, and their artefacts emerged from these socio-political markers in India's freedom struggle. As Kawlra explains looking at the colonial spatialisation of 'tradition' in the context of Kanchipuram saris (this volume), the place-based typology of traditional craft in India was part of the wider trend in the making of nationhood through a presumed congruence between state and culture on the international stage.

Crafts, textiles, and cotton, as material objects and raw materials, were suitable for long-distance trade, and transformable into profitable products back in England. For the performing arts, however, there was no equivalent potential for monetary capital accumulation. Only a small number of Indian performers travelled to the West, and although the emerging recording industry was connected to the colonial extractive economy of shellac (Devine 2019), the scale was insignificant in comparison to the raw cotton and manufactured textiles circuit. Nevertheless, the recording was an important source of income for numerous artists and, as Neuman examines in his chapter, through its ability to separate performer, voice, and product, affected how listeners encountered traditional hereditary performers and their place in national culture in the twentieth century.

What became known as the classical and semi-classical arts were not just insignificant to the colonial government or nationalists in terms of economy, but were presented by reformers in terms of non-industrious decadence of India's feudal rulers. Entwined with this view was the perceived immorality of the *nautch* ('dancing') girls and *devadasis*. While handicrafts, as well as catering to elite consumption, provided everyday objects for personal domestic use, professional performing arts were associated with public contexts that began to be seen as distinctly unwholesome in the early twentieth century (Kumar 1988). The reformist discourse surrounding such performing was, therefore, in many ways antithetical to that of crafts whose value lay in the basic toil and productivity of India's rural economy.

The most influential reformers of classical performing arts were upper-caste Hindus whose thinking was shaped by orientalist ideas tracing high arts back to ancient 'classical' India and Sanskrit *shastra*s (treatises) (Bakhle 2005; Weidman 2006). Many members of the upper-caste Hindu urban intelligentsia themselves became artists of these adapted arts, as Williams explores in this volume in the context of the resulting relationships of hereditary artistes with their patrons-turned-performers. An overarching discourse of reviving or saving classical performing arts from the traditional performers, ostensibly for the new nation, shaped this process (Morcom 2013; Soneji 2012; Srinivasan 1985; Weidman 2006). As elaborated by Leucci's contribution to this collection on South Indian *devadasi*s, hereditary female performers faced the most drastic change, losing forms of valued performing labour to which they had long-standing rights. Also, as Sachdeva and Neuman (this volume) explore in different ways, North Indian courtesans adapted as emerging technologies and mediatised performing contexts brought new opportunities. Ultimately, however, female hereditary performers became starkly marginalised. The classicisation process also included a strong anti-economic thrust whereby those for whom performing was a profession and a livelihood were looked down on, notably, the mostly Muslim male hereditary performers. Visible payment of classical musicians became seen in negative terms, and performing as a spiritual pursuit was asserted as the ideal (Morcom this volume). This ambivalence still exists to some degree and has established a pattern of not thinking about performing in terms of sustainable livelihoods.

Although the performing arts of village India did have a place in the lives of royalty and aristocracy, they were not associated with waste and decadence. Colonial officers and early colonial folklorists, who worked with local upper-caste Indians, studied these low-status artists and produced the category of 'folk,' romanticising rural and local performing arts while also denigrating them (Babiracki 1991; Fiol 2017). Crucially, most so-called folk musicians and instruments carried stigma, and the middle classes and upper castes did not, therefore, appropriate folk arts and bring them into urban, modern India on a major scale (Fiol 2017). In terms of theatre, the leftist Indian Peoples Theatre Association (IPTA), formed in 1941, did to some degree involve urban Indians with folk arts in certain parts of the country, as it sought to mobilise the populace against colonial rule through traditional art forms. However, unlike crafts, village forms of performing arts creativity were not widely valorised, with no movement equivalent to *swadeshi*, and many hereditary performers have left their profession. Fiol engages with these issues of the dignity of work in the context of Dalit drummers in the ritual and capitalist economies of today's village India in Uttarakhand, and de Bruin in the context of the intense physical labour of Kattaikkuttu (both this volume).

It was, thus, the pan-North and South Indian classical traditions that became iconic of Indian culture rather than folk arts. It is also interesting to note that no equivalent of 'classical' emerged in the world of crafts. Elite artists did develop fine art and sculpture in India, but it never became a significant force ideologically or economically, as the *Swadeshi* narrative took mainstage (Lal 2023).

The impact of partition in 1947 on the creative economies of craftspeople and performers has barely been studied. The massive migration shifted patterns of making and trading for many years, with *karkhaanas* (workshops) divided, supply chains disrupted, and crafts left languishing (Bilgrami 2020). For North Indian musicians, the impact was severe, with many musicians and wealthy patrons migrating to Pakistan (Saeed 2008–2009). While there is a scarcity of research on crafts and performing arts in relation to partition in post-partition India, there is even less accessible literature on Pakistan and Bangladesh.

## Institutionalisation and the Growth of Mechanisation, Globalisation, and Capitalist Systems of Production Post-independence

In the early decades following independence in 1947, handicrafts had become an important sector of the economy, second only to agriculture in terms of employment in India (Liebl & Roy 2003). India established national, state, and regional or village-based committees and commissions, notably the All India Handicrafts and Handloom Board, Khaadi Village Industry Commission, the Khaadi Village Industry Boards, the All India Spinner Association, the Central Cottage Industries Exposition, and the State emporia. These supported, promoted, and showcased regional crafts.

Traditional performing arts were not seen in terms of economy or industry, and while structures that engage and promote production, consumption, and exports were efficiently put in place for crafts, this was not the case for music and performing arts. Nevertheless, the latter were important to notions of heritage and culture, and certain state institutions were set up to preserve and promote them, notably, the national-level Sangeet Natak Akademy (SNA) and the Indian Council for Cultural Relations (ICCR), as well as regional-level institutions (Cherian 2009). All India Radio became crucial for broadcasting classical and semi-classical music and provided jobs for musicians. These state institutions also supported folk performing arts, codifying and promoting them in urban areas. In addition, broadcasts reached many people back in villages and were immensely important, although this separated the arts from rural contexts in terms of production (Fiol 2017). State, and more recently, non-government organisations have also provided some support for certain folk forms in the context of rural education. This little-explored aspect of numerous regional performing arts is a central focus of Basu's chapter, looking at women of the Chitrakar community in Bengal who traditionally make scrolls but also perform in the verse-duelling *kobigaan* song-theatre (this volume).

Overall, state support for folk performing arts genres is not proportionate to the quantity and diversity of musicians and traditions. Folk performing arts have neither a middle-class audience base nor status as an economic sector to draw attention from commissions and development projects. Skilled performers spend much time doing other forms of work, and great indignity of labour remains (de Bruin, Fiol, and Prakash, this volume). They also increasingly compete with mass-mediated forms of vernacular pop music and DJs, which have a modern allure, and are mostly produced by upper castes (Fiol 2017). As de Bruin describes in her chapter on *Kattaikkuttu*, performers in addition contend with new forms of financing, payment, and loans that are exploitative, resulting effectively in bonded labour.

We can see further imbalance of provision of the state infrastructures that promote the development and growth of the creative sector. Educational institutions have become very widespread for the classical and semi-classical performing arts, as well as, more recently, for Western and commercial music, providing livelihoods for many musicians. However, these institutions prioritise classical, semi-classical, and now Western music over folk music, though some regional music schools teach certain traditions. Similarly, there are few institutions that teach traditional craft making, though numerous ones exist for fine art. It is also notable that while awards or accolades for classical performing arts and fine arts are abundant, they are limited for crafts. These oversights suggest that traditional crafts are not valued as real art, and the same is true for folk performing arts, which have a limited presence in urban India. The difference here is of coded versus tacit knowledge

(Polanyi 1966). Notably, while the classical performing arts and fine art are presented as national (despite the existence of clear geographical contours in their prevalence and institutionalisation), folk performing arts and crafts are viewed as regional.

National policy interventions secured the economic position of crafts in the decades after independence. Programmes aimed at vocational training, capacity building, livelihood generation, and poverty alleviation focussed on craft making. Also, development actors and international donors invested in this sector. The export of handicrafts from India grew from INR 3.86 billion in 1986–1987 when the Handicrafts Exports Council was set up, to INR 252.7 billion in 2019–2020. At this time, the role of women, and the inclusion of them as producers of profitable crafts, also became key drivers for policy. The connections between home-based incomes, women's development, indigenous knowledge, and crafts facilitated the recognition of the role of crafts in generating livelihood across South Asia. Crafts have become more visible in contemporary, urban areas since the 1990s, with the setting up of international craft fairs (such as at Dacchi and Surajkund) and open-air crafts markets where craftspeople can sell their crafts, such as Dilli Haat (Delhi) and Lok Virsa (Islamabad). These draw people from across the socio-economic spectrum. They also enable craftspeople to promote their skills and highlight the spectacle of making as performance.

In the 1990s, liberalisation and rapid technological progress brought changes in the consumption of crafts. A growing middle class aspired to buy into the authenticity of handmade products through shops like Dastakar, Anokhi, FabIndia, Behbud, and Sungi in India and Pakistan. Export of handmade goods increased as both nations built reputations as producers of traditional products of high quality. Designers from India's fashion schools and Pakistani art schools also worked with craftspeople, bringing the potential for star and celebrity value to crafts, but also concerns with appropriation. Indeed, echoes of the inequities of *jajmani* and patronage systems can be seen. Such an elite appropriation of crafts in a sense parallels what happened earlier with classical music.

In the decades after Independence, the advent of new technology in the form of cassettes had an immense impact on music at many levels. There was an explosion of recorded regional music industries in the 1980s, whereby folk music gained wider circulation (Manuel 1993). Performers adapted to new formats, audiences, and patrons, and women, albeit not easily, have been able to break into previously male domains (Basu, this volume). However, not many traditional low-caste musicians have been able to substantially capitalise on technology. As Fiol (2017) explores in Uttarakhand, it is 'folk elements' more than artisan folk performers who have featured aurally and visually on recordings and videos. There have been attempts to break this pattern in recent urban-based collaborations with folk artists, such as the wave of Sufi music in urban India and Pakistan (Manuel 2008; Virani 2016). Coke Studio in Pakistan has been particularly prominent in this. Tourism that helps traditional performers has developed in a handful of states only, with Rajasthan a notable example. Opportunities have emerged more recently in large-scale folk festivals, sometimes overlapping with those featuring classical artists. But, like trends with crafts, these festivals typically benefit a relatively small number of artists in traditional performing communities (Virani 2016). The major change in the world of performing arts in India following liberalisation has been the dramatic expansion of the middle-class zone of performing arts from classical genres to Bollywood, which has increased the challenges for many traditional performers (Morcom 2013). In addition, as Rudisill's chapter in this volume explores in the context of reality TV dance shows and dancing in the 'Kollywood' Tamil film industry, these worlds *of middle-class performers* are divided in terms of kinds of labour and status.

With crafts, the movement of people, skills, and goods into the capitalist structures of a newly liberalised India of the 1990s fused the concepts of tradition and culture. Music and performing arts, in contrast, have continued to be framed by narrow definitions of classical, folk, and popular, marking class- and rural-urban-based divides. There is an increasing softening of high vs. low and folk vs. popular distinctions, especially in the world of Bollywood and vernacular pop music. However, this has not affected the fact that village-based or folk performing arts barely connect with shifting capitalist structures. In terms of resilience and adaptation, there is no equivalence of traditional performing arts to crafts as a pillar of not just national identity but economy. Although in certain villages or regions, there are success stories, it is overwhelmingly classical performing arts, and now popular or Bollywood music, dance, and cinema, that are iconic of India and arguably on a par with handicrafts in terms of international reach, soft power, and industry. Despite the infrastructure to support commercialised craft making and the recognition and appreciation of skills locally and overseas, most craftspeople remain on or below the poverty line. They show little interest in passing their skills onto their children, and dream, rather, of mainstream education for them along the professional lines of doctors, engineers, lawyers – anything, but craft makers. Generations of craft producers, to this day, recognise the love they have of making, but also the compulsion to make, as they possess no other skills, and lack the education and social status to make the shifts upwards within society.

As so many chapters in this book explore, despite the increased profile of crafts in urban areas and the phenomenon of certain star folk performers, fundamental problems for traditional performers and craftspeople are still prevalent: poverty, the pervasiveness of stigma, and a reluctance for social reproduction and continuity of practice in future generations. For many craftspeople and folk performers, pride in their traditions is being erased by abject poverty, a lack of economic mobility for creative producers, and continuing stigma. Disenfranchisement, persistent and systemic exclusion, stigma, and erasure have been profound for some traditional creative workers in particular, for example, the female hereditary performing communities, as well as leather product makers and repair and renewal workers like *rafugars* and *mochis*.

It must be noted that the COVID-19 pandemic has severely impacted or destroyed the livelihoods of many performing artists who rely on performance and teaching, apart from a minority able to teach and perform using online technology. Crafts have also been dealt a major blow as all fairs and markets were cancelled. The repercussions of this are only beginning to be explored, and are beyond the scope of this volume.

## An Interdisciplinary Approach to Creative Practice and Culture

Amidst a plethora of academic work on crafts and performing arts, our aim is to create a new, interdisciplinary context for considering a more unified notion of creative practice and culture by examining craftspeople and performers side by side. This book reveals interconnections and also makes apparent the different emphases of the scholarly traditions of crafts and performing arts.

As evidenced by many of the chapters, there has been a far greater focus on the economies and development issues of contemporary crafts than on the performing arts, with Wilkinson and De Nicola, Mirza, Raina, Kaul, and Lanzillo all focusing on crafts in this way. There is comparatively far greater understanding and documentation of crafts than folk or rural performing arts, where the majority of scholarly attention is on classical performing arts, and, recently, popular culture. While this volume includes chapters on contemporary popular and mass culture creative labourers (Rudissil, notably), it places great emphasis on the creative economies and predicaments of contemporary traditional performers in chapters by de Bruin, Fiol, Morcom, and Prakash, with de Bruin and Basu looking at the work of non-profit organisations with such artists. Leucci, Sachdeva, and Williams all explore historical performers with a comparable focus on livelihoods and labour. Scholarship on performing arts, in comparison to that on crafts, provides a far richer illumination of aesthetics, arts, and knowledge, though, predictably, largely for the classical genres. However, in this volume, Raina examines the value of tacit uncoded knowledge to women who make crafts in conflict-ridden and fragile locations.

Crafts that have not been a part of *Swadeshi* are also understudied. Thus, while there is a large body of work around textiles, many others amongst India's 177 officially registered Geographical Indicator for crafts (Government of India 2019) have little documentation or scholarship on them. In this volume, Lanzillo brings focus to colonial-era trades that were never a part of *Swadeshi* efforts, exploring how metal-working and weapon artisans have negotiated economic marginalisation while asserting community identity and status. In addition, Chambers and Kaul both focus on woodworking craftspeople.

Following John Clammer's work (2014) on culture and international development, we emphasise in this book that culture is always an economy, and is also a question of human lives, social structures, and thus, social transformation. The 18 chapters in this book encompass performing arts and crafts of radically different kinds and at historical periods from the late nineteenth century to the present day, exploring the lived, human, and material circumstances of cultural and artistic production. Most of the chapters focus on present-day India, spanning the south and north, with two on present-day Pakistan. The authors consider the multidimensional aspects of survival and continuity for creative labourers in connection with the challenges and opportunities of colonialism, nationalism, capitalism, and mechanisation, as well as issues of caste, class, gender, and religion.[1]

Creative practices have withstood the shifting sands of time over centuries, ebbing, flowing, and adapting. Some have faded away into nothing. The economics of colonialism and the intensification of capitalism from the later nineteenth century saw forms of creative practice set on significantly different trajectories, with many facing marked threats. The trails of these trajectories continue to indicate deep fault lines in the way creative practices are understood, accepted, appreciated, promoted, and also marginalised. The core issues for craftspeople and performers, despite the differences, remain the same – unsteady incomes, lack of educational skills, notions of pride and dignity of labour, and the ever-present question of sustainability and resilience juxtaposed with the commitment and drive to create. This is what we aim to highlight in the book as creative economies of culture.

## Note

1 We would like to note that while we have made images in this book conform to the regulations of the publisher, which prevents full faces from being shown without explicit permission in writing, this questions the agency of those who wish to be photographed, the integrity of research processes, and can result in the erasure of people with lower levels of education or technological access. This is particularly significant to this book given the marginalised and deeply unequal status of a majority of traditional artisans and performers.

## References


Ayyagari, S 2022, *Musical resilience: performing patronage in the Indian Thar desert*, Wesleyan University Press, Middletown, CT.

Babiracki, C 1991, 'Tribal music in the study of great and little traditions of Indian music,' in B Nettl & P Bohlman (eds.), *Comparative musicology and anthropology of music: essays on the history of ethnomusicology*, University of Chicago Press, Chicago, IL, pp. 69-91.

Bakhle, J 2005, *Two men and music: nationalism in the making of an Indian classical tradition*, Oxford University Press, New York.

Bilgrami, N 2020, 'A timeless journey: reflections on the crafts heritage of Pakistan,' *Journal of Heritage Management*, vol. 5, no. 2, pp. 121–43.

Catlin-Jairazbhoy, A & Jairazbhoy, N 2008, *Music for a goddess*, Film, Apsara Media for Intercultural Education, Van Nuys.

Cherian, A 2009, 'Institutional maneuvers, nationalizing performance, delineating genre: reading the Sangeet Natak Akademi reports 1953–1959,' *Third Frame: Literature, Culture and Society*, vol. 2, no. 3, pp. 32–60.

Clammer, J 2014, *Art, culture and international development: humanizing social transformation - rethinking development*, Routledge, London.

Devine, K 2019, *Decomposed: the political ecology of music*, MIT Press, Cambridge.

Dewan, Saba. 2019, *Tawaifnama*. Chennai: Context.

Edwards, E 2005, 'Contemporary production and transmission of resist-dyed and block-printed textiles in Kachchh District, Gujarat,' *Textile*, vol. 3, no. 2, pp. 166–89.

Fiol, S 2017, *Recasting folk in the Himalayas: Indian music, media, and social mobility*, University of Illinois Press, Urbana-Champagne, IL.

Government of India, Ministry of Textile, 2019, *A compendium of geographical indications handicrafts of India*, Development Commissioner Handicrafts, New Delhi.

Hansen, K 2002, 'A different desire, a different femininity: theatrical transvestism in the Parsi, Gujarati, and Marathi theatres,' in R Vanita (ed.), *Queering India: same-sex love and eroticism in Indian culture and society*, Routledge, New York, pp. 163–80.

Kumar, N 1988, *The artisans of Banaras: popular culture and identity, 1880–1986*, Princeton University Press, Princeton, NJ.

Lal, V 2023, *Insurgency and the artist: the art of the freedom struggle in India*, Roli Books, New Delhi.

Liebl, M & Roy, T 2003, 'Handmade in India: preliminary analysis of crafts producers and crafts production,' *Economic and Political Weekly*, vol. 38, no. 51/52, pp. 5366–76.

Manuel, P 1993, *Cassette culture: popular music and technology in North India*, University of Chicago Press, Chicago, IL.

Manuel, P 2008, 'North Indian Sufi Popular Music in the Age of Hindu and Muslim Fundamentalism,' *Ethnomusicology*, vol. 52, no. 3, pp. 378–400.

Mason, K 2013, 'Musicians and the politics of dignity in South India,' in P Bohlman (ed.), *The Cambridge history of world music*, Cambridge University Press, Cambridge, pp. 441–71.

Morcom, A 2013, *Illicit worlds of Indian dance: cultures of exclusion*, C. Hurst and Co, London; Oxford University Press, New York.

Narayan, K & George, K 2017, 'Tools and world-making in the worship of Vishwakarma,' *South Asian History and Culture*, vol. 8, no. 4, pp. 478–92.

Neuman, DM 1992, 'Patronage and performance of Indian music,' in BS Miller (ed.), *The powers of art: patronage in Indian culture*, Oxford University Press, New Delhi, pp. 247-258.

Polanyi, M 1966, *The tacit dimension*, Doubleday, Garden City, NY.

Qureshi, RB 2002, 'Mode of production and musical production: Is Hindustani music feudal?' in RB Qureshi (ed.), *Music and Marx: ideas, practice, politics*, Routledge, New York, pp. 81–105.

Ramaswamy, V 2004, 'Vishwakarma craftsmen in early medieval peninsular India,' *Journal of the Economic and Social History of the Orient*, vol. 47, no. 4, pp. 548–82.

Saeed, Y 2008–2009, 'Fled is that music,' *India International Centre Quarterly*, vol. 35, pp. 238–49.

Schofield, K 2007, 'The social liminality of musicians: case studies from Mughal India and beyond,' *Twentieth-Century Music*, vol. 3, no. 1, pp. 13–49.

Sherinian, Z 2014, *Tamil folk music as Dalit liberation theology*, Indiana University Press, Bloomington.

Soneji, D 2004, 'Performing Satyabhama: text, context, memory and mimesis in Telegu-speaking South India,' PhD thesis, McGill University.

Soneji, D 2012, *Unfinished gestures: devadasis, memory, and modernity in South India*, University of Chicago Press, Chicago, IL.

Srinivasan, A 1985, 'Reform and revival: the devadasi and her dance,' *Economic and Political Weekly*, vol. 20, no. 4, pp. 1869–76.

Upadhyay, MN 1976, *Handicrafts of India*, Swarajya Printing Works, Sucunderabad.

Virani, V 2016, 'Find the true country: devotional music and the self in India's national culture,' PhD thesis, University of California, Los Angeles.

Wade, BC & Pescatello AM 1977, 'Music "patronage" in Indic culture,' in N Pirrotta (ed.), *Essays for a humanist: an offering to Klaus Wachsmann*, The Town House Press, New York, pp. 277–336.

Walker, M 2014, *India's kathak dance in historical perspective*, Ashgate, Farnham.

Weidman, AJ 2006, *Singing the classical voicing the modern: the postcolonial politics of music in South India*, Duke University Press, Durham, NC.

# 1 Musical Unfreedom and the Drummers' Dilemma

## Cultural Labour and the Value of Music in Indian Caste Society

*Brahma Prakash*

### Introduction: Places of Value

Traditional caste-based forms of music in South Asia may be both the most and least valuable services in Indian society. Any attempt to make sense of the value of music becomes an enigma shrouded by factors such as taste, location, and labour, as well as the larger context in which music and performers are located in a caste feudal society. In this chapter, I situate the value of music in relation to the social values it engenders for marginalised communities. In these contexts, music creates a condition of what I would like to term musical unfreedom in which to drum or not to drum – to produce or not to produce music – becomes a political question. However, to drum or not to drum is not always a choice but is a service condition in which performers need to be located. In a paradoxical situation, so-called lower castes must perform caste services that will further enslave them. Music becomes the social marker and immediate mode of identification for the caste and communities of performers. For instance, one who plays a musical instrument called a *baja* becomes a Bajaniya, and a player of a *pambar* or *mandar* becomes Panwariya or Manariya. It is important to ask what is the relationship between music and social? Performers not only produce music but, in the process, also produce themselves. The performers' relationship with the specific form of music produces marginality in which the performers become social (as they acquire some identity) and deviant (because they are not seen as normal) at the same time. Society considers Dalits and other low castes who engage in such music to be professionals even lower than their low-caste equivalents. Why do they get marginalised when they come in contact with music? What is the materiality of music that marginalises their social status further? What is the materiality of musical instruments that not only denigrates the instrument and its rhythm but also the individuals and communities who own and play them? Though these questions can be extended to the other performing arts such as dance and theatre, I argue that there is something very specific to music in its distinct politics and aesthetics. Most importantly, as Mason has written, 'the world music histories should also be told through the prism of labour and dignity' (2013, p. 442); this is my overarching focus.

Scholars have tried to analyse the drummer's dilemma in relation to the marginalisation of performing arts and communities in various contexts (Brown

DOI: 10.4324/9781351031028-2

2007; Kumar 2019; Manuel 2012; Morcom 2013; Qureshi 2002; Soneji 2012). Morcom (2013) explores the problem in the context of modernisation, looking at the politics of exclusion and inclusion from the colonial and bourgeois nationalist discourses to post-independent India that led to the erasure of courtesans and transgender female performers (p. 98). The author analyses the problem in relation to the bourgeois-nationalist ideologies of rights, liberalism, progress, and science, arguing that these ideologies have facilitated ignoring the sociocultural identity of performers and excluding them from officially sanctioned Indian culture. Working on the interface of popular culture and technology, Kumar (2019) discusses the production of new values in relation to vernacular music and technology. He analyses the problems as performative access and informality. These two authors focus on the field of encounters in which the values of music and the status of performers must be discussed in relation to exclusion and inclusion, or formality and informality. However, as I argue in this chapter, questions remain concerning the drummer's dilemma in relation to service and obligation in traditional caste society in which drumming becomes a trap as opposed to drumming as a loss of important skills and cultural heritage.

A caste society sees singers and musicians as the lowest of the low, but their music is considered both an ultimate offering and ultimate obedience. How is it possible that some cultural activities remain exceedingly musical, such as dancing and drumming, but dreadfully unfree socially? Brown describes this problem as 'the puzzle of musicians,' and studies musicians in terms of liminal status (2007, p. 13). However, while Brown's assertion can be true for some professional musicians and performers such as for the elite male musicians and courtesans, the same does not necessarily apply to musicians from the lower orders such as musicians and performers from Dalit or low-caste backgrounds. As I argue here, while an important concept, liminality as a framework often falls short in explaining the cultural phenomenon of the 'drummers dilemma.' From the situated social expectations, these performers are neither just liminal nor deviant. Their status is, instead, specifically defined in the hierarchical social and aesthetic norms. Hence, it is their fixed status rather than their statuslessness that is also the site of the problem. Liminality as a conceptual framework offers us a tool to unravel some of the complexities, but it also tends to obfuscate the problem of marginality in other ways. Therefore, it is not the liminality but marginality that seems to determine the status of Dalit, or low-caste community musicians, and the value of music in an Indian caste society.

I use cultural labour as a conceptual framework to discuss the problematic that produces this paradoxical relationship. The framework focuses on the problem in which the performance of marginalised communities, despite having enormous aesthetic potential, gets devalued in the hegemonic aesthetic regime. On various occasions, such performances lead to both the passionate production of values by the marginalised communities and the enslavement of the musicians as they become servants in performance. I term this problematic *musical unfreedom,* analysing it as a cultural process that involves freedom and unfreedom in a specific social context. It can be argued that the condition can affect the emotional and creative being of the artists, musically. In this system of control, one can appropriate the value of music by devaluing the performers. In other words, the value of music itself lies in the devaluation of the musicians. Qureshi describes a somewhat similar situation with elite male Muslim hereditary musicians dependent on feudal patronage, who 'continued to transmit and perform their art according to their oral tradition, sustained by ideals of feudal patronage and its aesthetic of connoisseurship and improvisation' (2002, p. 84). Each caste or community over a period of time also develops specific cultural expression in ghettoised spaces. In such a situation, the so-called untouchable castes, because of restrictions on movement, may still have some autonomous ghettoised space for their music that others may not have. Their performances in the feudal household and those they do for their family and communities are radically different in relation to the constitution of performance and the production of aesthetic values.

Some forms of music in comparison to others pose more stigma in the caste society. Drumming is one such profession in a caste society that carries a sense of defilement in the dominant aesthetic regime. The question one needs to ask is whether the music of the marginalised communities has the potential to abandon its servitude and transgress its unfreedom? If that is possible, then the value of music can change, along with the status of the musicians. New works on *oppari* and *dappu* have shown how performers can challenge their unfreedom by breaking their links from the service economy of the caste order (Gorringe 2016; Hons 2018).[1] The perception of hierarchy of musical taste is associated with social classes in various contexts. However, what is the constituent of music that privileges or marginalises it in different contexts? How do we explain the specific stigma associated with music in the Indian context? Does it lie in the social body, the performing body, or in the musical form or instruments? I locate the problem in the materiality of music.

## Three Dilemmas

Gordon R. Thompson (1991) makes an interesting observation about the Charans of Gujarat who are hereditary singers. He observes that while Charans feel comfortable with the *path* (recitation) part of the performance in which they perform genealogy, they do not seem comfortable with their identity as musicians. As Thompson underlines, 'musical behaviour is symbolically associated with a low-ranking social status by the Charans' (1991, p. 388). The Charans carefully maintain a distance from their musical behaviours, while at the same time asserting their identity as genealogists. They want to show themselves as poets but not as singers and musicians, and thus, they must carefully craft their identity in such a way that the identity they assert is not overshadowed by their association with music.

As singers, performers, and genealogists, Charans maintain three hierarchical identities: the poet, singer, and musician. While Charans do not have a problem with associating themselves with poetic histories, their associations with musical histories are problematic. Thompson (1991) cites an incident in which Charans gathered to celebrate their oral heritage (poems, songs, stories) in order to reaffirm their caste identity (p. 388). But when it came to associating their identity with music and singing, the communities were divided on whether or not they should celebrate that association. These Charans did not want to associate themselves with professional singing because the service of playing musical instruments and singing had been traditionally associated with Langhas and Mirs in the region of Gujarat. Charans consider Langhas and Mirs lower than themselves in the ranks of the caste hierarchies. The question one needs to ask, then, is whether the low status of Langhas and Mirs is related to the music, and the power of music to construct a social identity. Thompson observes,

> The reasoning of these Charans is based on the role of musicians in the old royal courts, where singers and instrumentalists were invited to entertain in the *raj darbar* (royal audience hall/ royal audience), but seldom to stay and offer advice. Charans by contrast are described historically as the confidants of their patrons, sometimes acting as oral couriers delivering poetic salutations or maledictions to the other rulers. They are often described as regaling Gujarat's royalty with stories recounting the bravery, loyalty and power of the ancestors of the hosts.
>
> (1991, p. 384)

Charans place themselves in the historic identity of singers in which they were considered entertainers with some status. In the present-day identity discourse, they tend to downplay their status as entertainers. Charans know that as entertainers and musicians they cannot make higher social claims. This problem is common among such singers and performers who downplay their musician and singer identities to achieve a recognisable social status in South Asian contexts. Drawing from Curt Sachs' distinction of 'singing professionals' and 'professional singers,' Thompson argues that Charans prefer to claim themselves as the 'singing professionals' than the 'professional singers' (see Sachs 1962). This perhaps explains the paradox of why traditional singers and musicians are trying to acquire an identity as poets rather than singers. This phenomenon can be observed in other parts of India. For example, in Bihar, singers prefer to call themselves *vyasa* (after the name of poet Vyasa, credited as having written the Mahabharata) instead of *gawaiya* (singer). This problem may relate to the politics of modernity in which poets have acquired special status due to the prominence of literature and literacy. However, it would be interesting to consider how these traditional professional singers see themselves in comparison to singers in the music industry. The second case in which I explore the drummer's dilemma relates to the status of *manariyas* in the region of Bihar and Uttar Pradesh. *Manariya*s, also known as *panwariyas* in other regions, are drummers, singers, and narrators who play an important role in lower-caste rituals. They form mixed-caste groups constituted largely of Dalits such as Chamars, Dusadhs, and Mallah (boatmen), as well as various non-Dalit low-caste groups. Dalits and low castes, unlike their upper-caste counterparts, do not tend to disparage *manariyas* as they also participate in their ritual and religious activities. This also happens because *manariyas* often create shared cultural memories and space between the

Dalits and the low-caste groups. These communities rather see them as genealogists who bring the deities and ancestors in dialogue with the communities. Also, these low-caste communities, though they maintain a hierarchy, do not maintain a distinction based on purity and impurity in a very strict sense.

Compared to the Charans, the materiality of music figures differently in the performance of *manariyas*, as the drum itself becomes the object of worship. Not surprisingly, *bhuiyan puja* (land worship), which *manariyas* perform, is also known as *manar puja* (drum worship) (Prakash 2019, p. 99). While in their everyday practices, low-caste groups still maintain some notions of purity and hierarchies; during the *puja*, these groups do not follow much caste restriction. What we find is an emergence of a liminal zone in which Dalits and low-caste groups come together in a shared space with a shared sense of memory and narratives. *Manariyas* acquire a special status along with the *shaman* (medium) and low castes would often treat them as community members. The communities believe that ancestor worship will not take place without the musical power of the *manariyas*. The communities believe that the singers can subdue shamans. After the puja, *manariyas* lay small children from the communities on the drum to get special blessings. Similarly, *manars* (drums) are worshipped by the household women, creating special status for the drums and the music produced from them. It is also crucial to note here that in most cases, *manariyas* are dependent on the patronage of Dalits and other low castes and not on that of upper castes. As *manariyas* most often perform for their own caste groups, their music acquires special value in Dalit and low-caste gatherings and is greatly appreciated. With these positive valuations, singers and musicians too acquire a special status. This shows how the status of drummers and the value of music change in relation to the social groups involved. One can read this special relationship as a case of liminality; however, the practices are strongly informed by the social hierarchies.

The third paradox relates to the performance of the Chamars of Bihar who play music on the inauspicious occasion of death?[2] Besides skinning dead animals and engaging in several forms of menial work, the caste also plays the drum on various occasions. Scholars such as Randeria (1989) and Gorringe (2016) have argued that the music of the Chamars, and other leather-working castes, is regarded as suspicious by mainstream society as it is performed on inauspicious occasions. However, the value of the music in these cases is in fact directly related to the status of the castes who perform this music. The communities often work as messengers on the occasion of death. Since they belong to an untouchable caste, the music they produce also becomes untouchable. In this case, it is the body and materiality of the caste that renders their music undignified. In addition, the music also acquires the value of the inauspicious event – death ceremonies in traditional Indian society. In a paradoxical situation, while the Chamars' musical services are needed, their bodily presence becomes a problem. In many parts of India, the drummers are referred to as *bajania* ('those who play') and their social identity gets reduced to a musical identity. In the formation of the social identity of Chamars, therefore, music and leather both mark their status. Death, inauspiciousness, and their caste association with polluting work contribute to the stigmatisation of both the music and the performers.

To summarise, in the first case, it appears that the dilemmas of Charans are the dilemmas of the values associated with music and modernity. But they also have to do with the authority of the textual and narrative tradition that gives performers a sense of hierarchy. While Charans identify themselves with song and poetry, instrumental music becomes a problem or is considered lesser. In the case of the *manariyas*, the values of music change according to the communities for whom they perform. Such music acquires a special significance when it is performed for the low-caste groups. This is not only about the liminal formation that comes with the music's ritual service, but it is also to do with the experiences of marginality that one caste group shares with other low-caste groups in demarcated spaces. Every caste has preserved its histories, genres, and embodied skills in their segregated spaces. Castes in demarcated spaces often share some common beliefs and cultural practices. *Manariyas* who come from Dalit and low-caste groups not only bring shared music and narrative of their locations but also a shared body in performance. In the case of the Chamars, mainstream society associates their music with impurity and inauspiciousness due to which performers are considered as unseeable and untouchable. The leather drum itself becomes a marker of the distinction. At the same time, a caste society tends to objectify the performing body at the instrumental level in a literal sense that marks musical unfreedom. It means it sees performers strictly in relation to caste and music. How can we interpret these three formulations? All three cases hint towards the production of social identity in relation to music. In all these three cases, musical service is involved, but the nature of the hierarchy remains different.

## Materiality of Music

What is the materiality of music in a caste society that marginalises musicians in these three contexts? Firstly, the materiality of music carries the performers' bodies, musical instruments, and the demarcated movements and rhythm. In the case of the Chamars, the drum itself becomes a metaphor for the human body and engenders its own physicality and loudness. Secondly, the music is performed by an already defiled body. Thirdly, tonality adds to this dimension. From the tonality of music, such as in the case of lament songs which generate a deep melancholic mood, one can recognise whether the music played is auspicious or inauspicious. The haunting rhythms associated with death also percolate into the defilement of musicians, as mainstream society views deaths and funerals as inauspicious. McGilvray (1983) argues that since the Chamars play the drum at funerals or to drive away evil spirits, its music is regarded as inauspicious. The materiality here lies in the object of engagement and the nature of the event. What is the object of engagement for music here? In the case of Tamil Nadu, the *parai* drum and Paraiya caste become a reference for each other. Even though not all Paraiyas play the drum, the communities are still perceived in the image of rhythm and instrument. Gorringe (2016) notes that for some Dalit activists, the sound of the *parai* reminds them of their degraded caste positions.

The formation of musical identity has also to do with sound. Loudness is another important element of materiality in music, the loudness that threatens the 'softness' and 'puritanical' taste of Brahminical music. Loudness also relates to the animality of music that is used in ritual. In this context, Ajith (2013) has argued that loud instruments are considered *asuravadyam* (demonic music) and those that sound like a soft charm are considered *devavadyam* (divine music). This suggests the erasure of certain kinds of bodily passion and sound from the dominant aesthetic regime. I have discussed these points in relation to the erasure of land(scape), bodily materiality, and viscerality in relation to the folk performances of the subaltern communities and their constant marginalisation (Prakash 2019). It is often through the performance of loudness and softness that mainstream caste society perceives music. The softness is not only about singing in certain scales and pitches, but is also about the cultivation and regulation of the body in a mode to accord with the Brahmanical aesthetic regime. It must be underlined that any scale can be sung loud or quiet. Softness is, therefore, not just about volume but also timbre, qualities such as smoothness and gentleness versus harshness and roughness. The focus of good music and institutionalised training has been on soft music in these senses. This is evident from the fact that the construction of instrumentalisation of Indian classical music has been done through the erasure of loudness and the reduction of bodily movements.

But is there a possibility to reconstitute music in a caste society with new values, outside of the notions of service and obligation? Some contemporary Dalit musicians indicate this possibility by reclaiming the body and materiality of the music. However, scholars like Gorringe (2016) question such resignification of existing humiliating caste service in a new form of art. The question arises of how marginalised communities can construct positive identities when their cultural memories and practices are inescapably associated with subordination? Thus, he questions the valorisation of *oppari* music as an art, citing several examples from Tamil Nadu in which the *parai* becomes a metaphor for stigmatisation. Gorringe is right to understand drumming as part of the genealogy of body, culture, and the possible formation of new subjectivity around musicians coming from Dalit and low-caste backgrounds. However, the transformative potentials of such music practices and their new values should not be undermined. It is often difficult to ascertain the materiality of music in direct reference to the bodies and musicality of performers.

Music in a particular society is socially located, so what counts as the values of music in a caste-based society differs from community to community; similarly, what musical behaviour is seen to say that poetic behaviour or acting behaviour does not say also differs. Why is musical behaviour such a complex issue for Charans? This lies in the particular kind of embodiment and corporeality of musical behaviour. The body is the centre of materiality and by denying the role of the body; the dominant regime of aesthetics also tries to designate certain music as low. The hierarchy of body and mind indicates how bodily movement is considered low and degraded in the regime of aesthetics. Ajith's observation (2013) is apt for understanding this problem of music.

> The textbooks on Carnatic music also say that a good musician should not make unnecessary body movements. This marks a division between the body (*Shareeram*) and the voice (*Shaareeram*). They say that voice is more

> important, and the body should not be given importance. If you look at the music reality shows on TV, there are performance rounds and melody rounds. There also there is a clear division between the body and the music.

The question of materiality can be extended to the timbre of the drum and other musical instruments. Groesbeck (2003) has argued that not enough attention has been given to timbre. Timbre in performance often creates a codified emotional state among spectators that is embodied in cultural and religious identity. Musical meaning and affect, according to him, 'were partially constituted through discourse on timbre and through the timbral aspects of performance itself' (Groesbeck 2003, p. 39). What Groesbeck terms timbral quality reveals the special power of listening. In the performance of Indian dance-drama Kathakali the left head of the drum represents demonic quality and the right head of the drum divine quality (48). This opens up the various aspects of identity and caste hegemony. It is the quality of timbre that also provides meaning and values that often become a site of contestation – the points of auspiciousness and inauspiciousness. We can say that without understanding the materiality of such music, it would be difficult to challenge the hierarchies and the low status of the performers.

## Between Freedom and Unfreedom

Scholars such as Arun (2007), Clark-Decès (2008), and Sherinian (2014, 2017) have shown how the contemporary drumming of Dalits can be different from that of the past. The music can articulate a positive Dalit identity in some cases that can be free from hierarchy. There has been a shift in the perception of folk performance and its political articulation in some cases. Dalit cultural struggles 'have deployed certain powerful modes of transvaluation in order to produce counter rejection through re-signification of what was previously stigmatized' (Guru 2009, p. 223). Singers like Gaddar, the popular balladeer from Telangana, have radically transformed the social identity of music genres and instruments. The increasing use of *dappu* and leather instruments in political protests shows how this positive assertion by Dalits and low-caste groups has become part of popular culture in the Telangana and Tamil Nadu regions. Mainly played at funerals, the mainstream caste society used to consider *dappu* (a type of hand drum) inauspicious and an untouchable's instrument but now the instrument has become a significant part of the socio-political movement in South India.

The question of the freedom and unfreedom of singers and musicians is implicated in the notion of service entrenched in the caste society. Therefore, only by severing this link can one articulate and produce new values of music. Despite its enormous creative potential, musical unfreedom remains an imminent danger through which creativity and passion embodied in the notion of service become the source of enslavement. The protest music of Dalits and Bahujans can be seen as de-service to the notion of ritual service. To give dignified values to music and singers, the marginalised community has to sever the link between music and ritual service. Although tourism industries and cultural festivals have opened up avenues for performers as part of the new creative economy, they have not necessarily left musical service. In many cases, the performers still carry the materiality of music in their behaviour and performance. The service of the caste system and the service of the neoliberal economy can go hand in hand without disturbing the link between social and caste hierarchies. Instead of feudal patronage, many performers have found corporate sponsorship but with a similar service condition. Mason (2013) cites the example of the Malayan caste of Kerala who earn a living and respect through participation in cultural tourism while they remain 'committed to the ritual responsibilities at home' (p. 447). Indeed, they gain authenticity by doing traditional service for their own communities. Cultural labour enters into the field of the creative economy, sometimes breaking but often retaining the link of a caste society.

## Conclusion

Labour in the form of service is very much part of musical production and consumption. In caste society, music is less about artistic production and more about services and obligation. It exists in the form of service to a deity, and it can also be a service to *jajmans* or patrons. It is a form of service to pay the ritual debt. And once music becomes an obligation, it also becomes an unfreedom. It may happen that as much as the communities perform and participate in such music, they produce their own enslavement. Thus, it can be argued that to drum or not to drum is not a matter of choice; it is rather a service condition of performance in which performers are placed. This service must be performed as part of the very maintenance of caste society. Music does not seem to have its independent existence outside of the service. Musical unfreedom is a problem that seeks aesthetico-political responses from performers, audiences, and academics. Performance becomes a trap, something that is inescapable while also being the only possible mode of articulation to think about freedom.

## Notes

1 *Oppari* is a traditional form of lament singing on the occasion of a death ritual in which performers use a leather drum *dappu*. The form has been recently used in Dalit cinema and political protest in Tamil Nadu and Telangana.
2 *Chamars* are considered one of the untouchable castes who work with leather and have been engaged in the occupation of tanning.

## References

Ajith, AS 2013, 'Caste in cinema and music: Kerala experience,' *Dalit Camera*, 29 June. https://roundtableindia.co.in/index.php?option=com_content&view=article&id=6705:caste-in-cinema-and-music-the-kerala-experience-part-2&catid=119:feature&Itemid=132

Arun, CJ 2007, 'From stigma to self-assertion: Paraiyars and the symbolism of the Parai drum,' *Contributions to Indian Sociology*, vol. 41, no. 1, pp. 81–104.

Brown, KB 2007, 'The social liminality of musicians: case studies from Mughal India and beyond,' *Twentieth-Century Music*, vol. 3, no. 1, pp. 13–49.

Clark-Decès, I 2008, 'The reinvention of Tamil funeral processions,' in KA Jacobsen (ed.), *South Asian religions on display*, Routledge, London, pp. 27–40.
Frith, S 1987, 'Towards an aesthetic of popular music,' in R Leppert & S McClary (eds.), *Music and society: the politics of composition, performance and reception*, Cambridge University Press, Cambridge, pp. 133–50.
Gorringe, H 2016, 'Drumming out oppression, or drumming it in? Identity, culture and contention in Dalit politics,' *Contributions to Indian Sociology*, vol. 50, no. 1, pp. 1–26.
Groesbeck, R 2003, 'Dhim, kam, cappu, pottu: timbral discourses and performances among temple drummers in Kerala, India,' *Yearbook for Traditional Music*, vol. 35, pp. 39–68.
Guru, G 2009, *Humiliation: claims and context*, Oxford University Press, New Delhi.
Hons, P 2018, 'Tamil Dalit art and identity: what to do with the drum?' *South Asia Research*, vol. 38, no. 2, pp. 140–55.
Kumar, A 2019, 'Informality in the time of platformization,' *Media Industries*, vol. 6, no. 2, pp. 117–32.
Manuel, P 2012, 'Popular music as popular expression in North India and the Bhojpuri region, from cassette culture to VCD culture,' *South Asian Popular Culture*, vol. 10, no. 3, pp. 223–236.
Mason, K 2013, 'Musicians and the politics of dignity in south India,' in PV Bohlman (ed.), *The Cambridge history of world music*, Cambridge University Press, Cambridge, pp. 441–72.
McGilvray, DB 1983, 'Paraiyar drummers of Sri Lanka: consensus and constraint in an untouchable caste,' *American Ethnologist*, vol. 10, no. 1, pp. 97–115.
Morcom, A 2013, *Illicit worlds of Indian dance: cultures of exclusion*, New York University Press, New York.
Prakash, B 2019, *Cultural labour: conceptualising the 'folk' performance in India*, Oxford University Press, New Delhi.
Qureshi, RB 2002, 'Mode of production and musical production: is Hindustani music feudal?' in RB Qureshi (ed.), *Music and Marx: ideas, practice, politics*, Routledge, London, pp. 81–105.
Randeria, S 1989, 'Carrion and corpses: conflict in categorizing untouchability in Gujarat,' *European Journal of Sociology*, vol. 30, no. 2, pp. 171–91.
Sachs, C 1962, *The wellsprings of music*, Da Capo Press, New York.
Sherinian, ZC 2014, *Tamil folk music as Dalit liberation theology*, Indiana University Press, Bloomington.
Sherinian, ZC 2017, 'Religious encounters: empowerment through Tamil outcaste folk drumming,' *Interpretation*, vol. 71, no. 1, pp. 64–79.
Soneji, D (ed.) 2012, *Unfinished gestures: devadāsīs, memory, and modernity in South India*, The University of Chicago Press, Chicago, IL.
Thompson, GR 1991, 'The Charans of Gujarat: caste identity, music, and cultural change,' *Ethnomusicology*, vol. 35, no. 3, pp. 381–91.

# 2 *Uḻaippu*

## Performance as Labour in a Tamil Theatre Tradition

*Hanne M. de Bruin*

'It's labour, hard labour.
Tying my crown really tight
to perform fast spins.
With a silver band and a strip of pearls on my forehead,
wearing ear and shoulder ornaments,
a shining breast pendant and strings of bells tied around my ankles
I perform tirelessly.
Is Kūttu art, they ask?
It's easy to speak of its shortcomings,
but only when you immerse yourself in it entirely,
will you be able to recognise its finesse.
Kūttu starts at ten at night.
It finishes when it gets light and
even then we should look fresh and focused.
Bigwigs, I tell you: It is labour, hard labour.
(Song written by P. Rajagopal for *Karnatic Kattaikkuttu*;
translated by Hanne M. de Bruin, First Edition Arts 2017)

### Art as Labour

*Kaṭṭaikkūttu* is a non-elite, rural, Tamil language-based, all-male form of total theatre that emphasises the heroic. Theatrical performances transmit aesthetic, cultural, and social information that comments upon how rural, non-Brahmanical Tamil society imagines itself.

The theatre derives its name from the fact that its principal characters, or *kaṭṭai vēṣams*, wear distinctive *kaṭṭai* ornamentation; the characteristic head, shoulder, and breast ornaments are made from the wood of the Indian Coral tree inlaid with mirrors. *Kūttu* means theatre in general and, in this case, encompasses acting, spoken word, vocal and instrumental music, and movement, as well as facial make-up, elaborate ornaments, and costumes, elements that are inseparable when producing a multimedia *Kaṭṭaikkūttu* event.

The song quoted above was written by Kaṭṭaikkūttu actor, director, playwright, and teacher Perungattur P Rajagopal. It was featured in *Karnatic Kattaikkuttu*

DOI: 10.4324/9781351031028-3

*Figure 2.1* Audience Marutam Village, Tamil Nadu; all-night performance of the Mahābhārata play *Dice and Disrobing* by the Kattaikkuttu Young Professionals Company, 2016. © Kattaikkuttu Sangam/A Sumanth Kumar.

(2017–2019), a collaborative production in which classical Karnatic concert music and folk *Kaṭṭaikkūttu* theatre met and spoke to each other on the same stage. Rajagopal, Karnatic vocalists TM Krishna and Sangeetha Sivakumar, and me, a theatre scholar and dramaturg, conceptualised *Karnatic Kattaikkuttu*. At the centre of the production, wedged between two episodes from *Kaṭṭaikkūttu*'s *Mahābhārata* repertoire was a musical conversation between Rajagopal and Krishna (Rees 2018). The conversation addressed, among other themes, the question of 'What is art?' from the perspective of a *Kaṭṭaikkūttu* performer and a Karnatic vocalist. Given the different economic, social, and cultural worlds *Kaṭṭaikkūttu* and Karnatic concert music inhabit, the answers to this question were quite different. While Krishna associated art with *ñāṉam*, or beauty and (spiritual) wisdom, Rajagopal related art to *uḻaippu*, which is hard labour, physical effort or exertion (de Bruin 2019, pp. 64–6).

Rajagopal comes from a low-caste Vaṇṇār (washerman) lineage some of whose male members were traditionally involved in the *Kaṭṭaikkūttu* theatre, while others washed laundry. For him, *uḻaippu* has both physical and social-emotional sides. *Kaṭṭaikkūttu*'s heavy *kaṭṭai* ornamentation, high-energy movement vocabulary, and open-throated singing, in combination with long, eight-hour performances, place great physical demands on the bodies of the performers.

Additionally, *Kaṭṭaikkūttu*'s epic *Mahābhārata* repertoire focuses on sacrificial battles that often result in the violent killing of one of two battle contestants and may give rise to possession-like states in performers and spectators alike (de Bruin 1999, pp. 124–42). It is the performers' job to lend their bodies and

*Figure 2.2* Duḥśāna (K. Radhakrishnan) and Draupadī (S. Tamilarasi) in *Dice and Disrobing*, Marutam Village, 2016. © Kattaikkuttu Sangam/A Sumanth Kumar.

minds to these heroic characters and recreate their violent confrontations in which *dharma* (righteousness, morally and legally right way of living) is at stake. In doing so, the performers take upon themselves the risk of becoming the potential sacrificial victims of these sacral battles if they were to fail to monitor their violent nature appropriately and their play crosses over into reality, minimising, or perhaps eliminating altogether, the fine line that distinguishes play from reality and self from character. Being of low caste makes *Kaṭṭaikkūttu* performers particularly competent to handle the danger posed by these sacral battles and the impurity of bloodshed and death to which these contexts may give rise, adding a dimension of personal vulnerability to their labour of performance.

Physical labour in India is associated with a low or no caste status and, consequently, with the handling of impurity – of real dirt and of ritual impure substances, such as blood, sweat, and faeces — as well as events of killing and death that are associated with impurity. Both physical labour and the handling of impurity are necessary to keep localised, rural caste systems and their hierarchical power structures intact. The outside world understands physical labour to be demeaning; involvement in it is a signifier of caste.[1] While it is impossible to gauge an individual's experience of what it means to be engaged in *uḻaippu*, and particularly in the labour of performing *Kaṭṭaikkūttu*, recent literature and personal accounts tell us that it involves feelings of exploitation, humiliation, and oppression, and may negatively affect the agency and self-identity of those involved.[2] As Guru and Sarukkai (2012) have pointed out, such experiences often are not recognised or verbalised by those involved in physical labour (pp. 148–9).

## The Last *Terukkūttu*

In a personal conversation, Rajagopal recalled an experience of humiliation in greater detail. It involved a *Terukkūttu* (literally 'street theatre') performance in Thenkalani in which he participated as a young child-actor of 13- or 14-years-old. Thenkalani is adjacent to Perungattur, the village where Rajagopal was born and raised. Rajagopal distinguished the practice of *Terukkūttu* from overnight *Kaṭṭaikkūttu* performances. While such overnight performances have a narrative structure, are demarcated by a well-defined performance space, and need three musicians and 10–13 actor-singers, *Terukkūttu* is mobile, has no specific narrative, and takes place during the daytime (de Bruin 1999, pp. 70–1; de Bruin 2023, pp. 37–8). The practice of *Terukkūttu* requires two actors – a male, *kaṭṭai* character and a female character – a mridangam player, and a leader or *vāttiyār* (Sanskrit, *upādhyāya*), who plays the hand cymbals. In this specific case, Rajagopal's father, C Ponnusami, headed the small *Terukkūttu* ensemble. Ponnusami was a locally famous, well-respected actor; he was also known to drink and have a short temper.

The practice of *Terukkūttu* and overnight *Kaṭṭaikkūttu* performances were part of a complex system – locally referred to as the *māmūl* system – that divided locality-specific occupational, ritual, and performance rights among the non-agrarian service and artisan castes. This system regulated interactions between the dominant landowning (cultivator) castes and the service and artisan castes to ensure the economic, social, ritual, and cultural functioning of a feudal, agrarian society. The hereditary *māmūl* rights were, at the same time, obligations that low-caste people could not refuse without upsetting this economic, social, and sacral local order (de Bruin 1999, pp. 62–3). Performing a *Terukkūttu* was a *māmūl* held by Ponnusami and others of his male, Vaṇṇār relatives.[3] The performance of a *Terukkūttu* was also a prerequisite to secure an overnight performance – the *Kaṭṭaikkūttu* proper – for the entire theatre company. The *Terukkūttu* took place on the second day of the Māriyammaṉ festival; the overnight performance on the third, and last, night of the festival. The *Terukkūttu* received no remuneration other than voluntary gifts; the overnight performance would be paid for and, consequently, was pivotal to sustaining traditional Vaṇṇār performers' precarious livelihoods.

The *Terukkūttu* ensemble preceded the processional icon of the goddess Māriyammaṉ, in this case symbolised by a pitcher or *karakam* decked with neem leaves and flowers. After the *karakam* had been decorated, the goddess was named and praised through songs (*varṇittal*) and lifted on the head of the bearer – three traditional tasks of the Vaṇṇār community in Perungattur – her procession would proceed through the streets of the caste village, halting in front of each house to allow the inhabitants to carry out an offering of light as well as of food items to the deity. Thereafter, the two *Terukkūttu* actors would dance in a small circle, circling around each other. They would sing songs specific to the *Terukkūttu* custom and perform well-known duets (*tarkkams*) between a male and female character from the overnight *Kaṭṭaikkūttu* repertoire, for instance between Karṇa and his wife Poṉṉuruvi (de Bruin 1999, pp. 63–70; de Bruin & Rajagopal 2001). On the occasion of the *Terukkūttu* led by Ponnusami Vāttiyār, Mani Gounder (pseudonym) was the headman (*periya kirāmaṇi*) of Thenkalani. After the *karakam* procession had come to a halt in front of his house for the customary light offer and after the two *Terukkūttu* actors had performed as usual, Mani Gounder gave Ponnusami 10 *paisa* (the equivalent of INR 5–7 today). Ponnusami felt this ridiculously small amount of money to be an afront to his honour (*mariyātai*) and to the group's labour. Enraged, he instructed his performers to discontinue the performance and told his son Rajagopal that this was the last *Terukkūttu* in which he would ever participate.

Without the *Terukkūttu*, the procession could not proceed – a situation considered potentially inauspicious for the village and its inhabitants. The *karakam* was offloaded from the head of the Vaṇṇār officiant and temporarily placed on a heap of rice on a wooden bench. Neighbouring Perungattur, acting on a complaint from Thenkalani and upset that their *vāttiyār* had been insulted, called for a *panchayat* involving several other villages. The *panchayat* concluded that even though Ponnusami Vattiyar was obliged to perform the *Terukkūttu* because he had accepted a *tāmpūlam*,[4] Mani Gounder had humiliated him and his name as an eminent actor by not properly endorsing his efforts with a more generous gift as he should have done in his position of headman of Thenkalani. Ponnusami stubbornly persisted in not performing, but finally relented by promising that he would lend local amateurs a set of *kaṭṭai* ornamentation and a male and female costume so that they could perform the *Terukkūttu* themselves. His refusal highlights that the relationship between low-caste performers and their higher-caste patrons was an interdependent, though unequal, one.

## Stigma

Listening in to performers' informal conversations, it seems that they have internalised the idea that *Kaṭṭaikkūttu* demands physical labour that is part of the theatre's aesthetics. Performers often take pride in the fact that an overnight performance would extend well beyond its conventional concluding time of around 6 a.m. While their boasting might be a way of coping with a reality of subservience, it also involves genuine pride in pleasing their local audiences through their art. This is not to say that performers deny the negative effects of *uḻaippu* and exhaustion on their bodily and mental constitution. Night-long performances deprive them of sufficient sleep; acting out violent deeds of combat and killing under the eyes of the goddess, who herself is thought to be in a heated state, cause 'overheating' of the body that actor-singers redress through dietary restrictions and oil baths. On the side of the patrons there also exists an expectation that performers exert themselves physically in order to receive gifts and make a (precarious) living, but even more so because it is their duty. Obligatory physical labour constituted part of *Kaṭṭaikkūttu's* profound and internalised stigma and the complex ways of managing what Erving Goffman (1963) called a 'spoiled identity.' Not only does *uḻaippu* mark performers as being of low or no caste, *Kaṭṭaikkūttu*'s stigma also sets rural performers apart as a group whose physical, cultural, and moral values do not conform to the dominant values of society. As elsewhere in the world, the general audience looks at actors, in this case *Kaṭṭaikkūttu* actors, with some suspicion, supposedly because they drink, disregard social rules, have illicit relationships, and are feared for using black magic (de Bruin 1999, p. 128).

*Kaṭṭaikkūttu*'s multifaceted stigma is reflected in the fact that most hereditary performers, including Rajagopal's own father, discouraged their sons from following in their footsteps to become professional performers. Today, abhorrence of physical exertion as an indicator of caste motivates some of Rajagopal's talented, young male students, who are educated and performed at a professional level when they were training under him, to opt for white-collar jobs rather than a career in the theatre (de Bruin 2023, p. 131). In 2002, Rajagopal and I established the Kattaikkuttu Gurukulam, a residential school offering rural children *Kaṭṭaikkūttu* training in combination with formal education and comprehensive care.[5] As the result of Rajagopal's advocacy and the fact that the Gurukulam offered a safe training space, *Kaṭṭaikkūttu* has opened to all genders. Rajagopal's students, thus, include a number of talented girls and young women. He taught them to perform female characters and *Kaṭṭaikkūttu's* typical male, *kaṭṭai* roles – therewith shattering the belief that women would not be able to do these physically demanding roles.

The introduction of young women into the profession was, and is, not a simple process and has social consequences for all involved. Very few female students have had the courage and drive on to go become professionals.

By going against the grain in a modern society that has deeply and systematically stigmatised professional women performers, they risk cutting off the all-important

*Figure 2.3* Draupadī (S. Tamilarasi) demands to know what happened during the game of dice; collaborative production Karnatic Kattaikkuttu, 2018 Festival of the Kattaikkuttu Sangam, Punjarasantankal. © Kattaikkuttu Sangam/PeeVee.

prospect of marriage that seals a woman's status as a 'good' woman. In contrast to high(er) caste and class women involved in classical performing art forms, female *Kaṭṭaikkūttu* performers face a double stigma: as actresses in a rural theatre that is looked down upon and as women who expose their bodies and sexuality in public, therewith defying the rules of propriety and bringing shame upon their families (e.g., Morcom 2017, p. 3).[6]

**Aesthetics**

Members of the urban arts establishment look down upon *Kaṭṭaikkūttu* and its performers. In their eyes, *Kaṭṭaikkūttu* does not have much to offer in terms of aesthetic satisfaction or meaningful value, while its low-caste, formally uneducated performers are felt to lack artistic literacy (de Bruin 2019, p. 55). The feudal context from which *Kaṭṭaikkūttu* emerged, in combination with the conditions of economic and social precarity under which hereditary performers operated, has shaped the theatre's aesthetics. Their low position within a rural caste-based hierarchy made it necessary for performers to attune their performances to the expectations of their principal patrons and spectators. This imbued *Kaṭṭaikkūttu* with an inherent flexibility that is reflected in the unwritten practitioners' rule that every performance should be *kirāmattiṉ iṣṭam*, which is 'according to the wish of the village' (de Bruin 1999, pp. 56–7; de Bruin 2023, pp. 39–40). Well-trained performers realise this flexibility by dexterously fitting many multimedia building blocks into a relatively fixed framework underlying each overnight performance (de Bruin 1999, pp. 223–67). In doing so the performers assemble unscripted, eight-hour-long, live events and fine-tune them to the demands and expectations of their patrons and audiences in and through the medium of performance (de Bruin 2023, chapter 2).

People who are unfamiliar with the form and those who are used to the codified aesthetics of, for instance, Karnatic music or Bharata Natyam, may perceive *Kaṭṭaikkūttu's* inherent flexibility as messy or a form of bricolage. Indeed, the performing body and voice of a *Kaṭṭaikkūttu* actor-singer are disciplined in ways that are quite different from those of a Bharata Natyam dancer or Karnatic vocalist. Over the last 200 years, these two art forms have been codified, institutionalised, technologised, 'purified,' and politicised. Exponents of these classical forms have adopted systematised training processes that deliver similarly trained bodies, visuals, voices and soundscapes that have come to define these forms as classical.[7] In contrast, the training of a *Kaṭṭaikkūttu* novice happens in a much more organic and individualised way; it is often non-verbal and non-analytical, takes place on stage, and the initiative is left to a young performer, rather than the guru, to work his way up by taking over the performance of principal roles from established actors senior to him.[8]

**Discourse of Contempt**

The stigma of the popular Tamil stage is reflected in a discourse of contempt that pervades local academic writing and the media from the end of the nineteenth century to the present (de Bruin 2023, pp. 8–10). Embracing Western, colonial ideas of what is legitimate theatre, Tamil theatre historians have blamed the deterioration of the Tamil stage on the lack of education and artistic integrity of its village-based actors without considering their economic and social circumstances. Highlighting the corporeality and viscerality of the low-caste performers, A.N. Perumal describes these actors in demeaning terms as 'shouting, hooting, hopping and leaping' (Perumal 1981, pp. 138–9). A Government of India publication plainly states that Tamil drama in the nineteenth century was something to be 'looked down upon for its lack of any intrinsic value' and goes on to question the integrity and morality of the performers (Gopalratnam 1981[1956], pp. 119–20). In their condemnation of the popular stage, academics, the arts establishment, and members of an emerging urban middle-class appear to have been pursuing a political agenda. They juxtaposed what they felt was a deteriorated popular theatre to a modern, or contemporary, bourgeois Tamil theatre that they themselves were in the process of creating. Anita Cherian has argued that the arts establishment fetishised the folk to represent the indigenous and the authentic as part of the newly constructed cultural identity of the young nation-state. According to the author, the folk was denied the ability to be modern or to modernise, because it had to remain authentic and static (Cherian 2007, pp. 29–30).

Against the background of the division between rural folk theatres and urban modern theatre, the difference between amateur and professional performers took on a new meaning (Dharwadker 2008, p. 43).[9] Members of an urban theatre elite that began to emerge during the late nineteenth and first decades of the twentieth century proudly referred to themselves as amateurs. This elite looked down upon professional performers who were engaged in the labour of performance to make a living. In contrast, amateur performers, many of whom were lawyers, businessmen, and government officials with sources of income elsewhere, pursued their passion in theatre during their leisure time and for art's sake only (de Bruin 2006, p. 87 and fn 11).

## Transition towards an Informal Performance Market

Rajagopal's memory of his last *Terukkūttu* in the 1960s coincides with the theatre's further dissociation from its organic embedding in the economic, social, and ritual *māmūl* system and, ultimately, its development into an autonomous genre. This process had far-reaching effects on the form and the practitioners: Earlier hereditary *Kaṭṭaikkūttu* performances were paid in kind (usually in the form of rice) by the village where they had *māmūl* rights to perform. Today, patrons commission a theatre company of their preference and pay them a lump sum in cash, which the performers then divide among themselves. Negotiations between performers and patrons about the price and quality of performances have encouraged greater competition among *Kaṭṭaikkūttu* companies. In addition, *Kaṭṭaikkūttu* performers also faced competition from the Drama or *Nāṭakam*, another popular theatre in the region. Whereas the boundaries between these two forms of theatre used to be fluid, *Kaṭṭaikkūttu* performers now began to emphasise the heroic nature of their performances to distinguish them from Drama performances. In addition, *Kaṭṭaikkūttu* performers appear to have monopolised festivals for the Goddess Draupadi to feature *Kaṭṭaikkūttu's* elaborate *Mahābhārata* repertoire. While *Kaṭṭaikkūttu* and Drama earlier appear to have shared performance elements, practices, repertoires, and performers, the boundaries became more sharply delineated, resulting in the development of two distinct genres (de Bruin 2023, pp. 41–7). Finally, *Kaṭṭaikkūttu* as a profession opened up to people for whom being a performer was a choice and not a caste-based obligation. These performers are largely drawn from the two largest caste groups in the region, Vaṉṉiyars and Dalits (or Scheduled Castes), whose members today dominate the field (de Bruin 1999, pp. 143–54).

## Advance

With the monetisation and commercialisation of the rural stage, intermediaries, called agents, made their entry, and with them, an advance system of providing loans, often against exorbitant interest rates, to performers. Agents broker the commissioning of performances, especially those of new or below-grade theatre companies that have not yet built their own clientele network. However, well-known companies refuse to use the services of these agents as they believe this to be below their dignity. These companies expect potential sponsors to approach them to commission a performance, and this is what continues to happen (de Bruin 2023, pp. 48–50).

*Kaṭṭaikkūttu* performers borrowed the practice of advance from the Drama genre, which, in turn, had copied it from the commercial Parsi theatre. Initially, owners-cum-actors would lend a small amount to co-performers in order to keep them in the company and help them bridge the lean season. However, with high returns on a high-risk, informal investment that does not require paperwork, *Kaṭṭaikkūttu* soon attracted financers from outside the profession. Since the 1980s, the practice of advance has become so widespread that today hardly any performer is not indebted to a financer. The amounts of advance have increased considerably and are often seen as representing the worth of a performer. The intricacy of this informal financial system speaks to the fact that financers are not interested in recovering the principal amount they originally invested. Instead, the advance system drives up the number of performances, allowing financers to recover the principal during or soon after a performer completes his first season with a particular company; thereafter, all additional interest recovered by the financer(s) is profit.[10] By not repaying, or not being able to repay, the principal amount, many performers knowingly have become bonded labourers. Their indebtedness prevents these performers from switching companies at the end of a season, as used to be the practice (de Bruin 2020, p. 8). This situation inhibits the circulation of artistic knowledge and skills within the profession, which is showing an impact on the quality of today's performances.

## Field of the Performing Arts

As active stakeholders and competitors, rural *Kaṭṭaikkūttu* performers try to maximise their share of the limited material and symbolic power generated by the field. In addition to vying for the favours of rural audiences, *Kaṭṭaikkūttu* performers compete for urban patronage, including from the government. The performers hope that this patronage can help them secure non-traditional performance opportunities at cultural festivals, engagements in which their dramatic medium is used to spread a particular message, pensions, and awards. Hereto, the performers need to actively negotiate access to the relevant power-structures. Bridging the rural-urban gap, representatives of *Kaṭṭaikkūttu* companies and individuals – company owners, principal actors, and financers – have lobbied bureaucratic and private institutions. Contemporary playwrights and theatre makers in turn have used *Kaṭṭaikkūttu*'s vocabulary and repertory to create new forms of urban theatre (Dharwadker 2008, pp. 318–51). In addition, political parties have used performers to promote their political interests.[11]

Furthermore, performers have set up their own organisations and organised their own cultural festivals. One of these organisations is the Kattaikkuttu Sangam near Kanchipuram. Founded in 1990 by Rajagopal together with 15 actors, musicians, and myself, the Kattaikkuttu Sangam is a not-for-profit initiative that aims to uphold the prestige and quality of *Kaṭṭaikkūttu*. As a democratically representative body, the Sangam unites professional performers across company boundaries and regional styles. Membership of the Sangam is on an individual basis. While some performers decided to become a member, others did not. On the occasion of its establishment, the performer-founders asserted the right to name the theatre on their own terms as *Kaṭṭaikkūttu* instead of *Terukkūttu*. The founders believed that this name was more appropriate as it identified the theatre by its visibly distinctive characteristic – the *kaṭṭai* ornamentation – and because they felt that this name carried greater dignity. Many performers have started referring to their profession as *Kaṭṭaikkūttu*, while rural spectators appear to have accepted the name unquestioningly. However, during a workshop organised by the Sangam in 1993, the name of the theatre became a topic of contestation between the Sangam and invited urban theatre workers and intellectuals some of whom felt that tradition should not be tinkered with, especially not by a foreign scholar, such as myself. This led to a split between those preferring to call their performances *Kaṭṭaikkūttu* and others, adhering to the name *Terukkūttu*, to refer to what are in fact the same narrative all-night performances in which the principal, male actor-singers wear *kaṭṭai* ornamentation. The debate reflects the dynamics of the Tamil field of the performing arts and the conflicting forces and vested interests at work within this competitive arena. Regarding the underlying linguistic problem of naming the theatre, there are other issues at stake. These issues concern the question of who can claim to be the theatre's legitimate representatives and who will ultimately decide on its form and content.[12]

## Conclusion

Even though *Kaṭṭaikkūttu* has moved out of a feudal system where performance was both a right and an obligation, *u̲laippu* remains very much part of the profession. However, its obligatory nature, which constituted its most demeaning aspect, has been renegotiated and has given performers greater agency, bargaining power, and an improved financial security. The fact that becoming a performer now is a personal choice represents a new kind of freedom. With the entry of *Kaṭṭaikkūttu* into a capitalist performance market, this freedom is being corroded by a new form of subservience represented by performers' indebtedness to financers with negative consequences for the quality of performances.

## Notes

1 For the intimate connection between livelihoods that are deemed unworthy because they require physical labour or identify a person as belonging to an oppressed caste, see Aparna Karthikeyan's introduction to her book on disappearing livelihoods in Tamil Nadu (Karthikeyan 2019).

2 Some of these experiences have found their way into regional language poetry and literature, making them (in an English translation) accessible to a wider audience (e.g., Sathyanarayana & Tharu 2011).

3 It is unclear if the practice of Terukkūttu was confined to members of the Vaṇṇār caste only. Paṇṭārams, one of the other castes whose members have been involved in Kaṭṭaikkūttu as hereditary artistes, were unfamiliar with the practice (de Bruin 1999, p. 70).

4 A *tāmpūlam*, consisting of betel leaves and areca nuts, is traditionally exchanged to seal an agreement or accompany a gift.

5 The Gurukulam had to close its doors in March 2020 because of the COVID-19 pandemic.

6 Susan Seizer analyses the strategies women artists use to cope with the stigma attached to their profession and their persona in a ground-breaking monograph on the Special Drama genre (Seizer 2005). In a co-edited volume, I have looked at the position of women performers in other Indian performance traditions (de Bruin 2011).

7 Invoking Diana Taylor's distinction between the archive and the repertoire, Shruti Gosh argues that the trained bodies of classical dancers can be treated as an archive that represents and preserves the dance tradition (Gosh 2018, p. 67). In the absence of systematised training, this observation does not work for *Kaṭṭaikkūttu*. Instead of a fixed archive, I have conceptualised *Kaṭṭaikkūttu*'s knowledge and know-how, which emphasises flexibility rather than fixity, as an oral reservoir or repertoire. The oral reservoir is located in the body-minds of the performers, who activate this knowledge in and through performance (de Bruin 1999, pp. 163–5).

8 For a description of the training process of a *Kaṭṭaikkūttu* actor-singer, see de Bruin (2020).

9 According to Brahma Prakash, culture acquired a new connotation with the rise of a bourgeois aesthetics as being something superior; something antagonistic to acts of labour (Prakash 2019, p. 17). The opposition of amateur and professional involvement in the arts seems to reflect a similar idea of culture as a transcendental experience that supposedly is no longer dependent on the body and on corporeal, physical work or *uḻaippu*.

10 I researched *Kaṭṭaikkūttu*'s advance system in 2007 in order to evaluate if microfinancing would be a better opportunity to financially support theatre companies.

11 See the Facebook picture showing *Kattaikkuttu* performers, including the late N. Ramalingam, in front of a BJP poster: https://www.facebook.com/photo.php?fbid=781847065215311&set=pcb.781848461881838&type=1&theater (accessed on 28 December 2020).

12 A detailed discussion of the naming debate can be found in de Bruin (2000).

## References

Cherian, A 2007, 'Imagining a national theatre: the first drama seminar report,' *Sangeet Natak*, vol. 16, no. 2, pp. 15–49.

de Bruin, HM 1999, *Kaṭṭaikkūttu: the flexibility of a South Indian theatre tradition*, Egbert Forsten, Groningen.

de Bruin, HM 2000, 'Naming a theatre in Tamil Nadu,' *Asian Theatre Journal*, vol. 17, no. 1 (Spring 2000), pp. 98–122.
de Bruin, HM 2006, 'Kaṭṭaikkūttu,' *Kalakshetra Journal*, vol. 4, pp. 73–104.
de Bruin, HM 2011, 'Contextualising women and performance in India: an introductory essay,' in H Brückner, HM de Bruin & H Moser (eds.), *Between shame and fame: performing women & women performers in India*, Harrasowitz Verlag, Wiesbaden, pp. 11–35.
de Bruin, HM 2019, 'Karnatic meets Kattaikkuttu: notes on an unusual cultural conversation,' *The Drama Review*, vol. 63, no. 3 (T243), pp. 50–73.
de Bruin, HM 2020, 'Becoming a Kattaikkuttu performer,' in PM Sarangapani & R Pappu (eds.), *Handbook of education systems in South Asia*, Global Education Systems in South Asia, Springer, Singapore, pp. 1–16.
de Bruin, HM 2023, *Kaṭṭaikkūttu: a rural theatre tradition in South India*, Methuen Drama Series edited by S Shepard, Bloomsbury, London.
de Bruin, HM & Rajagopal P 2001, *In their own words: the unheard history of the rural Tamil stage as told by four of its professional exponents* [Video documentation], International Institute for Asian Studies, Leiden.
Dharwadker, AB 2008, *Theatres of independence: drama, theory, and urban performance in India since 1947*, Oxford University Press, New York and Oxford.
First Edition Arts (FEA) 2017, Program book, *TM Krishna—Karnatic Modern II. Karnatic Meets Kattaikkuttu: a cultural conversation*, First Edition Arts, Mumbai.
Goffman, E 1963, *Stigma: notes on the management of spoiled identity*, Prentice-Hall, Englewood Cliffs, NJ.
Gopalratnam, VC 1956[1981], 'Tamil drama,' in *Indian drama*, Ministry of Information and Broadcasting, New Delhi, pp. 119–26.
Gosh, S 2018, 'I know it and I name it as I do it,' in P Chakravorthy & N Gupta (eds.), *Dance matters too: markets, memories, identities*, Routledge, London and New York, pp. 66–77.
Guru, G & Sarukkai, S 2012, *The cracked mirror: an Indian debate on experience and theory*, Oxford University Press, New Delhi.
Karthikeyan, A 2019, *Nine rupees an hour: disappearing livelihoods of Tamil Nadu*, Context, Chennai.
Morcom, A 2017, 'The cure is worse than the disease: Mumbai dance bars, and new forms of justice in the history of female public performers in India,' *Cultural and Social History*, vol. 14, no. 4, pp. 499–512.
Perumal, AN 1981, *Tamil drama: origin and development*, International Institute of Tamil Studies, Madras.
Prakash, B 2019, *Cultural labour: conceptualizing the 'folk performance' in India*, Oxford University Press, New Delhi.
Rees, S 2018, 'Conversation between T.M. Krishna and P. Rajagopal as part of *Karnatic Kattaikkuttu*,' Serendipity Arts Festival, Goa, 20 December 2018. https://youtu.be/m0niP6sxerQ
Sathyanarayana, K & Tharu, S, 2011, *No alphabet in sight: new Dalit writing from South India*, Penguin Books, New Delhi.
Seizer, S 2005, *Stigmas of the Tamil stage: an ethnography of special drama artists in South India,* Duke University Press Durham, NC.

# 3 Narratives of Craft and Power in Sindh, Pakistan

*Seher Mirza*

This chapter discusses notions of power and how we perceive empowerment in craft economic development. It highlights how power is interlinked with identity and culture that generate meaning in our lives leading to learning and transformation. This builds on my PhD work, *Threads of the* Indus (Mirza 2020), which is based on a hybrid project I set up in 2010 in Sindh, Pakistan which included a business initiative – Sjo.[1] This was intended to address the socioeconomic development challenges through design interventions. The research involved extensive fieldwork in Khairpur, Pakistan, with a village community of traditional women artisans who practice different textile crafts and specialise in needlework embroidery as part of their thriving material culture. In this chapter, I protect the identity of this community by referring to them as 'the women' or 'artisanal women' or by the initials AGJ, which is a practice identifier. In the project, I relied on a phenomenological approach that allowed for a deep understanding of the complex layers of relations between people and their making practices as well as the objects they make, looking at embodied knowledge of 'lived experience' (Merleau-Ponty 1962[1945]) or the 'habitus' (Bourdieu 1990) of craftswomen. The aim of the research was to improve power relations for marginalised rural women artisans by triggering agency. As a Pakistani woman, design practitioner, researcher, and facilitator, my project also involved shared practices of making. I reflect on how I used my own lived experiences of craft practice, including my training as a weaver, to mediate and collaborate with the women's embroidery, and to explore new meaning and mutual learning through this encounter (Figure 3.1).

## Textiles as Memory in My Childhood

One of the drivers of the phenomenological epistemology of my research is my relationship with textiles. Engaging in my own making, as well as that of the craftswomen, enabled an exchange of ideas that informed my thinking as well as methodology. This created positive memories and relationships for me and the women with whom I worked.

My first conscious interaction with textiles, as distinct from clothing, was my first sewing lesson with my *dadi ama* (grandmother), both hand and machine, at ten years old. In the house we shared, textiles covered everything, far more than

DOI: 10.4324/9781351031028-4

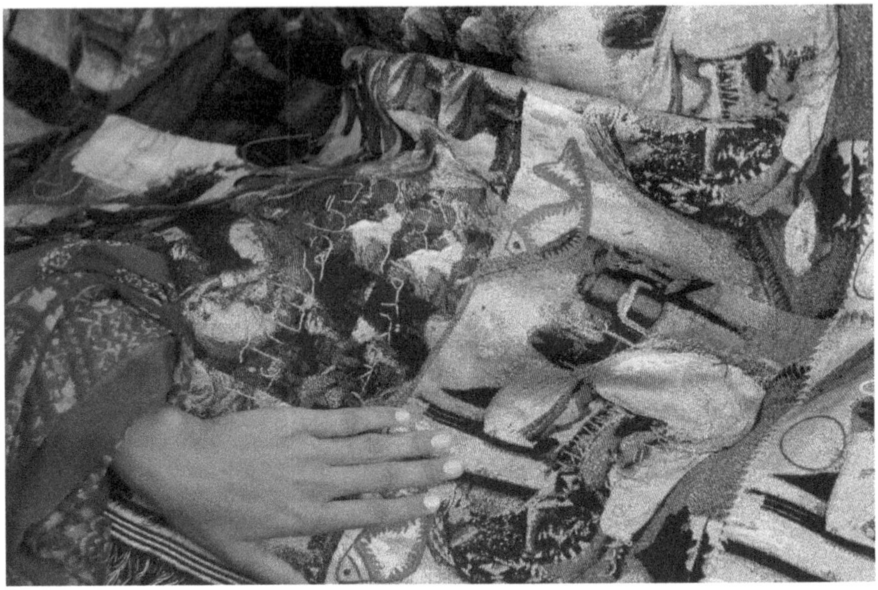

*Figure 3.1* Collaborative textile titled 'transformation' (Jacquard weave and stitch) from the 'Textile dialogue series' on power, author's PhD project. Photograph by author (2015).

in any of my friends' houses.[2] In one of our projects, my grandmother and I sewed decorative cloths to cover the metal bottom of the different-sized compartments of her *paan daan*, the box which stores betel nut and other things used to make *paan*, particular to the Indian subcontinent.[3] She changed these cloths regularly, while a damp cloth was used to keep the betel leaves fresh. As I grew older, my grandmother gave her grandchildren traditional clothing for special occasions that she often embroidered and that always carried a sweet cardamom smell that I associate with her. When I hold or wear a garment worn by my grandmother, it is always more special and cherished, perhaps enlivened by the smell, or touch, or sound that it makes, but most definitely due to the memory it evokes of another place and time. As a child, I did not realise my senses were constantly being bombarded by the sight, smell, and touch of textiles that occupied many spaces at home such as the *paan daan* cloths, tablecloths, sideboard coverings, wall hangings, and crocheted water glass covers weighed down with beads. There were all sorts of connections and relationships that textiles created around me, with me, with us as a family. My history with textiles and this very specific developmental aspect is thus embedded in my habitus, forming part of my syntax, language, and lexicon (Bourdieu 1984).

Interactions and activities like those between my grandmother and me make people's relationships stronger (Hyde 2012[1983]; Tilley 2006). Reflecting on the memories we had together and the things we shared, what stuck out to me, and was special to us was the time we spent sewing, as well as our conversations about textiles and sewing. It was our space that we shared through textiles and our love of making. I wanted to explore this memory of togetherness through the experience of craft activity in the work with artisanal women. There is a vast body of knowledge that connects memory to tactile practices at a young age (Millar 2012; Ricoeur 2004, p. 99; Jones & Stallybrass 2000). Marked by its everyday use and impregnated with the sweat and stains of everyday life, material cultures offer an understanding of how people make sense of the world through physical objects and material practices.

The research process that I undertook was influenced by these lived experiences of everyday interactions, engagement, and the immersive aspects of textiles that surround us. The research methods for my fieldwork were informed and shaped by this embodied understanding of textile practices of making, mending, and remembering collectively. These methods allowed me to explore my relationship with textiles. This practical crafting-based approach also helps define how practices of making inform, influence, and enhance agency. Here, I understand agency as the potential of making as a means of enacting embodied knowledge for exploring difference and self-recognition, for allowing a range of voices and opinions to be heard, and enabling socioeconomic transformations that begin with the self.

## Generating Meaning in Craft Encounters: Deconstructing Subtle Power

The values for making and the forms of creativity used in my research practice are derived from the experiences of those present within it as participants – craft makers at AGJ and also the researcher-maker-participant. In the context of craft, my phenomenological epistemology includes reflection on the perceptions of the practice of making by both the participants and myself as the researcher. The starting point was to consider how a bond between participants could be achieved through their crafts, as well as what makes a textile special and highly valued as something human and emotional in addition to having transactional value. To develop this method, I began by observing and reflecting on my own embodied experiences of textiles, craft, and making, creating space for participants to understand how the nature of human and material connections is subjective and affects human development (Bronfenbrenner 1979; Merleau-Ponty 1962[1945]; Tilley 2006).

The participants spoke about their use of embroidery for the making of household textiles and their traditional attire called *gajj*,[4] which they refer to as their *pehchaan* (material and cultural identity). These are intricate, heavily embroidered, multicoloured textiles that are handmade by the women in Sindh. These embroidered textiles are identity markers of the women of this community and are usually made for use within the domestic space, and for exchange as gifts within the family. This is something they hold in common with other women makers in developing countries who also use embroidery to display and define their identity. The *gajj* that a woman makes or wears is usually not available for sale. The *gajj* delineates the community's journey as originally Balouch and now settled in Sindh for the last few generations. The overall pattern of the *gajj* draws on the *pashk* of Balouchistan; here the stitches used to fill the design pattern have evolved over generations to a mix of Indigenous Sindhi and Balouchi embroidery styles. Although South Asian embroidery styles correspond to the region (Frater 1993), migratory influences are visible through similarities in styles of embroidery between Sindh and Balouchistan, and between Sindh and Kutch and Rajasthan in India. These spaces that lie in between geographies, ethnicities, and religions are merged through textile embroidery practices, which create their own hybrid aesthetic identities. These women live within rural remote villages of Sindh, distant from the rapid developments that surround larger urban metropolises.

The importance of power in the context of lived experience and habitus is seen as 'a cultural and symbolic creation' that is constantly reaffirmed through the subtle interplay of agency and structure that shapes our behaviour (Pettit 2020, p. 73). This behaviour is internalised in a subconscious and embodied way to generate and replicate structures in society. For communities with a strong material culture legacy, their traditional craft is one such cultural and symbolic creation. The making of traditional textiles in Sindh represents forms of identity, local knowledge, familiarity, belonging, memory, and emotion. It is impacted by years of interaction of the community, within local governance structures, and external development actors.

Rural communities, especially of women, struggle to access state resources on their own merits and instead rely solely on systems of power and patronage (Weiss & Khattak 2013). Thriving feudal landowner hierarchies ensure that the marginalised social position of communities such as the women of AGJ remains unchanged, while local education systems that could aid rural development and social change are fraught with problems (Agha et al. 2018; Lall 2011; Rahman 2012). This is commonly visible across large swathes of South Asia and other developing nations and in part informs sustainable development goals 1 and 5 (poverty and gender).

During fieldwork, I noted that local philanthropists, NGOs, and government's view craft practice as a means of generating income for women in rural areas and for this reason build craft development and women's empowerment programmes. However, these initiatives are, oftentimes, seen to replicate hierarchies and perpetuate inequities between rural craftswomen, markets, and design innovation. This manifests in a variety of subtle yet significant ways and is culturally ingrained through socially conditioned behaviours that respond to perceived authority and domination. This was seen during a workshop I conducted with the AGJ crafts group in which a local non-governmental organisation visited. The workshop's seating arrangement was reorganised by mid-level staff in anticipation of an executive's short visit and the women were told to sit on the floor. This was done without any consultation with me as the workshop facilitator, whilst the executive stayed only for 20 minutes without sitting down at all. This physical lowering of position is significant because of the posturing of power. In other contexts where authority might be present the women might automatically sit on the floor, whilst those perceived with authority sit higher up on wooden/jute beds *charpois*. This inequality of status in terms of gender and rural context is so deeply ingrained that it is seen as tradition and not indicative of power inequalities. Such inequalities are evident throughout design-driven interventions that are used to empower and develop craft making. Often these inequalities are visible in the subjugation of village communities through interventions that make them reliant on others for changes in their lives, with highly skilled craft communities subjected to being seen as labour without creative independence. Designers from urban cities, educated and qualified, are introduced to craftswomen, who are then asked to work on the creations of the designers, to be sold outside their rural locations. This creates a disconnect among knowledge, crafts making, trade, and value when traditional artisans are repeatedly subjected to outside designer interventions in which craft making is reduced to just skilled labour.

Designers often introduce products that have no local provenance to be replicated in exact specifications by craft communities (Cohen 1989). During my work in Sindh, I observed designers providing foreign and unfamiliar design briefs that required only the technical skills of artisanal makers. One example was a designer working remotely who gave the AGJ women specific instructions for technical construction and measurement for cathedral patchwork for a cocktail dress. This design bore no resemblance to the women's own patchwork or applique quilts. Cohen (1989) terms this 'encroaching commercialization,' in which a commercial business with economic motives utilises and exploits abundant local skills for the 'hand-made' production of standardised products that have little if anything to do with vital native material culture (p. 163). The idea may be alien to the craftspeople involved, and require standardisation and mass production from a hand-crafting culture. This disregards the social tenets that keep these communities together. In AGJ, making quilts for the bridal trousseau is a community activity charged with meaning. Making everyday patchwork quilts provides a constructive activity for older members to still contribute to their community. However, these skills and practices are often viewed by designers external to the context as sources of income and profit making only. This often results in separating the meaning of the making from its external monetary value. These physical and symbolic experiences leave a mark through actions and inactions that contribute to narratives of power and agency in local communities. This has a largely negative impact over a longer period of interaction on the community and their skills. The removal of meaning, value, and a human connection to making, strips this down only to exchange value in financial terms. These external design interventions cause damage and should be reconsidered when engaging with craft-making communities.

## The Values for Making and Forms of Creativity

At the start of my study, young women of AGJ appeared to emulate urban fashion in their clothing instead of wearing their traditional *gajj* styles of dress. There was limited use of traditional stitches and techniques in their own attire as compared to the older generation who predominately wore the *gajj.* Over time, I realised that mainly married women wore the *gajj* and unmarried younger ones did not. However, seeing some of the younger women marry revealed that the new generation was wearing the *gajj* less as compared to the older generation, and were therefore not making use of their skills or techniques in their clothing. The choice being made by younger women for their personal attire indicates a wider shift at play, an imperceptible shift that exchanges tradition and heritage in favour of the contemporary and modern for a range of reasons, not least access to information and images through technology. These preferences for different, modern, non-traditional clothing by the women of Sindh are in line with theories of fashion, dress, and body and their complex relationship with youth around the world, across centuries.

In my previous field trips for an NGO, I found pieces that reflect personal relationships, such as trousseau pieces for young brides made by the mother and family, often demonstrating high quality of workmanship and detail. Such pieces are not intended for commercial purposes and no monetary gain is anticipated, but makers lavish their attention on them and invest their efforts in making outstanding pieces which remain in the family for generations. The associative emotional value of these textiles seemingly gives them meaning both for the maker and for the receiver.

Values such as creative freedom, emotional connection, embodied experience, and associated memory all generate meaning, reinforcing the importance of forming meaningful, equitable, and reciprocal relationship spaces between artisanal women and facilitators like myself for making together. These multiple meanings prove to be more engaging for young women, and for the quality of the relationship with their identity, dress, and practice. This can be seen as the first stage of meaning between the maker and the object; when this intimate relationship and its value to the maker are communicated to people outside of the community who buy these embroidered textiles, it adds another layer of meaning for them too contributing to the value of the piece. This is described particularly eloquently by Frater (2002): 'embroidery is a personal expression of community, subcommunity and status within the community' (p. 158).

## Material Culture and Identity

The AGJ women describe their craft (practice) as giving them two forms of identity: an established identity that refers to identity in their material culture, as in their traditional clothing; and an emerging identity that they employ for purposes other than their own personal clothes, that bears their mark of making, representing them as the maker. When I enquired about how the women felt about their practice, they predominantly described their work, their craft, as *humari pehchaan hai* or 'as their [representative] identity.' Over the years of engagement, this led to questions about the shaping of this distinct idea of identity, what triggered it, and how it contributes to self-definitions and othering of objects made using Sindhi skills, for people outside the community. I recognised here the interplay of value and practice across intersectional identity lenses of women from the community. Somewhat differently aware, travelled, more literate younger women had shown a lack of engagement with the making of the *Gajj* and therein lies the dynamic nature of material culture and identity.

These craftswomen have a complex relationship with their craft that is evident when they trade in hand-embroidered textiles. The women wear their *gajj* every day as a marker of their identity. Three women recounted their experience of selling Sindhi embroideries in India at a fair, where they were asked to sell their own personal outfits that they wore on the day. They did have a change of clothes and could have parted with the *gajj* but chose not to. Marvi, Ghulam Zohra, and Naz described their responses to others wanting to buy their traditional outfits in India,

> [T]hey loved our *gajj* so much they asked to buy them but we said we don't have any to sell, so they asked us, just give us the ones you are wearing, and we said no, we cannot. We had other [changes of] clothes but we did not want to sell our *gajj*.
>
> (Mirza 2020)

These women did not see their personal *gajj* as a commodity for sale, and felt attached to the *gajj* they had made for themselves. This is indicative of the *gajj* being associated with emotion and their identity, and, in this case, therefore considered more important than earning an income as a transactional object. Martin (2016), co-founder of IDEO, provides insight into western development ideology in such a context, stating, 'we mistakenly assume that there's no way a person can or should possibly worry about self-esteem if they're hungry' (p. 1).[5] This decision to not sell and the concept of poverty and need are discussed well across a wide range of literature that uses Maslow's nineteenth-century theory of human motivation and needs (1958).

Another example of this relationship was noted while conducting workshops when the accompanying NGO staff member asked an AGJ artisan to show me the work[6] the women were completing for a well-known Pakistani Fashion designer through the homeworkers group, Pakistan

> Shereen hands me the sample and once I see it, I remark, 'it is very nice and well done' to which she replies, *'kaam tau hai, humara kaam nahin hai'* translated it means 'its work, it's not 'our' [traditional] work. The stitches were satin stitch and it appeared more contemporary but looked more like work from northern Pakistan.

This alongside my extensive fieldwork observations strongly suggested to me that the women prefer to do their own traditional stitch (Mirza 2020, Doctoral fieldwork).

Designers who work with these and other similar craftswomen in an attempt to enhance their ability to sell craft-made goods for sustainable incomes often introduce new ideas, designs, styles, and stitches. Women who do such work are able to sell a wider range of craft-made goods. However, these interactions with women from AGJ indicate that the women have a clear demarcation of what is 'theirs' and what is perceived as labour for trade under the guidance of an external designer. This poses larger questions about culture and development. And about the clash of development for economic needs with the desire of women to hold onto the practices which they value and embody.

## Barriers to Agency: Local Craft and Women

In a context such as Sindh, communities have been accustomed to subordination in relation to the landowning class, development projects, organisations, and local authorities, which leads to a diminished sense of self-worth and confidence. This lack of self-worth creates an obstacle to believing that individuals in rural societies can do something on their own that enhances their lives and wellbeing (Bandura 1995; Chambers 1983; Mirza 2020). This is because knowledge hierarchies place the artisan communities at the bottom of the pyramid with experts, such as the top tiers of management, social superiors, outsiders, and designers being on the top. This leads to the social conditioning of the marginalised in relation to the class structures in place and their capacities, thus limiting their agency (Sachs 2008; Zimmerman 2000). In addition, there is little participation of communities in the processes (or the decision-making behind the processes), which inhibits development outcomes that can build confidence in craftswomen's abilities and enable action for positive change.

The traditional artisan's value of handmade craft is attached to his or her person because it is something he or she (as part of a community of makers) can do and can relate to doing as part of the local material culture (Frater 1995). Parker (2010) notes that makers may internalise the values that the outside world places on their work. Gauntlett (2011), Sennet (2008), and Tilley (2006) all note that our social and material capacities as humans are interrelated, particularly those of craft makers, while Gillow notes that 'the needle is the cheapest way to embellish or decorate something locally, due to lack of resources' (Gillow, personal communication with author, January 2010).

There is a need for a pause for reflection here on the notion of knowledge, in its wide range of formats and hierarchies, as well as how it is valued by the community. This practice of making involves a breadth of knowledge, lived experience, creative agency, local inspiration, decades of visual exposure, and all the tacit and non-tacit aspects of making, as resources. The women are the definers, interpreters, and custodians of their craft practice; this value, in a traditional or economic context, contributes to how they feel and what they represent. For these women, their craft is a space in which they see a reflection of themselves. Herein lies the agency that craft provides to women who make hand-embroidered textiles in Sindh. Whilst their knowledge may not be in the form of formal educational qualifications, their pride in it, their understanding of it, and their willingness to engage in the trade of it should not be seen as a weakness. Any engagement with crafts making that external actors get involved with should be with the intention of co-production and collaboration, which boosts the ability of each partner to work towards the best outcome for the makers and their practice.

## Interconnectedness of Craft and the Social Value of Making

In a collaborative environment, participants can learn visually and practically through the freedom of their practice through experimentation. By allowing for mistakes, and through equitable approaches of external facilitators, artisans can develop their skills and craft (Schon 1987). Gauntlett (2011) suggests that 'making is connecting because through making things and sharing them in the world, we increase our engagement and connection with our social and physical environments' (p. 2). Textile artist Fry (2013) points out the self-reflective process that occurs as a dialogue between a maker and their crafted object

> Drawing on the insights afforded through the process of reflection, I place emphasis on the co-dependency of interworked materials and my lived experience. This becomes cemented through touch and making. By being in dialogue with my artifact, the interweaving of thinking through material accentuates the ways in which my embroideries become, a direct expression embodying experience.
>
> (pp. 16–7)

Despite Fry's (2013) non-utilitarian context of making, this idea underlines the power that creative agency can afford to a maker who has the space for inquiry expressing the dynamic relation between lived experience and materials through craft practice. Sennett (2008) describes our capacities to form craft and human relationships as connected:

> The craft of making physical things provides insight into the techniques of experience that can shape our dealings with others. Both the difficulties and the possibilities of making things well apply to making human relationships. Material challenges like working with resistance or managing ambiguity are instructive in understanding the resistances people harbor to one another or the uncertain boundaries between people [...]. I argue no more and no less than that the capacities our bodies have to shape physical things are the same capacities we draw on in social relations.
>
> (pp. 289–90)

These ideas on craft suggested to me that the processes of craft making create another dimension to the relationship with others and our own perception and contribute to the development of self through our practice. A useful approach is one that deals with the social, economic, and material aspects of rural craft communities simultaneously rather than focusing on one or the other. The understanding of empowerment for a marginalised community of makers with rich material cultures should be viewed as nuanced at all times, and must not be generalised or simplified with a one-size-fits-all approach to development.

## Articulating Agency through Craft

The AGJ women, although articulate about sharing techniques with others within their community, were less aware of their own creative process and the development of their ideas. Whilst they have a clear method of making design decisions, these have not been formally coded in any way or documented in any format. They show an intuitive understanding and unconscious aesthetic; Polanyi (1966) defines their knowledge as tacit. According to Polanyi, people who possess tacit knowledge cannot explain the decision rules that underlie their performance; this knowledge is personal, and people often have the 'power to know more than they can tell' (p. 336).

The ability of an individual or group to be heard does not have to rely on linguistics; makers can express themselves or make themselves known through their craft practice. Textile writer and curator Nasreen Askari notes the strong visual identity of textiles in Pakistan

> I came across a woman draped in a beautifully embroidered *Chadar* [shawl] at the hospital, awed by its intricate work, touching it I asked her where it was from. She slapped away my hand angrily and walked away. The next day I saw her and she told me, 'this shawl tells you which clan I belong to, that my husband is a carpenter and my family ancestry. It represents my identity. Do not talk to me asking where it is from, everything you need to know is right here on my *Chadar!'*
>
> (Askari personal communication with author, September 2014)

Echoing Askari, Frater (1995) notes, 'the style with which a folk embroiderer expresses herself is not chosen, but assumed' (p. 18). The kind of power described here is visual, subtle, and a syntactic language of textiles as a form of agency. This complex and nuanced form of power is often undervalued, overlooked, or unused in development initiatives which are focussed on rural livelihood generation for women in developing nations. However, it is a vital aspect of their identity and practices and should be seen as a key cornerstone for any future endeavours to enhance rural women's social and material lives.

## Notes

1 S jo is a small-size business initiative set up by the author with the research group of craftswomen in Sindh, which enabled her to address the economic concerns of the community and to understand the complexities of commercialising traditional craft practice. She was a participant observer in this initiative and an integral part of the phenomenological approach.
2 The textile coverings included pillowcases, some of which she embroidered herself; tablecloths of all sizes for every table and sideboard embroidered by her, for her, or bought by her.
3 This is an ornate metal box, often made of silver, with special compartments to keep various things that go into the making of the betel leaf wraps that are usually eaten by older ladies and men.
4 The *gajj* which the AGJ women wear is a traditional tunic similar in pattern and style to a *pashk* worn by Balouch women with a heavily embroidered front.
5 Based on Maslow's hierarchy of needs pyramid in 'A Theory of Human Motivation' (1943).
6 For a purchase order.

## References


Agha, N, Syed, GK, & Mirani, DA 2018, 'Exploring the representation of gender and identity: patriarchal and citizenship perspectives from the primary level Sindhi textbooks in Pakistan,' *Women's Studies International Forum*, vol. 66, pp. 17–24.

Bandura, A 1995, *Self-efficacy in changing societies*, Cambridge University Press, New York.

Bourdieu, P 1984, *Distinction,* Routledge Kegan & Paul, Abingdon, Oxon.

Bourdieu, P 1990, *The logic of practice*, Polity Press, Cambridge.

Bronfenbrenner, U 1979, *The ecology of human development: experiments by nature and design*, Harvard University Press, Cambridge, MA.

Bronfenbrenner, U 1995, 'Developmental ecology through space and time: a future perspective,' in P Moen, GH Elder, Jr, & K Lüscher (ed.), *Examining lives in context: perspectives on the ecology of human development*, American Psychological Association, Washington DC. pp. 619–47.

Chambers, R 1983, *Rural development: putting the last first*, Pearson Education, Harlow.

Cohen, E 1989, 'The commercialisation of ethnic crafts,' *Journal of Design History*, vol. 2, no. 2/3, pp. 161–8.

Frater, J 1993, 'Elements of style: the artisan reflected in embroideries of Western India,' in N Fisher (ed.), *Mud, mirror and thread: folk traditions of rural India*, Mapin Publishing, Ahmedabad, pp. 66–109.

Frater, J 1995, *Threads of identity: embroidery and adornment of the nomadic Rabaris*, Mapin Publishing, Ahmedabad.

Frater, J 2002, 'This is ours: Rabari tradition and identity in a changing world,' *Nomadic Peoples*, vol. 6, no. 2, pp. 156–69.

Fry, G 2013, 'Characteristics of practice: embroidery as data,' *Text: For the Study of Textile Art, Design and History*, vol. 40, pp. 16–20.

Gauntlett, D 2011, *Making is connecting*, Polity, Cambridge.

Hyde, L 2012[1983], *The gift*, Canongate, Edinburgh, London.

Jones, RA & Stallybrass, P 2000, *Renaissance clothing and the materials of memory*, Cambridge University Press, London.

Lall, M 2011, *Pakistan and its diaspora: multidisciplinary approaches*, Palgrave MacMillan, New York.

Martin, P 2016, 'Turning Maslow's hierarchy on its head,' *Bright Magazine*, viewed 9 January 2019. https://brightthemag.com/@patricemrtn

Maslow, A. H. (1958). A Dynamic Theory of Human Motivation. In C. L. Stacey & M. DeMartino (Eds.), *Understanding human motivation* (pp. 26–47). Howard Allen Publishers. https://doi.org/10.1037/11305-004

Merleau-Ponty, M 1962[1945], *Phenomenology of perception*, Routledge, London.

Millar, L 2012, *Cloth and memory*, Direct Design Books, Kent.

Mirza, S 2020, 'Threads of the Indus: the subtle forms of power in craft development in Sindh, Pakistan,' PhD thesis, Royal College of Art, London.

Parker, R 2010, *The subversive stitch*, I.B. Taurus, New York.

Pettit, J 2020, 'Transforming power with embodied practice,' in R McGee & J Pettit (eds.), *Power, empowerment and social change*, Routledge Taylor and Francis, London, pp. 68–82.

Polanyi, M 1966, *The tacit dimension*, Doubleday and Co, New York.

Rahman, T 2012, *The class structure of Pakistan*, Oxford University Press, Karachi.

Ricoeur, P 2004, *Memory, history and forgetting*, London, Chicago, IL.

Sachs, W 2008, 'Climate change and human rights,' *Development*, vol. 51, no. 3, pp. 332–7.
Schon, D 1987, *Educating the reflective practitioner*, Jossey-Bass, San Francisco, CA; London.
Sennett, R 2008, *The craftsman*, Penguin Books, London.
Tilley, C 2006, 'Objectification,' in C Tilley, W Keane, S Kuchler, M Rowlands, & P Spyer (eds.), *Handbook of material culture*, SAGE Publications, Thousand Oaks, CA, pp. 60–73.
Weiss, AM & Khattak, SG 2013, *Development challenges confronting Pakistan*, Kumarian Press, West Hartford.
Zimmerman, MA 2000, 'Empowerment theory,' in J Rappaport & E Seidman (eds.), *Handbook of community psychology*, Kluwer Academic/Plenum, New York. pp. 43-63

# 4 Artistic Labour at Stake

## The Case of South Indian Courtesans' Changing Patterns of Professionalism in Colonial and Post-Colonial India

*Tiziana Leucci*

> Patrons, lovers, youth, beauty, wealth and health abandon us and go away. Jewels can be stolen or be lost forever, but our Art nobody can take away from us. As a sincere friend (*sakhī*) never will disappoint, leave or betray us, no matter if we are rich or poor, Art will always accompany our lives till the end, faithfully, until our last breath.

These words were told to me by an aged *devadāsī* I interviewed in Chennai in 1998 (she did not want her name to be revealed due to the social stigma). She lived alone in a poor basement when we met. This lady showed me an old photo of herself young and fully decorated with precious stones. She had lost everything since then and that photo was the most precious object she had. However, despite her miserable condition, she did not 'feel destitute and lonely' as 'her art was always with her, making her rich, but not in a material way.' Very proud of her past profession as an artist, she wished in her next life to be reborn again as a dancer. During our meeting, I was moved by the depth of her touching memories and by her dignity and self-confidence while referring to her life. She described her artistic training and performances as both her work and duty, along with the joy and the struggles she underwent in her youth in order to master her art. In her own words, dance was her 'breath' and her 'job' too, allowing her to live and get appreciated and respected for her talent. A few months later the aged *devadāsī* passed away. I encountered similar attitudes from the other hereditary performing artists I met and with whom I learned dance in India (VS Muthuswamy Pillai, his son KM Selvam Pillai, and the Mysore court dancer Kadur Venkatalakshamma). Their profession was for these artists both a form of art and handicraft during the learning, performing, and teaching processes, as well as a source of delight, personal gratification, and accomplishment, as well as being also a remunerated form of highly specialised labour.

In this chapter, I focus on artistic labour as described by Indian hereditary performing artists and in two medieval South Indian inscriptions. To contextualise my argument, a few introductory notes will be useful. *Bharatanāṭyam* dance today is the reformed and nationalised descendant of a more varied choreographic and ritualistic tradition practised till the first half of the twentieth century by female dancers, who were also courtesans, performing for the deities in temples (*devadāsīs*),[1] and for the kings and the nobles in the courts (*rājadāsīs*).[2] These

DOI: 10.4324/9781351031028-5

dancers also performed in their own salons and when their patrons invited them to their residences for special socio-religious occasions. The custom of consecrating girls to the local deities,[3] and the presence of dancers in both temples and royal palaces, intrigued many European travellers in India.[4]

Meanwhile, these performers also aroused the contempt of Christian missionaries, who could not understand and accept the presence of courtesans in the local liturgy and within the temples' precincts. Since the end of the nineteenth century, a segment of the Indian urban élite integrated the values and puritanical morality of the missionaries and began to criticise the ancient custom of dedicating dancers to temple deities and royal courts. After a century of legal debates, in November 1947, the *devadāsī* institution was abolished in the Madras Presidency (encompassing at the time a large portion of South India). It was not the British colonial rulers who did this, as people often believe, but Indian reformers, and three months after India won its independence. Even before the legal abolition of their status, all temple and court dancers and their community, including their accompanying musicians, singers, and dance masters (Tamil: *naṭṭuvaṉārs*), had property previously allotted to them by the temple authorities confiscated. The hereditary dancers and their profession were criminalised as licentious and immoral, a stigma that unfortunately endures in contemporary Indian society. Yet, the *devadāsīs*' poetic repertoire of songs and dance, and its erotic and devotional dimensions, was imbibed by Bhakti cults. In those songs, the male deities were addressed as the singers' own patrons and lovers, and sometimes also as their own parents or children, in accordance with lyrical conventions (Leucci 2016; Peterson 1989). In addition, since the 1930s, the knowledge of these artists has become a form of part-time activity for Indian urban upper-class girls who rarely dance professionally.

In 1987, 40 years after the Devadāsī Act, I got a scholarship in Chennai to study South Indian dance. I was intrigued by the artistic and socio-religious status of *devadāsīs* and *rājadāsīs* in the past, and astonished by the consequences of such a harsh legislation on these hereditary artists. After initial training at the Kalakshetra College of Fine Arts, I decided to learn the repertory of music and dance directly from them. During the classes and discussions I had with them, I was struck by the pride they took in their art and their past profession, even though their community was despised and marginalised since the late nineteenth century. It is noteworthy that most of the former temple and court artists I interviewed in India spoke of their profession as an art and a craft entailing a specific duty, status, right to do a qualified work (Sanskrit: *dharma*; Tamil: *muṟai*), comparable to the professions of other castes.[5] Here, I focus on their artistic and ritualistic forms of labour as described to me by them and as mentioned in some medieval texts.

To illustrate this, I have selected two eleventh-century Tamil epigraphic inscriptions. It is particularly interesting that they list many performing artists, including singers, dancers, musicians, music, and dance masters, along with several categories of craftspeople, whose work was closely connected with performances in the temple. These inscriptions are a precious source of information for musicologists and dance scholars because of the names, professions, and rich variety of musical instruments mentioned. They also recount the specific allowances and grants for the qualified professional work of the people employed in the shrine, making their content an open-air archive recording more than 800 names, honorific titles, and places of belonging, as well as the functions and wages of each artist and craftsperson working in that temple. Such recordings are similar to the administrative records of contemporary theatres in which the names, functions, type of contracts, and salary of each artist, craftsperson, and technician engaged are registered.

I was amazed that the Tamil word *muṟai* that twentieth- and twenty-first-century hereditary artists have used to define their professional work was exactly the same as the term found in these eleventh-century Tamil inscriptions. It denotes 'the duty to do a qualified work' and the right of the artists and craftspeople to perform a specific type of labour in the shrine in exchange for which various types of allowance the king and the temple authorities allotted to them according to their particular working status and professional competence. Consequently, the term has been used from the beginning of the eleventh century till today in the inscriptions and by artists and craftspeople, to define their highly qualified labour and their own right and privilege to perform in temples and royal courts. Burrow and Emeneau (1968, p. 5015) and the *Tamil Lexicon* (1982, p. 3300) translate the term *muṟai* as:

> order, arrangement, system, regularity, turn by which work is done, time (as once, twice), birth, manners, custom, approved code of conduct, relationship by blood or marriage, justice, antiquity, fate, nature, what is binding, law, duty, turn, relation between kin, propriety, virtue, relationship, manner, plan, course, system, routine.

Thus, these meanings denote an established order, a well-structured and planned time, a binding relationship between two parties, and a work schedule. *Devadāsīs* I met employed the term *muṟai* to define the work done in rotation associated with the Tamil word *paṇi* ('service in a temple').

## Rājarāja I, Patron of Poets, Performing Artists, and Craftpeople

Rājarāja I (947–1014 CE) became king in the year 985 CE. During his reign, he conducted successful military campaigns through which he expanded the Cōḻa territory remarkably. Once emperor, the monarch renamed himself Rājarāja ('King among the kings'). During the 29 years of his reign, Rājarāja devoted himself to consolidating his kingdom's socio-religious structure by employing a complex network of political diplomacy, strengthening the economic and financial administration, thus providing his subjects with a period of relative peace, and building anew a temple in his capital city of Tañjāvūr. This imperial shrine was completed in the year 1010 CE, and it was the largest temple ever erected in India at that time. As suggested by Inden (1990, pp. 230–1), its construction was at once a religious and a political act, asserting the Cōḻa king's supremacy as a worthy emperor ruling over the defeated kings. In his imperial shrine, Rājarāja took great care to detail the donations he, his queens, the members of his royal family, and his aristocratic retinue made to the deity. This collection of texts is not only dated precisely but they also provide historical information regarding the donors, the people, and the gifts donated to the deity and employed in the shrine. Temples were the centre of a host

*Figure 4.1* Two Apsaras, celestial counterparts of the dancing girls referred to in inscription no. 66 as *taḷiccēri peṇṭukaḷ*, 'the ladies (residing) in the temple quarters'. Mural painting in the ambulatory passage around the *garbhagṛha* of the Rājarājeśvaram temple, Tañjāvūr (11thcentury). Courtesy C. Nachiappan 2004, pl. XVIII.

of activities, political, cultural, and economic, as they housed the state treasury and acted as institutions for taxes, tributes, and money lending. The texts also reveal the court and the temple's social structure and administration, as well as how the shrine functioned financially, liturgically, and artistically.

Two inscriptions are particularly interesting for this case study. The first relates to the emperor's order to engage singers and musicians to chant daily in the temple the Tamil Bhakti hymns and the Śaiva saint-poets (Tamil: *nāyanmārs*) composed. The second concerns the employment of 400 dancers, several dance masters, accompanying musicians, artists, and craftspeople. Thus, the two inscriptions are important as they inform us how these performers were remunerated for their services and how their royal patronage functioned.

## Rājarāja I's Inscription No. 65

In this inscription, Rājarāja has ordered 48 singers and 2 musicians to be appointed to chant the Tamil sacred hymns (*Tiruppadiyam*) to Śiva in the temple. I quote here part of the inscription, from the Hultzsch et al.'s translation (pp. 256–9), to which I have added some transliterated Tamil terms:

1 Hail! Prosperity! … Srī-Rājarājadeva, who … — to the lord Srī-Rājarājadēva had given, — for reciting the *Tiruppadiyam* before the lord of Srī-Rājarājēsvara – 48 musicians [*pidārar*], one person who should beat the

small drum [*hudukkā*] in their company, and one person who should beat the big drum [*kotti-mattalam*] in their company. These 50 persons were to receive from the city treasury of the lord a daily allowance [*nibandha*] of three *kuruni* of paddy each … Instead of those among these persons, who would die or emigrate, the nearest relations of such persons were to receive that paddy and to recite the *Tiruppadiyam*. If the nearest relations of such persons were not qualified themselves, they were to select [other] qualified persons, to let [these] recite the *Tiruppadiyam*, and to receive that paddy. If there were no near relations to such persons, the [other] incumbents of such appointments were to select qualified persons for reciting the *Tiruppadiyam*, and the person selected was to receive the paddy in the same way, as that person [whom he represented] had received it. Accordingly, [the names] were engraved on stone, as the lord Srī-Rājarājadēva had been pleased to order.

2 To Pālan … three *kuruni* of paddy per day.

3–49 (Paragraphs 3–49 list all the other 47 singers of *Tiruppadiyam* appointed in the temple, mentioning the quantity of paddy, (three *kuruni*), granted to each one.

50. For beating the small drum, to Sūryadēva-Kramavittan, alias … Vidanga-Udukkai-Vijjādiran '(he who resembles) a Vidyādhara (in beating) the small drum,' … three *kuruni* of paddy per day.

51. For beating the big drum, to Gunappu(ga)r Marudan, three *kuruni* of paddy per day.

Rājarāja, the King/God (Tamil: *Ko*) in his majestic palace/temple (Tamil: *koyil*), as a monarch in his court, surrounded by attendants, ministers, courtesans, and performing artists, is presented here as the protector of the artists, providing them with proper occupations, grants, and allowances in exchange for their ritualistic performances. Thus, the 48 singers and 2 drummers received from the city treasure, as daily allowance, a quantity of paddy for their services. As the Sanskrit term employed here (*nibandha,* relating to 'those who received an allowance') highlights, such allowance implies not only a payment for work done, but establishes a close link (*bandha*) between the King/God as royal patron and the artists as performers and as his servants/devotees. For substitution in the case of death, departure, or working shift, preference was given to their nearest relations, suggesting the system was already at that time hereditary, and a family tradition of a particular community. However, professional skills remained required to get appointed for the service in the temple. Hence, when competent people were not found among the family, the inscription states that candidates of professional merit were chosen from elsewhere. These lines also suggest an urge to fill up vacant posts, likely to guarantee uninterrupted liturgical service of chanting hymns in the temple.

The *ōtuvār* singers, affiliated to the *devadāsī*s and *naṭṭuvaṉār*s, kept the tradition of *Tiruppadiyam/Tēvāram* songs in the Śaiva temples alive until today. That Rājarāja I was fond of *Tēvāram* songs is confirmed by the scenes depicted inside the temple *vimāṉa*[6] (Dehejia 2000; Leucci 2013a), by the sculptured panels of the saints' lives, and by the story narrated in the fourteenth-century version of the

*Tirumuraikantapurānam* by Umāpati Civācāriyar. The tale describes how Rājarāja found some palm-leaf manuscripts containing the *Tiruppadyam* texts in the Śiva temple at Cidambaram (believed to have been lost since the period of their composition by the three major Tamil saint-poets, Tirunānacampantar, Appar, and Sundarar) and how he rescued them from the ravages of time and white ants (Shulman 1992, pp. 101–2). After listening to some verses of these hymns, Rājarāja was so moved that he decided to find the entire corpus. Shulman (1992, p. 102) suggests that Rājarāja had help in his mission to find and restore the texts and music of the hymns. Those who aided Rājarāja included Nampi Āṇṭār Nampi, author of the *Tirut toṇṭtar tiruvantāti* and compiler of the *Tēvāram* hymns, as well as the temple priests and a female descendent of the artist who set the hymns to music. Most probably, this female was a 'temple woman' proficient in music and therefore able to restore their tunes, a task impossible for those not acquainted with the specific tradition of *Tēvāram* singing. This detail is important as it implies that the knowledge of singing *Tēvāram* hymns was a hereditary profession, preserved by the members of a community of temple artists in which singers, musicians, dancers, and teachers were all related by family ties, confirming what has been suggested by inscriptions and ethnographic studies. For example, *devadāsī*s told me they used to sing Tēvāram hymns, and Kersenboom-Story (1987, pp. 147–8) mentions TA Swaminatha Pillai, *naṭṭuvaṉār* at the Tiruvalaputtur temple, who told her how *Tēvāram* hymns were sung by both *ōtuvār*s and *devadāsī*s.

Inscription 66 shows that only temple women were allotted houses within the temple quarters, whereas no male musician, singer, or dance master got those grants. I propose that such a peculiarity was due to a customary practice, common until recent times, in which most male members of the *devadāsī* community (musicians, singers, and *naṭṭuvaṉār*s) resided in the homes of their mothers or sisters. Located close to the temple precincts, royal and religious authorities assigned houses to the officiating *devadāsī*s as part of their rights and privileges (*muṟai*), and in exchange for their ritual and artistic services offered to the gods (*paṇi)*. It may be that since the reign of Rājarāja I, or even earlier, temple dancers, *Tēvāram* singers, musicians, and dance masters were all considered members of the same community, following the systems of matri-locality and soror-locality, customary among them (Leucci 2012).

## Rājarāja I's Inscription No. 66

This is the lengthiest medieval inscription found so far in South India. I quote part of it from the translation by Hultzsch et al. (1984, vol. 2, pp. 260–303), to which I have added the original Tamil terms:

1 Hail! Prosperity! The lord Srī-Rājarājadeva had given and transferred temple women [*taḷiccēri peṇṭukaḷ*], from [other] temple establishments. To [the dancing girls] shares [*paṅku*] were allotted as allowance [*nibandha*]. ... In place of those among these shareholders, who would die or emigrate, the nearest relations of such persons were to receive that

allowance [*kāni*] and to do the work [*muṟai*]. If the nearest relations were not qualified themselves, [they] were to select [other] qualified persons, to let [those] do the work, and to receive [the allowance]. If there were no near relations, the [other] incumbents of such appointments were to select qualified persons from those fit for such appointments, and the persons selected were to receive the allowance. Accordingly, [the names of these persons] were engraved on stone, as the lord Sri-Rājarājadēva had been pleased to order: —

2 The temple women (were the following): —

3 To [*nakkan*] (ś)ē(ra)maṅ(gai), a girl of Lōkamahādēvi-Īsvara at Tiruvaiyāṟu, [who resides in] the first house of the southern row [*śiṟagu*] of the temple street on the south (*of the temple*), one share.

Paragraphs 4-402, list the names of the women [*taḷiccēri peṇṭukal*], the temples and places where they were attached before being transferred to Tañjāvūr, and the houses and shares allotted to each one of them.

[The list follows of more than 800 names of the dance masters, musicians and other artists, craft-masters and temple attendants.]

The artists' names are accompanied by honorific titles attesting to their merits. The inscription also lists the names, functions, and grants given to the craftspeople, such as tailors for the costumes, jewellers, astrologers, potters, bards, torch bearers, and garland makers, connected with the artistic activities in the shrine. Thus, the inscription seems also to suggest that those artisans were closely related to the communities of the temple performers. Rājarāja's royal palace, built of bricks and now lost to time, was located close to the temple and its magnificence had been the subject of a theatre-play, as mentioned in an inscription (Hultzsch et al. 1984, vol. 2, p. 67). Similarly, 400 dancers were each allotted a house located in the streets adjacent to the shrine, known as the temple quarters, and are referred to as *taḷiccēri peṇṭukaḷ*.

To understand its Tamil meaning, we must go back to the girls' dedication ceremony to the temple. From ethnographic studies, including my own interviews with *devadāsī*s and *naṭṭuvaṉār*s, important elements emerged in their descriptions of this ceremony (Leucci 2016, 2023). Firstly, whether a king, a queen, a member of the royal family, or anybody else donated a girl to the deity (Sanskrit: *devadāna*), it was considered a definitive act believed to bestow welfare, and high religious merits (Sanskrit: *puṇya*), upon the donor, the person donated, and their communities. Like any other offering to the gods, such as fruits, flowers, food, and jewels, the girl had to be spotless. After the approval from all concerned, the dedication ceremony took place on an auspicious day the temple astrologers selected in accordance with the girl's horoscope. The rite changed the girl's status whose life, from that time onwards, was devoted to the deity's service. The *devadāsī*s and *naṭṭuvaṉār*s I interviewed said that when a girl was 'donated' to the temple, she left her family and integrated into the 'god's lineage' (Sanskrit: *devakula*). Consequently, the temple became her home and the deities her parents. Such affiliation to the gods clarifies why in the Tamil epigraphic texts she was called *tēvaṉār makaḷ* ('daughter of god'), *patiyilār* ('she (whose) home is the temple') (Tamil Lexicon 1982, p. 2474), and, as in inscription 66, *taḷiccēri peṇṭukaḷ* ('the lady of the temple quarters'). After the dedication ceremony, the girl joined her new community. She then began long and strenuous training in dance and vocal and instrumental music. The courtesans were the most sophisticated women in India, and the young *devadāsī*s had to also learn poetry and master several languages and related literature in order to fulfil their duties and functions. Being legally adopted by an elder *devadāsī*, at her mother's retirement or demise, she got hereditary rights and privileges (*mānyan* and *inām*), such as the house, lands, paddy, and food, given by the temple authorities as allowance (*nibandha*) for the work (*muṟai*) done as a service (Tamil: *paṇi*; Sanskrit: *seva*) to the deity, according to the modality described by inscription 66.

Thus, the dedication ceremony marked the beginning of the girl's training under the *guru* and her affiliation to his own artistic lineage (*gurukulam*), implying that the girl became a member of her master's family, not only as a pupil, but because she was instructed in the *naṭṭuvaṉār*'s family tradition of dance and music repertory peculiar to her temple of affiliation. Such a repertory, of which her *guru* was the custodian and the transmitter, consisted of songs, dance, and rhythmic sequences, as well as hand gestures narrating the deeds, loves, and miracles of gods, saints, and heroes according to the myths and legends of the shrine (*sthalapurana*). All the *devadāsī*s and *naṭṭuvaṉār*s I met used to refer to this tradition as *bhāni* (Tamil: *pāṇi*), 'mode, a musical style or family tradition' (Pesch 1999, p. 294). This word literally means 'stores, provisions' or 'word, speech.' It therefore implies the idea of a casket of songs, stories, dances, and melodies, representing the wealth and artistic property of a specific family tradition and its identity. As Kersenboom-Story (1995) observed, 'To be part of such a transmission is no small or light matter. It brings riches and privileges, but also strong restrictions and responsibilities to entire genealogies' (p. 96).

The holders of this tradition had the duty of passing it on to the next generation of natural and adopted children, being all part of the same 'god and teacher's lineage' (*dēvakulam* and *gurukulam*), and enriching the family patrimony with new compositions to preserve their artistic knowledge. Being imparted by oral transmission and not having a standardised notation, if a generation of artists stopped practising and teaching their repertory, it would have been irremediably lost. Hence, the importance of the *pāṇi* as a specific artistic style and a family tradition. Consequently, the inscriptions referring to the urge to replace temple artists and craft-people, in case of their transfer or demise, appear clear and pertinent. Such precautionary measures aimed to prevent any interruption of service in the temple by preserving the transmission of its knowledge to future generations.

All the *devadāsī*s I interviewed said that their work was done by rotation, and that each family had specific rights and duties for their service to the gods (again designated by the terms *muṟai* and *paṇi*) to be performed at precise times of the day and on certain occasions, such as ceremonies and processions. Their service was remunerated with grants by the temple authorities and regulated by meticulous calculations undertaken by the temple astrologers, combining the horoscopes and periods of impurity of each *devadāsī*, such as menstruation, sickness, post-natal seclusion, and mourning periods, as well as the liturgical calendar, and inauspicious times (Tamil: *Rahu kalam*), such as sun and moon eclipses. If a dancer was in a state of impurity and ritualistic pollution, another dancer replaced her so as to ensure uninterrupted service in the temple. Their presence was necessary at occasions such as coronations, royal weddings and births, diplomatic visits, socio-religious festivals, as well as at rituals to prevent or reverse critical and dangerous situations, such as drought, flooding, famine, and epidemics. The *devadāsī*s were also invited to dance in wealthy homes for rites of passage or for private concerts. Each of these occasions earned them costly presents. They also received regular gifts from their patrons and lovers, who vied by means of wealth for their favours, such relations are a matter of prestige for both parties (Leucci 2009).

Under colonial rule, missionaries and reformers from Europe and America led anti-*nautch* ('anti-dance') campaigns precisely attacking the patronage of these artists. The colonisers criticised the fact that every socio-religious festival was accompanied by courtesans. The campaign succeeded and led to the magistrates and reformers of a free and independent India, having internalised colonial puritanical morality, passing the Devadāsī Act. In one fell swoop, the law erased a rich artistic and cultural institution, as well as a corporation of women once powerful, scholarly, rich, and largely emancipated in comparison to the rest of the female population of the time. Obliged to marry, without ever again being able to practice the now denigrated theatrical arts, there was no longer room for *devadāsī*s in the new Indian nation, which was often symbolised as a submissive wife or as Mother India, with sacrificial overtones.[7] Courtesans were therefore reduced to their all-too-public immorality and legally criminalised. They were banned and erased from the social, artistic, and political fields in the now-independent country, and were replaced by non-professional practitioners from the Indian urban upper-caste élite. Finally, the proud, dignified, and excellent artists I met were right when they defended their own artistic profession and way of living as their own community's duty (*dharma*), specific type and right of labour (*muṟai*), and highly qualified work as service to the temple (*paṇi),* but unfortunately, their voices have been unheard, despised, and silenced.

## Notes

1 *Devadāsī* ('servant of gods') is a generic Sanskrit term defining a class of artists and courtesans attached to the temples where they performed various artistic and ritualistic tasks.
2 *Rājadāsī* ('servant of kings') is a generic Sanskrit term defining a class of female musicians, dancers, poetesses, and courtesans, attached to a royal court.
3 I employ the term 'consecration' here with the original Latin meaning of 'transforming, making, rendering somebody or something sacred,' 'to sanctify.' Some medieval Sanskrit texts mention the initiation ceremony (*dīkṣā*) of those courtesans dedicated to Siva's temples (*rudragaṇikā*s).
4 See Bor (2007); Leucci (2005, 2013b).
5 'The use of the term 'caste'(*jāti*), in relation to the *devadāsīs* is misconceived; according to the *devadāsīs* themselves there existed a *devadāsī* way of life or professional ethic (*vritti, muṟai*), but not a *devadāsī jāti.* The profession of *devadāsī* was hereditary, but

it did not confer the right to work without adequate qualification' (Srinivasan 2010, p. 139).

6 The Tañjāvūr *vimāṉa* is the towerlike shrine symbolising Mount Kailāsa, Śiva's abode that hosts the temple's main deity's statue. See Nachiappan & Srinivasan about the mural painting in this shrine 2004.

7 See Soneji (2010, 2012); Morcom (2013).

## References

Bor, J 2007, 'Mamia, Ammani and other Bayadères: Europe's portrayal of India's temple dancers,' in M Clayton & B Zon (eds.), *Portrayal of the East: music and the oriental imagination in the British Empire, 1780–1940*, Ashgate, Aldershot, pp. 39–70.

Burrow, T & Emeneau, MB 1968, *A Dravidian etymological dictionary*, Clarendon Press, Oxford.

Dehejia, V 2000, *Indian art*, Phaidon, London.

Hultzsch, E, Venkayya, RBV & Sastri, RSH (eds.) 1984, *South Indian inscriptions. Tamil inscriptions of Rajaraja, Rajendra Chola, and others in the Rajarajesvara temple at Tanjavur (1895–1913)*, vol. II, Parts III, IV & V, Navrang, New Delhi (first published by Archaeological Survey of India, Madras), trans. E Hultzsch, RBV Venkayya, & RSH Sastri.

Inden, R 1990, *Imagining India*, Basil Blackwell, Oxford.

Kersenboom-Story, S 1987, *Nityasumangalī: Devadāsī tradition in South India*, Motilal Banarsidass, New Delhi.

Kersenboom-Story, S 1995, *Word, sound, image: the life of the Tamil text*, Routledge, New York.

Leucci T 2005, *Devadāsī e Bayadères: tra storia e legenda: le danzatrici indiane nei racconti di viaggio e nell'immaginario teatrale occidentale (XIII–XX secolo)*, CLUEB Bologna.

Leucci T 2009, 'Du DāsīÂttam au Bharata Nātyam. Ethnohistoire d'une tradition chorégraphique et de sa moralisation & nationalisation dans l'Inde coloniale et post-coloniale,' PhD thesis, EHESS, Paris.

Leucci T 2012, 'South Indian temple dancers: "donated" to the deity and "donors" for the deity. Two Tamil inscriptions on music and dance in the Rājarājeśvaram temple at Tanjāvūr (11th century),' in A Murugaiyan (ed.), *New dimensions in Tamil epigraphy: historical sources and multidisciplinary approaches*, CRE-A Publ., Chennai, pp. 209–53.

Leucci T 2013a, 'Scenes of music and dance in the mural paintings at the Rājarājeśvaram temple (Tanjāvūr, 11th century): Inter-textual & multidisciplinary analysis,' in L Giuliano (ed.), *Ajaṇṭā e oltre: la pittura murale in India e Asia Centrale*, Museo Nazionale d'Arte Orientale 'Giuseppe Tucci', Artemide, Roma, pp. 95–118.

Leucci T 2013b, 'Between seduction and redemption: the European perception of South Indian temple dancers in travelers' accounts and theatre plays,' in F Kouwenhoven & J Kippen (eds.), *Music, dance and the art of seduction*, Eburon-Chime, Delft, pp. 261–87 (text), 421–9 (notes).

Leucci T 2016, 'Royal and local patronage of Bhakta cult: the case of temple and court dancers,' in E Francis & C Schmid (eds.), *The archaeology of Bhakti II: royal Bhakti, local Bhakti*, IFP / EFEO (Indologie), Pondichéry, pp. 257–302.

Leucci T 2023, 'Usages and instrumentalisations of the Sanskrit derm '*dāsī/dāsa*' (servant-slave) in pre-colonial and colonial South India: the case of the *devadāsīs* and *rājadāsīs*,' in JAB Hegewald (ed.), *Embodied dependencies and freedoms: artistic communities and patronage in Asia*, De Gruyter, Berlin, pp. 143–94.

Morcom, A 2013, *Illicit worlds of Indian dance: cultures of exclusion*, Oxford University Press, New York.

Nachiappan, C (photos by) & Srinivasan, PR (text by) 2004, *Magnificent mural paintings: Sittanavasal, Panamalai, Tañjāvūr early Cōḻa paintings & Karana sculptures of Tamil Nadu*, Kalakshetra Publications, Chennai.

Pesch, L 1999, *The illustrated companion to South Indian classical music*, Oxford University Press, New Delhi.

Peterson, IV 1989, *Poems to Śiva. The hymns of the Tamil saints*, Princeton University Press, Princeton, NJ.

Shulman, DD 1992, 'Poets and patrons in Tamil literature and literary legend,' in BS Miller (ed.), *The powers of art: patronage in Indian culture*, Oxford University Press, New Delhi, pp. 89–119.

Soneji, D (ed.) 2010, Bharatanatyam. *A reader*, Oxford University Press, New Delhi.

Soneji, D (ed.) 2012, *Unfinished gestures: devadāsīs, memory, and modernity in South India*, The University of Chicago Press, Chicago, IL.

Srinivasan A 2010, 'Reform or conformity? Temple "prostitution" and the community in the Madras presidency,' in D Soneji (ed.), *Bharatanatyam: a reader*, Oxford University Press, New Delhi, pp. 139–59.

*Tamil Lexicon* 1982, 6 volumes, University of Madras, Madras, p. 3300.

# 5 Women, Crafts, and Landscapes

## Acknowledging Cultural Rights for Sustainable Development

*Zahra Hussain*

### Introduction

Within the context of the 'great development failure' (Scott 1998, p. 37), globalisation has been critiqued for its adverse effects on nature and the environment, as well as on indigenous populations and their cultures (Ehrenfeld 2003; Klein 2007; Mander & Tauli-Corpuz 2005). Development interventions and the effects of globalisation in remote regions and areas, such as mountain communities, have been seen as destroying cultural landscapes, including languages, practices, oral histories, and objects, and disturbing the fragile balance that indigenous cultures have maintained with their environment for generations (Hirsch 2001; Lieber & Weisberg 2002). The local cultural landscape and its contextual reality are often ignored in development projects and programs, which results in failed projects and an angered community (Fedorak 2013). It is thus important to take the cultural landscape into account when planning development interventions, especially when the lives of the inhabitants, as well as their material culture and products, are entwined with everyday life in their locality. Cultural landscapes are constituted through a range of practices carried out by inhabitants as they engage with the landscape to 'make it relevant for their own lives, strategies and projects' (Rose 2002, p. 457). Most importantly, identities are performed in lieu of a certain sense of belonging within the home and community, and these practices play an integral role in who people are, and consequently, how everyday life is lived (Stevens 2012, p. 588).

In the debates on development and sustainability, it is crucial to engage with cultural landscapes, while keeping in view the cultural rights of communities, as well as the protection of indigenous knowledge and ways of being in the world. The practice of craft making is integral to the development and maintenance of cultural landscapes and considered a key manifestation of the cultural expression of communities (Clammer 2014). In this chapter, I explore the relationship between cultural expression and sustainable development. I will discuss the value of understanding cultural landscapes, especially the process of crafts production in the Laspur Valley located in the northwest mountains of Pakistan. This exploration of the cultural landscape of Laspur Valley focuses on the craft of carpet weaving, including how this practice enables women to perform an

DOI: 10.4324/9781351031028-6

identity, experience belonging, and manage their socio-cultural lives. In addition, I examine how current forms of access in Laspur Valley have the potential for developing sustainable livelihoods within the region and exercising 'integral development' (Clammer 2014).

## Development, Cultural Rights, and Sustainability

The importance of local and indigenous cultures has received critical attention in the prelude to the Convention on the Protection and Promotion of the Diversity of Cultural Expressions, where UNESCO asserts, 'the need to take measures to protect the diversity of cultural expressions, including their contents, especially in situations where cultural expressions may be threatened by the possibility of extinction or serious impairment' (Convention on the Protection and Promotion of the Diversity of Cultural Expressions 2005). Local processes of self-expression, such as craft making, have declined in remote areas as the inhabitants have acquired access to mass-produced products at affordable prices. In addition, top-down crafts development initiatives introduced in underprivileged localities often treat craftspeople as mere labour and exploit their rights to fair income, creativity, and expression (Gauer 2011).

Craft products are important not only as utilitarian objects but also because they are considered to be social forms that are entwined with the values, ideas, and everyday lives of communities (Ames & Schlereth 1985; Miller 2005). Crafts become repositories of wealth reflecting the time, labour, and effort invested in their production. In traditional societies, crafts have been used as items of everyday use in the house, for decoration, as memorials, and for exchanging gifts. In the process of exchanging craft goods as gifts, craft producers become agents in the maintenance of social networks, relationships, dependencies, and obligations (Mauss 1990). At an individual level, craft also signifies how craft makers express themselves in the world, and in the process of gifting these crafts they not only give the object but also something of themselves with it (Gregory 1982; Ingold 2001). In this sense, craft goods in traditional societies become in-alienable possessions to be kept and exchanged within certain social groups rather than sold (Weiner 1992). Craft making is therefore a socio-cultural process embedded in the cultural landscape as well as a personal, experimental process through which craft makers express their creativity.

Clammer (2014) reviews the process of creativity, expression, and cultural development, advocating for a kind of development that he calls 'holistic' or 'integral.' It is about the participatory approach to development that is based upon the worldviews, values, and practices of local people for whom development is intended. This idea of development is deeply connected to freedom (Sen 2014). Clammer (2014) discusses the importance of holistic development and asserts that such a view 'sees culture at the core of human being-in-the-world' (p. viii). The author emphasises the value of cultural expression (arts, music, and crafts) in the maintenance of cultural landscapes. In response to UNESCO's calls for developing 'creative industries' based on indigenous cultural production (folk arts, music, crafts), Clammer argues that economic benefit as a primary concern in such development interventions results in the degeneration of the local cultural expressions as well as identity and creativity of local peoples, suggesting,

> [D]evelopment, while certainly aimed at meeting the basic needs of the poor, should also concern itself with the 'humanization' of people generally, by seeking to enhance their needs for expression, creativity and conviviality; … it should be endogenous and self-reliant and must be in harmony with the environment.
>
> (Clammer 2014, p. 41)

This debate is crucial for the once-remote regions that are being rapidly connected to other regions via roads, ideas, and intervention. For example, the China-Pakistan Economic Corridor (CPEC) that is currently underway and connecting many northern regions of Pakistan to the south of the country has given rise to local tourism and industries in the mountain valleys (Manzoor & Wei 2018). However, the absence of policy in the crafts sector has led to the degradation of crafts as well as the exploitation of craftspeople. Literature suggests that lack of policy in the crafts sector contributes to crafts being undervalued and also undermines the agency of craft persons (Pereira et al. 2006). In addition, the craft initiatives NGOs introduced in northern Pakistan contribute to the degradation of this sector as the environment in which they operate is 'characterized by false promises, disappointments and subjection to charity' (Kulick 2015, p. 4).

These factors have played an important role in the development landscape of northern Pakistan and it is thus important to speculate on the possible models for sustainable, bottom-up, and self-reliant development. Firstly, during such projects, craftspeople are usually employed as labour, while artists and designers carry out the creative process, resulting in reduced autonomy for the craftspeople (Banks 2010). Secondly, if intermediaries, such as middlemen sellers or organisations, are involved in the process because craftspeople lack access to the market, their autonomy is further undermined. The autonomy of craftspeople is a cultural right that is important to protect in order to ensure the longevity of cultural expression and hence sustainable development. In both circumstances, the relationship between the craft and craftspeople is important to investigate so as to determine the aspects of creative autonomy and cultural expression that are vital for the sustainable development of the crafts sector.

I now turn to the case of Laspur Valley where I carried out research in August 2018 and January 2019 to understand how local women have managed to keep the craft of carpet weaving alive amidst the development drive that infiltrated the northern valleys in Pakistan in the last two decades and the recent surge of infrastructural development in the wake of CPEC. The research consisted of three week-long trips to the valley where I conducted interviews and a scoping workshop on crafts enhancement. During these engagements, women shared their views and stories about carpet weaving and why they continue to practice it.

## Laspur Valley: A Contextual Overview

The valley of Laspur is nestled in the high mountainous region of northwest Pakistan (see Figure 5.1), which has remained an important locality on the route connecting the Karakorams (71°–79° E, 35°–36° N) and HinduKush via the Shandur Pass. To its east is the province of Gilgit-Baltistan, southeast is Swat Valley, in the northwest it borders the Wakhan Corridor, and to the west, the Nuristan and Kunar provinces of Afghanistan. The lives of communities in Laspur are dominated by the geographic topology, consisting of glaciers and ice cover in the upper region, the largest outside the polar zones, while the lower areas and valley bottoms form bare rock and barren slopes as well as gradual slopes purposed for farming. In summer, the livestock and a few inhabitants from each household relocate to temporary abodes in the high pastures for a period of four to five months. The other members of the family stay in the permanent homes and tend to the fields and orchards. In winter, the valley receives heavy snowfall restricting access to 'down country' as well as other adjoining valleys. Harsh winters and the snowfall that usually occurs between December and March confine inhabitants to their vernacular abodes when temperatures drop down to −20 °C to −30 °C, restricting the mobility and communication of inhabitants across the valleys. Among other indoor activities, this confinement is used by women to practice knitting and weaving.

## Crafts as a Relational Object and Practice

In Laspur, it was evident that creative practices are used for self-expression and for a sense of belonging, as well as to maintain social and familial relations between women and their extended families. For example, women in Raman village in Laspur Valley describe how they feel a certain sense of belonging to their house through practices such as 'painting coloured patterns on the wall' (see Figure 5.1), which they do afresh each year. Hence, through the repeated practice of painting, and the process of creative expression, the women experience a sense of belonging to their home. The women in these mountain communities also experience belonging through collective activities, such as collecting firewood and cutting grass, as well as craft making, weaving, and stitching.

In the Laspur Valley, carpet making, known locally as *qani qori*, is an important creative practice through which women express their culture. As part of the Laajverd Visiting School program, a series of conversations were carried out with local craft makers to understand how craft features in their lives. Fouzia Yaftali, a young local woman, shared,

> This practice was introduced in the valley circa 1950 by the tribal leader, my great grandfather, who brought a craftsman to weave carpets for our household. Local women in the village began to take interest in this and learnt to weave carpets under the mentorship of the craftspeople, and eventually only women were interested in continuing this practice in their homes.

During discussions, a local woman explained how carpet weaving is a pleasurable endeavour, and that when she is busy doing other household tasks, 'the carpet calls out

*Figure 5.1* Painted wall of a house in Raman Village, Laspur Valley. 2018. Retrieved from LVS 2018 Photo Archives.

to me "come and weave me". It is so difficult to not weave carpets' (Beena, Fieldwork notes 2018). Another woman exclaimed how she yearns to work on her loom and to keep weaving until the final product is ready because it is a 'source of joy' for her. A young woman mentioned how this activity of carpet weaving is 'intoxicating' for her because she finds it very hard to leave her loom and do any other work; therefore, she spends her day looking forward to the time when she will go back to her weaving. These carpet weavers also explained how the carpet reflects their selves and it is their 'thoughts, passion, and effort' that accumulate in the form of the carpet. The women explained how each carpet consists of the 'design we think in our heads and [we] bring it out in each weave, so we look forward to how it will look once it is completed' (Sana, Fieldwork notes, 2018). Conversations with craft weavers showed how the practice of weaving is an important part of their being and identity, as well as being a source of pleasure and pride. Moreover, this practice allows women to express their creativity, thoughts, and ideas and bring them into the world in the shape of a 'beautiful form' (Aimon & Zakia, fieldwork notes, 2018). In this sense, the self of the maker is extended and displayed in the form of the crafted product (Ahuvia 2005; Belk 1988).

## How Relations Are Renewed and Maintained through this Practice

Carpet making is more of a collective than an individual process in this region. During a session with craft women in Laspur, a local weaver explained how the

*Figure 5.2* Local women weavers showing their crafts and carpets during a session in Laajverd Visiting School. Retrieved from LVS 2018 Photo Archives.

process begins with collecting goat hair and wool from the sheep, which is later cleaned and sorted (see Figure 5.2). The process of thread making, locally known as *gidoi,* involves the presence and efforts of ten women who gather in the evening and work throughout the night in order to spin yarn for a single carpet. During this process, the women share stories, sing songs, and drink tea until dawn after which the yarn is ready. Indigenous rituals and processes around the practice of carpet making also play a role in the continuity of this craft, making it a socio-cultural practice rather than simply an individual endeavour. Once the yarn is ready, female weavers are supposed to set up the loom to begin weaving the carpet. Until two decades ago, it was believed that if the loom is set up by a male member of the household, the carpet will be strong as it will derive the strength of the man. However, this notion has faded away as more women became involved in the practice of weaving and helped each other set up looms.

Carpets are always woven by two or three women who are neighbours or are related to one another. The women collectively decide on the design patterns and colour scheme and take turns weaving the carpet. When inquired about the time it took to weave a carpet, they responded 'we don't keep track of time – a few days or a few nights we spend together doing it, we don't count.' This illustrates the logic of time associated with craft making, which is not counted by the hours (labour and profit) but rather by the time spent together. When starting a new carpet, women from the family of the weavers and neighbouring households come together to celebrate with traditional food and songs. An older woman explained how this ceremony is meant to bring good luck to the weavers because,

> the most pious woman from our gathering is requested to be the first to step inside the door of the room in which the carpet will be woven. Her good character is meant to bring good luck to the weavers and the carpet.
>
> (Bushra, Fieldwork notes, August 2018,)

In this sense, carpet weaving is a communal practice that women endorse and celebrate by gathering and eating together.

In previous times, during the process of weaving a carpet, the host woman ensured the well-being of the weavers by providing them with tea and food. During my conversations with the weavers, they shared how weavers would demand food on behalf of the carpet by saying, 'you hear the sound of the loom – as one wooden piece knocks the other wooden piece, this means the carpet is hungry and wants food' (Aisha, Fieldwork notes, August 2018). These stories and rituals around the practice of carpet weaving show how the carpet assumes a character in correspondence to the humans involved in its making; it is strong if a man sets the machine, it will be a good piece if a pious woman walks into the room, and it will be completed in time if the weavers are well fed. In this sense, the carpet becomes alive for the makers and women revere the practice of carpet weaving as a personal endeavour as well as a socio-cultural gathering formed through stories and keeping kith and kin. Moreover, the practice of carpet weaving becomes a mode of self-expression for women and a means of asserting their way of being in the world. Most importantly, this practice draws its strength from the collective efforts of the many women involved in preparing for, caring for, and celebrating with the weavers.

*Qani qori* is thus an amalgamation of individual and communal practices that are performed repeatedly each winter and is deeply tied to how women assume an identity, perform socio-cultural activities, and exercise their right to self-expression. Moreover, these carpets become carriers of relations as they are made for one's own house and kept in a daughter's dowry; at home, the carpets are a source of joy for the woman, while the ones in the dowry are meant to strengthen relations with the in-laws. The in-laws expect at least two or three carpets to be gifted in the dowry and mothers and sisters thus weave these carpets together to ensure proper quantity is gifted, which is not uncommon for most textile-based crafts that are women centric. Craft goods thus assume a life of their own as meanings are inscribed in their forms and they circulate in various ways within a context and locality (Appadurai 1988). In this sense, the craft of carpet weaving and sustainability are intricately connected through the collective process of creating and maintaining socio-cultural relations while using natural materials, and ultimately gifting and/or using the carpets in homes as in-alienable possessions (Weiner 1992).

## Temporality, Technology, and Integral Development

Laspur Valley can be accessed through a rocky, dirt road from Chitral City, and is the last village before the Shandur Pass at 3,700 meters, where the highest polo ground in the world is located. Due to the poor conditions of the road, as well as the State's general neglect of cultural economies in the Upper Chitral region, Laspur received little attention in terms of the development of community crafts initiatives and enterprises. Mobility and access to this valley from southern cities remain an issue until the CPEC is completed. A few shops, such as a general store, an apparel shop (filled with Chinese goods), and some basic household materials shops are located on the main road in Laspur Valley. Dairy products, meat, and chicken are consumed from one's own farm, while women in the household make apparel such as knitted woollens, although jackets and other clothing are bought from the markets in Chitral. Since physical access to Laspur is a challenge, only a few shops and limited items are sold, and inhabitants in the village do not rely on them. Women are the caretakers when it comes to kitchen gardening and keeping the animals for dairy products. In this sense, the cultural landscape and creative expression of local communities have remained almost entirely intact, unlike other mountain towns in northern Pakistan where cheap apparel and items (usually made in China) found their way into the valley through road networks, making the local practices of craft making redundant. For example, the practice of *qani qori* is highly valued by the older women in Laspur Valley who continue to make carpets despite access to markets in Chitral.

Despite this, in the last two years, the practice of carpet weaving has started to be at-risk of degeneration. Women themselves identified several reasons for this during our conversations. First of all, educated younger women and daughters in the house are not interested in taking up this activity. Some have also discouraged their mothers from this practice because the wool and hair cause breathing problems. Secondly, a crafts enterprise was introduced in the valley recently in which women were hired for a daily wage to weave carpets; the business owner would provide the design and pattern and sell the carpets the women produced. However, this initiative was not successful due to issues of trust and responsibility between the business owner and the women weavers.

Within this context, another point of view also emerged, as Fauzia Yaftali explained, 'we need to safeguard this practice ourselves, why should we give it into the hands of others?' Although physical access to Laspur remains a challenge, this somewhat remote mountain community was recently connected to the World Wide Web through mobile phone access and internet. This has introduced interesting dynamics in the valley, in which the educated young women realise the value of protecting cultural expression. Fauzia explained how access to mobile phones and internet has also provided access to new ideas and online markets. In this sense, Laspur Valley is operating in a unique temporality to other mountain towns that got access to road networks much sooner. For young women, access to the internet and technology at a time when the craft-making practice is still alive opens up a whole different set of opportunities for developing livelihoods and strengthening the practice of craft making.

The temporality in which Laspur Valley finds itself has the potential to nurture what Clammer (2014) calls 'integral development,' in which an intermediary or middleman is no longer required. A few young women who have received undergraduate level education in the social sciences are aware of the power dynamics in terms of labour, skills, and livelihoods. They also realise the value of craft making and the potential of technology in building a self-led and autonomous crafts development program. Although these women lack training in business development, they understand the crucial temporality in which they are operating and benefits they can derive from it. The intervention of externally led enterprises may take away skilled women, and the development of CPEC will bring opportunities as well as challenges to the village. In this situation, it is crucial to develop a locally led program that will enable women to continue exercising their agency and autonomy in the process of carpet making, rather than becoming mere skilled workers paid a daily wage. Alongside this, the opportunities that will come with the road in the form of increased accessibility, products, and tourism will also affect local business in different ways. Given the situation, Fauzia's priorities are clear,

> I have deferred my plans of doing an MPhil and only want to focus on setting up this crafts enterprise. I will work with weavers and show other young girls that this practice is important for protecting and promoting our cultural heritage.

A year on from these conversations, Fauzia reflected on the challenges related to establishing a locally led crafts enterprise and emphasised the need to raise awareness of the processes involved in setting up a business. She elaborated, 'craft women require money upfront, before they even start weaving because they don't trust the process or the market – they are too disassociated from it.' She explained how women required surety regarding the income they could generate before investing their time and energy. Moreover, the uncertainty also contributed to creating mistrust between Fauzia and the women weavers, which could potentially lead to conflict if her mother had not intervened and used her status and relations within the community to settle the dispute. Women continued to weave carpets for their homes and families, but resist making and waiting for these to be sold in an unknown market. In this context, 'integral development' (Clammer 2014) would require raising awareness; if women are aware of the process and have sufficient knowledge about the market, they will be able to decide for themselves and understand the value of their work.

*Qani qori* is a collective practice in which women support each other, and their mutual trust and social relations must not be tainted by a business enterprise or program. Moreover, when initiating a program, care must be taken to ensure that social relations between craftspeople in a locality remain intact and flourish as this is an important aspect of cultural sustainability. With the required guidance and skills, a locally led enterprise in Laspur Valley will enable local women to protect and strengthen the practice of carpet weaving and derive economic benefits from this, while access to the internet can facilitate links to urban and global markets. In this business model, two factors are in the mix: local awareness of cultural protection and locally led processes of crafts development. These factors ensure sustainable development in three ways:

- a Protecting the indigenous practice of *Qani-qori* (using wool and goat hair from local animals rather than buying yarn from the market), which older women deem important, 'that no material should be wasted, and must be used in creation of something else' and hence retain a relationship with the natural landscape.
- b Protecting and strengthening rights to cultural expression that are intrinsically linked to one's identity and sense of belonging in the world, which will

ensure that local communities continue to thrive in their geographic and cultural landscapes.

c Craft enterprises must allow local social and familial relations to flourish rather than create mistrust and conflict between communities in a locality.

## Conclusion

This chapter explored the cultural economy of carpet weaving in Laspur Valley, focusing on its significance in the everyday lives of women living in this mountain community by drawing out links between the natural landscape, cultural practices of everyday life, and social relations that communities maintain. I discussed the challenges to this practice within the current scenario of infrastructural development and the potential of developing this as a sustainable and locally led model for cultural protection and economic development. *Qani-qori* craft is a culturally specific, historically contingent, and geographically emplaced practice; hence, a contextual responsive strategy is required to maintain this practice along with its social and cultural attachments. With recent access to the internet and mobile phones, as well as the development of the road infrastructure, this valley is bound to undergo rapid changes and challenges. Amidst this scenario, it is clear from engagements in the field that the value of cultural expression is still intact. However, careful approaches are required in order to make this process economically viable, culturally feasible, and experientially meaningful for the communities in order to achieve sustainable development.

## Acknowledgements

The Laajverd Visiting School field program, 'Etho-ecologies; building shared futures,' held in 2018 in Laspur Valley enabled the research for this chapter. I am especially thankful to Fauzia Yaftali and local women weavers for giving their time and sharing their ideas and experiences.

## References

Ahuvia, AC 2005, 'Beyond the extended self: loved objects and consumers' identity narratives,' *Journal of Consumer Research*, vol. 32, no. 1, pp. 171–84, https://doi.org/10.1086/429607

Ames, KL & Schlereth, TJ 1985, *Material culture: a research guide*, University Press of Kansas, Lawrence.

Appadurai, A 1988, *The social life of things: commodities in cultural perspective*, Cambridge University Press, Cambridge.

Banks, M 2010, 'Craft labour and creative industries,' *International Journal of Cultural Policy*, vol. 16, no. 3, pp. 305–21, https://doi.org/10.1080/10286630903055885

Belk, RW 1988, 'Possessions and the extended self,' *Journal of Consumer Research*, vol. 15, no. 2, pp. 139–68, https://doi.org/10.1086/209154

Clammer, J. 2014. 'Art, Culture and International Development: Humanizing social transformation (1st ed.). Routledge. https://doi.org/10.4324/9781315775555

Clammer, J. and Vickery, J. 2020, 'The Sociology and Culture of Sustainable Development: an interview with Professor John Clammer,' *Journal of Law Social Justice and Global Development* [Preprint], (25). https://doi.org/10.31273/lgd.2019.2501.

Convention on the Protection and Promotion of the Diversity of Cultural Expressions, 2005, UNESCO, Paris.

Ehrenfeld, D 2003, 'Globalisation: effects on biodiversity, environment and society,' *Conservation and Society*, vol. 1, no. 1, pp. 99–111.

Fedorak, SA 2013, *Global issues: a cross-cultural perspective*, University of Toronto Press, Toronto.

Gauer, MAN 2011, 'Crafting identities: female crafters and their expressions of identity through crafts,' Master's thesis, University of Oslo, Oslo.

Gregory, CA 1982, *Gifts and commodities*, Academic Press, Cambridge, MA.

Hirsch, P 2001, 'Globalisation, regionalisation and local voices: the Asian Development Bank and rescaled politics of environment in the Mekong region,' *Singapore Journal of Tropical Geography*, vol. 22, no. 3, pp. 237–51, https://doi.org/10.1111/1467-9493.00108

Ingold, T 2001, 'Beyond art and technology: the anthropology of skill,' in MB Schiffer (ed.), *Anthropological perspectives on technology*, University of New Mexico Press, Albuquerque, pp. 17–31.

Klein, N 2007, *The shock doctrine: the rise of disaster capitalism*, Metropolitan Books/ Henry Holt, New York.

Kulick, G 2015, *Conducting design research in Pakistan's craft sector: opportunities and limitations*, no. 6, Nordes 2015, Design Ecologies.

Lieber, RJ & Weisberg, RE 2002, 'Globalization, culture, and identities in crisis,' *International Journal of Politics, Culture, and Society*, vol. 16, no. 2, pp. 273–96, https://doi.org/10.1023/A:1020581114701

Mander, J & Tauli-Corpuz, V 2005, *Paradigm wars: indigenous peoples' resistance to economic globalization*, Journal of Sociology and Social Welfare.Vol 35, Iss.2, Article 25.

Manzoor, F & Wei, L 2018, 'A review of China-Pakistan Economic Corridor and Tourism Opportunities,' in E Editor (ed.), *Proceedings of the third international conference on economic and business management,* Atlantis Press, pp. 79–82, https://doi.org/10.2991/febm-18.2018.18

Mauss, M 1990, *The gift: the form and reason for exchange in archaic societies*, trans. WD Halls, Routledge, London.

Miller, D 2005, 'Materiality: an introduction', in D Miller (ed.), *Materiality*, Duke University Press, London, pp. 1–51.

Pereira, T, Shackleton, C, & Shackleton, S 2006, 'Trade in reed-based craft products in rural villages in the Eastern Cape, South Africa,' *Development Southern Africa*, vol. 23, no. 4, pp. 477–95, https://doi.org/10.1080/03768350600927235

Rose, M 2002, 'Landscape and labyrinths,' *Geoforum*, vol. 33, no. 4, pp. 455–67, https://doi.org/10.1016/S0016-7185(02)00030-1

Scott, JC 1998, *Seeing like a state: how certain schemes to improve the human condition have failed*, Yale University Press, New Haven, CT.

Sen, A 2014, 'Development as freedom,' in JT Roberts, AB Hite, & N Chorev (eds.), *The globalization and development reader: perspectives on development and global change*, Wiley Blackwell, Hoboken, NJ, pp. 525–48.

Stevens, P 2012, 'Towards an ecosociology,' *Sociology*, vol. 46, no. 4, pp. 579–95, https://doi.org/10.1177/0038038511422586

Weiner, AB 1992, *Inalienable possessions: the paradox of keeping-while giving*, University of California Press, Oakland.

# 6 The Performance of Payment

## Differentiating Devotional, Erotic, and Classical Performing Arts in India

*Anna Morcom*

In this chapter, I look at a particular cultural pattern of paying performers by giving spontaneous gifts of money or valuables during or just after a performance. This traditional practice in South Asia spans diverse forms of music-making such as *shehnai* (shawm) players in Hindu temples, singers of *Qawwali* or Hindu devotional music, *Ghazal* singers, and cis- or transgender-female erotic performers. Tipping also used to be a norm in what became the classical performing arts as they were performed in courts and salons. As I explore in this chapter, tipping is not just a simple matter of payment. While different genres may feature the same basic practice, it is manifested in vastly different ways, and with vastly different meanings. Exploring how tipping is enacted allows us to look at the role of money in different cultural economies, and how it embodies and mediates value, exchange, social relationships, and social status. I focus on three contrasting genres: *Qawwali*, bar dancing, and classical music.

A now extensive anthropological and sociological literature teaches us that money is social and cultural rather than an impersonal measure or medium of value or exchange (Dodd 2014; Hart 1986; Maurer 2006; Zelizer 1994). Although money is defined to some degree by abstraction, notably, 'the reduction of incommensurable qualities to measures of quantity,' this is by no means total (Keane 2008, p. 28). As I explore here, even though the cash that performers are tipped with is a widely exchangeable medium of value, the ways in which it is done inscribe radically different social worlds, or, to use Appadurai's term, 'regimes of value' (1986). Money can act as a token as well as holding a quantitative or cash value and can move between these two statuses. It is always semiotically mediated, and its meaning is, thus, precarious to some degree (Keane 1996). As Nigel Dodd (2014) multifariously explores, money is a process of gargantuan social proportions, involving the interconnection of states, and markets, as well as many other social and cultural contexts and forms of authority. In addition, it must be remembered that cash is just one of the forms that money takes. For example, Marx (1904[1859]) saw money as existing in a pyramid with 'fictitious capital' at the top (speculative financial products where money is apparently self-expanding), credit money in the middle, and hard cash at the bottom (see Dodd 2014, p. 58). Thus, the use of money does not necessarily imply commercialism, and even when it does, its role and value are not entirely constant or predictable.

DOI: 10.4324/9781351031028-7

In order to understand money and its multiple cultural and social meanings in performing arts, it is necessary to place it in a broader context of value production and exchange. Nancy Munn (1986) and other scholars argue compellingly that value is essentially produced through actions rather than residing in things. Money cannot hold value independently from human actions and exchanges. As Marx (1993[1939]) emphasises, money must circulate to maintain value (Dodd 2014, p. 52), and as Jane Guyer (2004) explores, monetary exchanges are performative. Rather than seeing money given to performers simply as payments, I analyse the forms and manner in which these payments are made. What are the gestures involved with visible cash payments? Is money given, showered, sprayed, thrown at performers' feet, handed to them, or handed to someone to give to them? How is it received by the performers? Is it acknowledged, and if so, how? What makes receiving money as tips seem cheap, or commercial, or lowly, and what makes it a respectful appreciation? Thus, in this chapter, I look at the enacting of tipping (or its absence) as a part of an overall performance event that characterises genres, and inscribes different social statuses such as class, caste, and gender. First, I describe the giving of spontaneous gifts of money in *Qawwali*, bar dancing (and other erotic genres), and historical classical performing arts in court and salon contexts. I then analyse more closely how gifts of money engender social and cultural meanings and values in these genres. Finally, I discuss classical music in the present day and the absence of visible, spontaneous payment.

## Gifts of Money in *Qawwali*, Erotic Genres, and Historical Classical Music

*Qawwali* is a genre of Sufi devotional music performed mostly by hereditary male Muslim musicians known as *qawwal*s at the *dargah,* or shrine, of a Sufi saint. As Regula Qureshi (1995[1986]) describes, the purpose of the genre is to praise the saint, to elucidate matters of spiritual wisdom through poetry, and to arouse spiritual love in listeners in the assembly. As the *qawwal*s sing, people give money, known as *nazr* or *nazrana,* in smaller or larger amounts. The giving of *nazr* is traced to rituals of Mughal courts and courtiers, where it was used extensively. This practice entailed 'the articulation or submission and allegiance to a superior by means of a gift or offering (*nazr*), which once accepted, entailed an obligation to confirm benefice on the donor' (Qureshi 1995[1986], p. 90). In a performance, a path is kept open amongst the listeners so people can come forward to give *nazrana* without distracting from the singing but within view of everyone present. It may be given to the Sufi leaders who then pass it on fully or in part to the *qawwal*s as a reward for their singing (Qureshi 1995[1986]; Johnston 2000, pp. 90–1). It may also be given directly to the *qawwal*s, who may keep all or part of it (Johnston 2000, pp. 90–1). Practices differ, and the giving of *nazrana* is just one aspect of the highly interactive performer-audience relationship of *Qawwali*. It tends to become more intense as a performance proceeds and listeners become more spiritually aroused (Johnston 2000, p. 90).

Strictly speaking, *nazrana* should be given with the utmost respect, placed on upturned palms held together and pointed towards the recipient.[1] However, people with less knowledge of these codes also throw money over the seated *qawwal*s, hand it to them, or place it on the harmonium. Amounts given are usually small bills, but large sums or valuables are sometimes given ostentatiously. *Qawwali* is also performed in concerts and parties, where the giving is typically more extravagant. Still, the performers acknowledge gifts with a gracious *salaam*, raising the right hand, palm to the face, and head slightly bowed. As I witnessed at the *dargah* in Fatehpur Sikri, and in a concert of these same *qawwal*s in the UK, the acknowledgement is the same; however, the money is given and whatever the amount, there is no attention to the money itself.

Bar dancing and the comparable erotic genres of salon *Mujra* and *Lavani* exhibit the same basic phenomenon of spontaneous monetary gifts of a non-fixed amount and a highly interactive relationship of performers and listeners of which these gifts form a part.[2] In *Mujra*, the term *nazrana* is used, or *bakshish*, but in dance bars, the English word 'tips' is used, possibly because the larger context is the hotel and restaurant industry. The *qawwal* community, courtesans (who are the foremothers of a large proportion of bar girls), and North Indian classical music are historically connected.[3] However, *Qawwali* is, of course, also a world away from the erotic genres in today's India, and the ways in which gifts of money are given and received are part of what shapes these differences.

In dance bars and today's *Mujra*, the purpose is erotically-laced enjoyment of music and dance, and the giving of money is intensely conspicuous.[4] Customers exchange large bills for wads of small bills to extend the moment of giving, heightening its visibility, and some also give large bills. Customers may stand close to a dancer and shower notes on her, dropping them one by one, or they may spray the money by propelling a wad of notes into the air in a stream, which is particularly dramatic with swirling dancers in glittering dresses and flashing lights. The sexualisation of this is not hard to miss; Mazzarella (2015) terms it an 'ejaculation' (p. 488). In Maharashtrian *Lavani*, a practice of giving money to dancers lips-to-lips existed in the past but was stopped.[5] In all these genres today, men often sit with wads of money visibly in their hands, fingering the notes, and anticipating the act of giving. Money is, thus, a focus of the interaction in dance bars. *Mujra*s are similar. I went to a *kotha* (salon) with two female companions in 2018. The dancer had been taking *farmaish* (requests) from us, and a male customer who had come in after started to become irritated. She then took a *farmaish* from him and he sprayed notes over her in a long stream. As she performed his second *farmaish*, he lay on the sofa, sprawling, with a pile of Rs 20 notes, and threw them at her. Her dancing became more seductive, interacting with him more intensely, and she touched his leg a couple of times and came very close. He gave her a pile of notes, and she herself threw it in a shower, and then, in a flirting manner, took some more notes from him.

In contrast to the performance of both *Qawwali* and the erotic genres, in today's classical music and dance, payment is strictly behind the scenes. The idea of giving money to a classical performer as they perform, let alone showering them with bills, is so inconceivable that the few people I put the idea to reacted with amusement. Some also added, in serious tones, that it is 'that *Mujra* style' and not done in classical music. Instead, a cheque or cash is given behind the scenes. Historically, money and valuables were given during or just after performances in the same basic format of spontaneous appreciation, reciprocation of value, and audience interaction as found in *Qawwali* and erotic traditions. Again, the historical connections must be emphasised – *qawwal*s and *tawaif* (courtesans) were central to what became today's classical performing arts. The *Akhbarat* chronicles of the early nineteenth-century Mughal emperors provide many references to musicians – *qawwal*s, *tawaif*, and *kalawant*s (high-status male soloists) – being given gifts and sums of money, often in auspicious multiples of 7 or 11 rupees (Pernau & Jaffrey 2008). The musician Vilayat Husain Khan also mentions such incidents in the nineteenth or early twentieth centuries in his book. Khan writes, 'The rulers of Rampur, Mysore and Kolhapur … invited [Bawali Bai] often and used to listen to her with pleasure and presented her with diamonds and precious metals' (cited in Wade 1984, p. 93). In a film about the legendary singer Kumar Gandharva, an eyewitness recalls him being given abundant gifts, including money, by members of the audience at one of the all-India music conferences in the early twentieth century where he performed as a child prodigy (Virmani 2009). Nevertheless, while courtesans and *ustad*s (male master musicians) were given spontaneous gifts of money or valuables in performance, written and oral sources reveal that this was enacted in a much more formal and restrained manner than in dance bars, today's *Mujra*, or contemporary *Qawwali* concerts. Indeed, Mamaji, a male elder from a family of *deredar* courtesans based in Mumbai involved in bar dancing, told me that in the old style of *Mujra* that he remembered, there were rules prohibiting touching, limiting the sexualisation of the exchange.[6] Similarly, Sureshwar Dhari Sinha, an elderly man from a former landowning family in Bihar, told me of the strict etiquette of *mehfil*s in their home that featured courtesans or male musicians, including how an uncle who showed up inebriated was instantly ushered out.[7]

## Money and Value in Performance

In this section, I examine gifts of money to performers in more depth, looking at the significance of visibility and ostentation. I also explore how such tips form a part of exchanges and relationships between humans and the divine that entail, to greater and lesser degrees, expectations, demands, or obligations.

### *Visibility and Ostentation*

In *Qawwali*, it is important that listeners visibly give money, as it is a medium of blessing for the spiritual supplicant and a mark of respect for the performers. However, it should not be an ostentatious show of wealth, and tips are acknowledged graciously, if briefly, whatever the sum and however they are given. This is principally because in Sufism, as Johnston (2000) points out, wealth is internal and measured in terms of closeness to the beloved – Allah, the prophet Muhammad, a saint, or one's spiritual guide (p. 278). The amount one gives cannot alter the amount of divine blessing or reward one receives, which is beyond quantification anyway.

Similarly, while spiritual states are visible externally in such actions as weeping, dancing, and twirling, the experience is essentially interior and should not be a show. Johnston (2000) describes an occasion in a *dargah* in Hyderabad that crossed these lines for many listeners. A *qawwal* from a prestigious lineage from Delhi had come to sing. He was dressed in a fancy manner and sang in virtuosic style and had attracted some wealthier listeners.

> One listener sat close to the lead singer and paid particular attention to the music, gesturing and shouting out frequently. During the course of the evening, he got up twice to place impressively thick gold chains around the singer's neck. Several other affluent listeners got up to offer thick stacks of 100-rupee notes during the hour-long performance. Notably, the listeners were not offering the money with the typical devotional-style gesture: two hands held together with the money in the hands which is then dropped or placed on the top of the harmonium in front of the singer while he gestures salam … in thanks. Rather the money was frequently given with a flashy show of bills thrown high in the air. The money was casually strewn around or thrown down in a waterfall or cascade effect, bills scattering down on top of the singer and front row of listeners.
>
> (Johnston 2000, pp. 355–7)

This style of giving money is more like that of the dance bars, where tipping is a kind of potlatch (Morcom 2015), or what Appadurai (1986) has termed a 'tournament of value' (p. 21). In dance bars, rather than being measured in spirituality, wealth is measured largely in money, the key basis of class in capitalism and a hegemonic form of value. Giving money to dancers in front of other customers to mark prowess and status is one of the main points of going to a dance bar, and can play a significant role in *Qawwali* performed for private parties, but should not take place in a shrine. However, I would add that more visible ways of giving money to *qawwal*s can also be viewed within a spiritual framework, with throwing money at their feet as indicating that wealth has no meaning.[8] As Keane (1996) has emphasised, meaning in these money gifts is semiotically mediated and, thus, unstable, and there is inevitably variation in different places.

Although there is scarce research on historical practices concerning classical music, the visible giving of money or valuables to performers by royal patrons was a way of displaying wealth and prestige (Qureshi 2002), and admiration for a performer. Such conspicuous consumption showed the patron's status as a landowner, someone who did not have to engage in productive labour, but took surplus from the labour of others (Veblen 1994[1899]). However, there is no question of the patron having to compete with others present as men of the largely lower-middle classes do in the potlatching of dance bars.

Visible gifts of cash are not just a marker of status in dance bars and formerly in classical music. They also constitute spontaneous responses to the pleasure and effect of the music, which can be unpredictable or overwhelming, and hence, gifts that are not of predetermined sums are appropriate (Morcom 2020). In dance bars, the experience is sexually inflected, and with *Qawwali*, spiritually so. I would add that although there has been much emphasis on the sexualisation of tipping in dance bars, it should not be reduced to this. I have attended *Mujra* in various places, performed with great skill and graciousness. Community elders or dancers encouraged me not just to tip but to keep tipping, exchanging large bills for small ones to draw the process out. It was not sexual, and I certainly did not shower or spray money. Indeed, *Mujra* dancers I talked to in Mumbai said they actually preferred to be handed money, as it was more respectful, though they must go along with what happens now.

### *Expectations, Reciprocity, and Obligations*

Historically, patronising musicians and visibly giving them monetary rewards indicated, among other things, the hierarchical relationship of service provision. The patron gained status from keeping performers who were obligated to perform; in return, the performer received basic, paternalistic support from the patron and extra gifts when the patron was so moved (Qureshi 2002). However, given the intimacy of patron-performer relationships and the potency of music, the hierarchy was not entirely clean-cut. Schofield (2007) has described the status of such performers as liminal.

In the dance bars, customers explicitly expressed how they felt themselves to be like the patrons as they tipped dancers (Dalwai 2012, p. 144). Closer scrutiny of giving and receiving, however, reveals the gulf between the twenty-first century largely lower-class male customers and former aristocratic or royal patrons. Dalwai (2012) describes bar girls as having a 'regal stance' in a way that exceeded even the liminal power of courtesans (p. 131). Unlike court musicians, bar girls have no obligation to serve or even pay a particular customer attention as a customer is not a patron. Dalwai observes that bar girls could greet tips with a 'not bothered by money' attitude, though they knew how to keep customers tipping through enough eye contact, attention, flirtatiousness, and sensual dance moves (p. 131). They could also seductively gesture for money from customers, or teasingly grab it.

Crucially, giving tips did not enable customers to 'buy' bar girls for sex or relationships. As Dalwai (2012) observes, it is well known that 'a woman cannot be purchased [in a dance bar] but must be won or earned' (p. 148). In fact, men became angry when giving vast amounts to bar girls did not result in sexual liaisons, and some even complained to the Bhartiya (Indian) Bargirls Union. The intensely visual giving of large amounts of money performatively manifests emotional abandon and unlimited desire, intensifying the mood of the Bollywood songs to which the girls danced. But these dramatic emotional and monetary gifts (which occasionally wiped customers out financially) were part of an exchange in which reciprocity was unpredictable. Some customers knew it was a game, others did not. This explosive cocktail of money, music, eroticism, and love gave the bar girls considerable power over their customers and was one of the drivers of a ban on dancing in bars in 2005. Regulators had earlier made attempts to temper these exchanges. For example, a rule was established that money should be given to stewards rather than directly to bar girls. The ban was successfully contested in the High Court in 2006 and Supreme Court in 2013, but the government has continued to produce stringent or impossible conditions for bars to regain performance licenses. In 2018, one such rule was the outlawing of money showering.[9]

Tipping in *Qawwali* is enacted in a way to enshrine very different expectations of reciprocity and obligation. In the *dargah*, *qawwal*s would not make demands of people for *nazrana*. *Nazrana* is 'a necessary payment for [the musicians] and a spiritual blessing for those making the offering' (Johnston 2000, p. 88). However, as Saleem Hasan Chisti, the senior *qawwal* at the *dargah* in Fatehpur Sikri, said, they would never request a particular amount from someone or question whether they were giving 10 or 20 or 100 rupees and to demand money would be 'very wrong.' He continued,

> People who come to this *darbar* [court] in which we are sitting, they come to ask from this *darbar* [i.e., from the saint], so why should we sit in this *darbar* and make demands from these people. No. If we are to ask then we will ask only from Him.

As he and his son repeatedly emphasised, everything they have is given by Baba Sahib, the saint. They are nothing without him and have no right to demand or expect.[10] *Nazrana* is given in cash, but its quantitative value is played down, making it more of a token (Keane 1996). However, beyond the moment of giving and receiving, the monetary amount is important to *qawwal*s. This is especially so given many are very poor, and in today's India, social value is increasingly measured by material wealth.

Ultimately, it is the duty of the *qawwal*s to serve the saint as a court musician would serve a patron, as well as the Sufi elders. Unlike in dance bars, the hierarchy is clear. Money cannot change a *qawwal*'s status in the Sufi spiritual economy. Similarly, a court musician, even if well-rewarded, would still remain fundamentally a service provider, as status resided essentially in land, not money. Dance bars, however, are primarily located in a capitalist class society where there is mobility, and money is the key medium. Beyond the *dargah*, money does affect a *qawwal*'s status and *qawwal*s do negotiate fees for concerts and I have heard them talk proudly of being paid large sums, even naming specific amounts.[11]

## Invisible Payments and Fixed Fees in Today's Classical Music

As classical music moved from the courts and homes of the aristocracy to middle-class establishments, tipping was stopped or died out. Radha Kapuria (2015) writes of how it was disallowed at the Harvallabh festival following the involvement of VD Paluskar, a key reformer of Hindustani classical music. Reformers decried the 'decadence' of royal patronage in terms of financial squandering, courtesans, and a combination of the two (Kobayashi 2003).

In the decades after independence, middle classes, who became the main audiences and performers of classical music, lived generally frugal lives. Classical music was supported strongly by the state and presented much less lavishly than in feudal times. The role of extremely wealthy individual patrons with business or aristocratic backgrounds had been crucial earlier in the twentieth century but gradually waned. It has not disappeared entirely, but is increasingly replaced by corporate sponsorship. One way or another, Hindustani classical music requires large amounts of money and resources, being an extremely costly art in terms of the time one must spend to become a performer or an informed listener. Therefore, the discomfort about cash tipping is not really about the amount of wealth or other resources that go into Hindustani music, but instead about conspicuous consumption and the visibility of money.

In a middle-class context in which people subsist principally from earned rather than unearned income, conspicuous consumption can evoke waste and depravity (Veblen 1994[1899]). This does not mean that wealth no longer exists or is unimportant. In a very similar way to Western classical music, Hindustani music underwent a sacralisation, making it a transcendent high art controlled by middle-class elites.[12] In both cases, classical traditions were sectioned off from popular genres, which in India became known as 'semi-classical.' The sacralisation also involved framing art as antithetical to money, even though there would be no such art without large surpluses.

The unacceptability of visible tips of cash for the so-called classical arts can also be seen in terms of Marx's (1904[1859]) pyramid structure of money in capitalism, in which hard cash is at the lowest level. It is the money of poor people, those who may not have a bank account or credit cards, or who live hand to mouth. Such individuals do not access credit money, let alone the apparently self-expanding 'fictitious capital' (Marx 1904[1859]). It is, thus, unsurprising that while cash tips are now inconceivable, corporate sponsorship is acceptable in Hindustani music, though its visibility is to some degree limited to avoid the appearance of commercialism, such as by not allowing logos on stage. The dance bars where cash was highly visible were, notably, a lower-middle-class arena. Similarly, the practice of a groom wearing a garland of banknotes is a rural or nouveau-riche phenomenon and is mocked by Indian elites.

The incongruity of cash tips in today's classical performing arts is also because it would imply that the receiver is a service provider, subordinate to the giver. While this was the standard in feudal patronage, post-reform classical music became an increasingly enclosed elite middle-class zone, with low-status traditional performers marginalised, whether abruptly or gradually. In addition, in tipping, remuneration largely depends on how moved listeners are by the music. Reformists decried the idea that performers were subject to the whims of patrons (Kobayashi 2003). In contrast, a fixed, agreed-upon fee puts the performer at the centre of the valuation and is consistent with a bourgeois model of the performer as an artist who performs ultimately for art or for God. In today's classical performing arts, rather than tips, spontaneous gestures and exclamations of appreciation are prominent as a non-monetary medium of value responding to the unpredictability of what a performer 'gives' you (Morcom 2020). Thus, we see how money's value and meaning are performative, and determined by its use.

## Notes

1 The *shehnai* player Satish Prakash Qamar also explained this to be the correct way to give *nazrana* to *shehnai* performers in temples (interview, 30 April 2017).
2 I was unable to witness bar dancing in India as a ban had been put in force in 2005, before I began my fieldwork in 2006. I went to various *Mujra* performances in Congress House and Foras Road in Mumbai; attended *Lavani* performances in Pune city and rural Maharashtra in 2007, 2008, 2010, 2017, and 2018; and visited Indian dance bars in Singapore in 2007.
3 See Schofield (2010) on the *qawwals* and *khyal*.
4 See Dalwai's (2012) descriptions of dance bars (pp. 131–2).
5 Varsha Kale, personal communication, 2017.
6 Interview, September 2008, Mumbai.
7 Interview, 16 October 2019, Delhi.
8 Mohsen Mohammadi, personal communication, 29 May 2019.
9 Personal communications with Varsha Kale since 2013.
10 Interview, 15 November 2017, Fatehpur Sikri.
11 See also Mason's (2013) discussion of gift and wage payments to hereditary performers of the Malayan caste in South India.
12 See Dimaggio (1982) on the sacralisation of Western classical music. In India, the sacralisation involved a subsuming of the newly named classical arts with Hindu religiosity.

## References

Appadurai, A 1986, 'Introduction: commodities and the politics of value,' in A Appadurai (ed.), *The social life of things: commodities in cultural perspective*, Cambridge University Press, Cambridge, pp. 3–63.

Dalwai, S 2012, 'Performing caste: the ban on bar dancing in Mumbai,' PhD thesis, Keele University.

Dimaggio, P 1982, 'Cultural entrepreneurship in nineteenth century Boston: the creation of an organizational base for high culture in America,' *Media, Culture and Society*, vol. 4, no. 1, pp. 33–50.

Dodd, N 2014, *The social life of money*, Princeton University Press, Princeton, NJ.

Guyer, J 2004, *Marginal gains: monetary transactions in Atlantic Africa*, University of Chicago Press, Chicago, IL and London.

Hart, K 1986, 'Heads or tails? Two sides of the coin,' *Man*, vol. 21, no. 4, pp. 637–56.

Johnston, SM 2000, 'Poetics of performance: narratives, faith and disjuncture in qawwali,' PhD thesis, University of Texas at Austin.

Kapuria, R 2015, 'The Harballabh festival of Punjab, c. 1875–1950,' *Social Scientist*, vol. 43, no. 5/6, pp. 77–91.

Keane, W 1996, 'Money as matter and sign,' *Etnofoor*, vol. 9, no. 1, pp. 71–81.

Keane, W 2008, 'Market, materiality and moral metalanguage,' *Anthropological Theory*, vol. 8, no. 1, pp. 27–42.

Kobayashi, E 2003, 'Hindustani classical music reform movement and the writing of history, 1900s to 1940s,' PhD thesis, University of Texas at Austin.

Marx, K 1904[1859], *A contribution to the critique of political economy*, Charles H. Kerr and Company, Chicago, IL.

Marx, K 1993[1939], *Grundrisse: foundations of the critique of political economy*, Penguin Books, London.

Mason, K 2013, 'Musicians and the politics of dignity in South India,' in P Bohlman (ed.), *The Cambridge history of world music*, Cambridge University Press, Cambridge, pp. 441–72.

Maurer, B 2006, 'The anthropology of money,' *Annual Review of Anthropology*, vol. 35, pp. 15–36.
Mazzarella, W 2015, 'A different kind of flesh: public obscenity, globalisation and the Mumbai dance bar ban,' *South Asia: Journal of South Asian Studies*, vol. 38, no. 3, pp. 481–94.
Morcom, A 2015, 'Terrains of Bollywood dance: neoliberalism and the transformation of cultural economies,' *Ethnomusicology*, vol. 59, no. 2, pp. 288–314.
Morcom, A 2020, 'Music, exchange, and the production of value: a case study of Hindustani music,' in A Morcom & T Taylor (eds.), *The Oxford handbook of economic ethnomusicology*, Oxford University Press, New York, pp. 1–21.
Munn, N 1986, *The fame of Gawa: a symbolic study of value transformation in a Massim (Papua New Guinea) society*, Cambridge University Press, Cambridge.
Pernau, M & Jaffrey, Y 2008, *Information and the public sphere: Persian newsletters from Mughal Delhi*, Oxford University Press, New Delhi.
Qureshi, RB 1995[1986], *Sufi music of India and Pakistan: sound, context and meaning in qawwali*, University of Chicago Press, Chicago, IL and London.
Qureshi, RB 2002, 'Mode of production and musical production: is Hindustani music feudal?' in RB Qureshi (ed.), *Music and Marx: ideas, practice, politics*, Routledge, New York and Abingdon, Oxfordshire, pp. 81–105.
Schofield, K 2007, 'The social liminality of musicians: case studies from Mughal India and beyond,' *Twentieth-Century Music*, vol. 3, no. 1, pp. 13–49.
Schofield, K 2010, 'The origins and early development of *khyal*,' in NDJ Bor & J Harvey (eds.), *Hindustani music: thirteenth to twentieth centuries*, Manohar, New Delhi, pp. 159–94.
Veblen, T 1994[1899], *The theory of the leisure class*, Dover Publications, New York.
Virmani, S 2009, *Koi Sunta Hai: journeys with Kumar and Kabir*, documentary, produced by Srishti, directed by Shabnam Virmani.
Wade, B 1984, *Khyal: creativity within North India's classical music tradition*, Manohar, New Delhi.
Zelizer, V 1994, *The social meaning of money*, Basic Books, New York.

# 7 Materialising Insurgency

## Walnut-Wood Carving and the Material Culture of Conflict

*Nikita Kaul*

At his shop, Suffering Moses, Sajid showed me a box that had been damaged in the floods that rampaged Srinagar in 2014. He informed me that this precious walnut-wood box was manufactured during his grandfather's time and was roughly a 100 years old. With some repair work and polish, Sajid and a group of craftsmen were able to restore this craft object to make it look like it had just been made. The carving on the box was intriguing. I had never come across this kind of intricate work during my immersive fieldwork with the craftsmen of walnut-wood carving. Sajid explained that the carving is called *nyuk kaam* (intricate work),[1] and was done 'back then, not anymore.' This craft object was certainly not a docile, decorative thing at the shop. It was symbolic of a time, practices, and social relations that brought it into being. It spoke about erstwhile training and practice of craftsmen, tools they used, and preferences of their customers. This made me ponder: Fifty years from now what would people, who look back into the artefacts of today, understand about Kashmiri society? What knowledge will these craft objects divulge about Kashmir and its people and what relationships would they unveil? Carrying forward this line of thought, this chapter focuses on the relationships that craft objects organise and mediate. It is based on an ethnography of walnut-wood carving craft practiced in Srinagar, Jammu and Kashmir, that I conducted for eleven months in 2014.[2] The objective of this chapter is to examine the convergence of two diverse worlds: of local Kashmiri craftsmen and armed personnel deployed in Kashmir for counter insurgency operations. While performing their tasks, the armed personnel also became craft consumers. Eventually, the walnut-wood carving craftsmen developed a much-defined range of artefacts that came to be known as military *kaam* (work produced for the military). In many cases, this relationship did not stay limited to them being mere producers and buyers of craft, but its benefits percolated into the personal lives of craftsmen who relied on their network with 'powerful army men' to grapple with everyday conflict in the valley. Relying on the framework of material culture, this chapter sheds light on the relationship between people and objects. It delineates the impact of insurgency and counter insurgency on the practices and relationships of walnut-wood carving craft. Secondly, it explains how craft objects mediate social relations between craftsmen and armed personnel deployed in the valley.

Walnut-wood carving is the practice of carving the native walnut wood that grows in different parts of Kashmir, especially the southern districts of Shopian and

DOI: 10.4324/9781351031028-8

Kupwara. The work of wood carving is traditionally performed by only men in a *karkhana* (workshop or factory),[3] and involves a hierarchical relationship between a master and his craftsmen. Objects carved from walnut wood are produced when craftsmen with three types of expertise come together: carpenter, carver, and polisher. Each of them undergoes a structured apprenticeship to acquire their respective expertise. The production of walnut-wood carving involves a wide range of objects for both utilitarian and decorative purposes. It includes jewellery boxes, wall hangings, furniture, fruit baskets, and flower vases on which the craftsmen carve traditional motifs of local flora and fauna. These motifs commonly encompass *chinar*,[4] rose, daffodil, forest, grapes, lotus, almond, and walnut, which are things of nature that the craftsmen commonly see around them. Sometimes the craftsmen also use an amalgamation of all these motifs, known locally as Punjabi design. The walnut-wood carved craft objects are produced for a vast clientele from across the world. Tourists, national and international buyers, and locals buy these objects, and their circulation in the market begins as soon as their production in the workshop is completed. The craftsmen either sell their craft objects directly to the customers or they depend on a mediation by traders or the state in case they do not have robust networks to facilitate sales. Hence, craft enters the marketplace through various possible networks between craftsmen-trader, trader-buyer, craftsmen-buyer, and craftsmen-state.

There has been an armed insurgency in Kashmir since the late 1980s. Historically rooted in the 1947 partition of Indian subcontinent, it gained momentum in 1989. A series of political and social events in Kashmir emboldened Kashmiri youth against India. The insurgency began with the demands of Kashmiris to separate from the Indian State or accede to Pakistan, a nation closer to the social and religious beliefs of most people in Kashmir.[5] This soon took the form of an armed struggle known to be morally and financially backed by international militant organisations. The armed struggle involved common men and women in the valley, both as victims of the struggle and its perpetrators. The slogans demanding *aazadi* (freedom) from the Indian state reverberate in all parts of the Kashmir valley. Strikes, shutdowns, assassinations, bomb blasts, stone-pelting, and damage to Government property continue to be a part of everyday life in Kashmir. As a response to this, the Indian state has been running an organised counter insurgency offensive, deploying army and paramilitary forces to occupy the city of Srinagar. The armed forces number 700,000 in the Kashmir valley, leading to an average of one soldier for every eleven civilians (Rai 2018, p. 1). Armed personnel in uniform are, thus, a common sight in the city.[6] They can be seen patrolling the streets, guarding government offices, marketspaces, banks, mosques, and temples. Bunkers are set up at many crucial locations in the city and army convoys conduct frequent rounds to ensure that the situation is always under control. They stand on duty across the city, agile with their guns, but are present in much higher numbers at volatile spots of the city in which incidents of violence commonly occur. One such area is downtown Srinagar, an older part of the city marked by bricked walls and a labyrinth of alleys within which are located *karkhanas* of various crafts commonly practiced in this part of the city like pashmina weaving, wood carving, and copper carving.

Securitisation of Kashmir has impacted everything in the region including employment, the mobility of people, availability of goods, and the reduced presence of tourists on which much of the economy heavily relies. My respondents, walnut-wood carving craftsmen, told me how they avoid going to work for fear of getting caught in a crossfire or a shoot-out. This creates a void in their workspaces. As there are fewer numbers of hands working in a *karkhana*, delays in order completion ensue. A sharp fall in the number of tourists and difficulties that traders face in transporting finished goods further exacerbates the problems.

The relationship between the armed personnel and local Kashmiris is hostile, rooted in the everyday experiences of people with random frisking, and cordoning off areas, as well as armed searches of individuals and their houses without prior warning or permission. The hostility of local Kashmiris is also rooted in atrocities committed by the Indian army (Batool et al. 2016; Mathur 2016) to which the Indian state and army have responded with either heightened aggression or participation in rescue and community works as well as development projects (Bhan 2014). However, there are also situations in which this hostility is transcended by acquaintance, friendship, and support as the armed personnel encounter the locals. While manning the public spaces, the armed personnel also temporarily become customers of the grocery shops, medical shops, or vegetable vendors that they visit for their everyday needs. One such friendship that develops is between craftsmen and armed personnel, which is mediated by the craft objects.

Armed personnel posted in the valley are important customers for walnut-wood carving *karkhana*s and shops. The craftsmen like Ghulam Qadir Sheikh, Sajid, and others I met during the ethnographic fieldwork were of the opinion that when the army came to Kashmir, they not only instantly took a liking for the craft of walnut-wood carving but also bypassed the traders to become their direct customers. The craftsmen felt that it was the army that brought the wood carving craft out of obscurity resulting from the politics of the region. They kept production going during the years when the insurgency was at its peak in the valley and tourism had reached its nadir. Kashmir is a non-family posting for armed personnel due to it being a highly volatile region. They bought craft for both personal and professional uses, for their offices and official residences. Walnut-wood carving craft objects became gifts to carry back home, souvenirs for the outgoing officers, or objects depicting symbols of their regiments while they served in the beautiful location of Kashmir, one of the more fantasised and romanticised places in India (Kabir 2009).

Serving the army and producing craft objects for them, the craftsmen invariably invite the irks of their neighbours who see them as traitors. However, the craftsmen also acknowledge the privileges of having army men as loyal customers. My respondents recall that amid curfews and cross-firing, jeeps would stop by their *karkhana*, often confusing their neighbours who were not sure if there was an arrest happening or a sale. Immediately after the armed personnel left, people would drop by to get assurances of the craftsman's well-being. The guns, attire, and the sound of screeching jeeps are the symbols of power that armed personnel display in Kashmir. With unrestricted mobility and freedom to shoot and arrest anybody at the slightest hint of suspicion, the power that the armed personnel hold is unmatched and unbridled. Thus, even though there is an apparent welcome offered to them at the craft shops, there is also a silent surrendering to the power that the armed personnel hold in Kashmir. This relationship between the armed personnel and craftsmen since the late 1980s has been shaped by politeness but embedded in fear and has shaped the material culture of conflict.

## The Material Culture of Conflict

Some objects are produced in the times of conflict, so much so that it is the conflict that instruments their making. Conflict is the only means to their existence and it is amid discontent and fear that works become meaningful. Material culture examines the relationship between objects and things. The objects that people use every day in a society reveals the historical, cultural, political, and social conditions of their origins. It reveals the skills, technology, and knowledge that were used towards the making of objects. Material culture provides a rich and unique form of access to the emotional and social dimensions of war and forced displacement, offering an insight into the lives of people who did not leave textual records (Auslander 2018, p. 7). It is a critical framework to understanding conflict and its aftermath. There are works that contribute to the study of material culture and memory of war like Cork (1994) focuses on a collection of war paintings produced in the West as an aftermath of World War I; King (1998) looks at the making of war memorials in Britain; and Al-Khalil (1991) examines war monuments.

Saunders (2000) talks about 'trench art' – objects of metal, cloth, bone, and wood made as souvenirs both during and after conflicts. The author describes trench art as including objects made by prisoners of war and soldiers, as well as civilians who were affected by the conflict. Saunders (2002) also talks about 'war objects,' such as bullets, tanks, or an entire landscape of battlefields. These objects could also be war weapons, memorials, or the ruins of a conflict. The trench objects and war objects, the author explains, evoke the memory of conflict and destruction and are traded as collectibles or displayed in museums as a heritage to promote tourism. In Kashmir, a new material culture in walnut-wood carving emerged as a subcategory of its own within the production chain, as conflict gave space to the building of new relations. The walnut-wood carved objects that craftsmen produce for the army and paramilitary personnel are distinctly called military *kaam*. Military *kaam* includes three categories of objects: trinkets or gifts, bulky furniture, and goods with insignia. These objects offer a view into the social and material world of conflict. The demand from the army emerged post-1989 and grew so much that it resulted in reorganisation of the production and circulation networks in walnut-wood carving. In certain parts of downtown Srinagar, there are workshops that specialise in catering to the demands of armed personnel clients.[7] These workshops regularly train groups of apprentices who specialise in producing military *kaam*. Their training is for a period of six months to one year, much shorter than the traditional apprenticeship that continues for a much longer period of eight to ten years. The apprentices in *karkhana*s that specialise in military *kaam* produce only one category of product (trinkets, furniture, or objects with insignia). These objects are then sold to the traders who either have a shop inside the barricaded cantonment area (which only approved traders can access) or have developed direct communication with the army officers. Assessing the interests of the armed personnel, the traders have developed catalogues with designs and products that match with their tastes.

The traders who have a shop inside the cantonment areas like Badami Bagh or Avantipora are most accessible to the army officers in and around that area. Such traders are considered to be a legitimate and reliable source of craft by the army customers. The shop has on display only a few pieces of walnut-wood carving objects, mostly smaller objects, but a catalogue with extensive possibilities gives their customers a glimpse at the range of craft work. These traders manage an entire network of craftsmen. Once they receive an order, they instruct the *ustad*, the master craftsman or owner of the *karkhana*, about the requirement, and determine the time needed for completion of work.

Craftwork produced for the military could be broadly grouped into three categories: bulky furniture, gifts or trinkets, and objects with insignia. Bulky high-value furniture items for home include dining tables, bars, sofa sets, wall hangings, or any other decorative item that occupies a space in the house of officers and moves with them when they are transferred to a different location. Gifts and trinkets are smaller objects that craftsmen mass produce, such as keychains, jewellery boxes, fruit bowls, and flower vases that also find their way into the tourist market spaces. The smaller objects mostly come from the Saharanpur wood carving industry.[8] The above two categories of military *kaam* do not have a distinct military identity and hence they easily merge with the regular, non-military craftwork. They do not have a distinct symbol of the armed forces and are mostly orders from armed personnels for their personal consumption. These objects are fluid and if the purchase by the original customer is not fulfilled for any reason, then a switch to other customers (non-military/civilian) can easily be made. The final category of military *kaam* is objects with insignia. These objects are distinct because of the symbols, and signage of the armed forces. They are used especially for display within official premises and include furniture and gifts to officers (to mark an occasion like a birthday, wedding, or anniversary) with a conspicuous logo of the regiment or battalion carved into the object. The regiment logos replace traditional motifs of walnut-wood carving. The objects with insignia formulate the distinct material culture of conflict, constituting a wide range of objects that do not fall into the traditional array of walnut-wood carving but were introduced because of insurgency. These commonly include paperweights, tabletops, wall hangings, and wooden sculptures depicting armed personnel in action in a battlefield (see Figure 7.1).

Even though traders commonly go between craftsmen and armed personnel, many armed personnel often bypass the middlemen to directly approach craftsmen, especially when they desire to commission a particular craftsman for their work. This also means that the personnel have better control over the time of delivery and substantially reduces the cost of the product. In cases of direct contact with the craftsmen, they pay a visit to a *karkhana* with a blueprint of the object they desire. Such objects are high value and large and they usually require a large sum to purchase raw materials as walnut wood is expensive. In a direct dealing between

*Figure 7.1* A table top with the regiment logo engraved in the centre and chinar motif on the edges produced for the regiment Sabre Killers 129 AD. Photograph by author.

craftsmen and officers, the commissioned work is, thus, paid for through a partial advance. In contrast, work that comes through a trader often involves no advance payment to the craftsman, requiring the craftsman to bear all the production costs himself to be reimbursed later. This gives rise to exploitative channels that craftsmen constantly strive to break by seeking direct contact with officers.[9]

Military *kaam* in walnut-wood carving has mediated a relationship between two diverse groups: local Kashmiri craftsmen and the armed personnel deployed in the valley. By developing a direct connection with the *karkhana*, the officers are able to form a personal relationship with the craftsmen. This association between a craftsman and an army man has benefitted the craftsman in some cases, especially in dealing with the instability linked to insurgency. A craftsman named Ashraf Ali Dar,[10] shared with me that in 2001, his 17-year-old nephew somehow managed to get in touch with the local militants and started working for them. During a stone pelting event, he was detained and taken to an unknown location. It was his craft links with senior personnel in the army for whom he had recently made a dining table set that helped Ashraf Ali Dar find his nephew and to vouch for his release. For his support, Ashraf Ali Dar gifted him an exquisite bar cabinet. In another instance, the son of another craftsman, Moin-ud-din,[11] began to show signs of supporting militants in the neighbourhood. Unable to pull his son out of this circle of influence, he called his brigadier customer, who visited them at their house in downtown Srinagar and spoke at length with his son. In a friendly conversation, the brigadier explained to him the risks of being caught as a militant or supporting a militant. There are many instances in which armed personnel have also supported craft traders by having their consignments move smoothly across the city border during shutdowns.

Beyond the materiality and novelty of craft, military *kaam* reveals a complex labyrinth of fear that shapes the objects. It reflects a personal relationship of trust between people whose desire to invest in their craft surpasses the fear of the armed personnel. However, producing for the army or trading with them does not require a craftsman to support the Indian army or the Indian nation state. The craftsman could easily be producing for the army and supporting insurgency at the same time, openly or clandestinely. Producing for the army also does not mean that one has put any faith in the armed forces or has a diminished wrath against them. A craftsman working in a conflict region may be able to disconnect himself from the object that he makes. The object ceases to represent the craftsman or his ideological stance on the conflict. While it unveils the connections between a craftsman and an army man, it also unveils the disconnection with the self that the maker crafts in the process.

## Armymen and Craftsmen: Shared Dispositions and Masculinities

Why is it that out of all the crafts, walnut-wood carving captured the interests of the armed forces? Why did some officers go as far as contacting some of the renowned craftsmen in the valley directly to purchase an exquisite piece of craftwork from them? Why do certain regiments see a walnut-wood crafted artefact as an appropriate gift or souvenir? While the rigour and training required by the military are paralleled in many craft-making practices, I found particular resonance in wood carving. During my fieldwork, I was selling a dining table set to a Colonel posted at Bandipora. He had visited Ghulam Qadir's *karkhana* after hearing accolades about his craftmanship.[12] It was during an interaction with him that connections between walnut-wood carving and the army became clearer as the colonel drew an interesting analogy, 'I find this craft interesting. It's sturdy, reliable and seasoned, much like us.' This suggests that the army men and walnut-wood carving craftsmen exhibit similarities in their dispositions and subjectivities. These are embedded in the training and practice that they (armymen and craftsmen) must undergo to become a certain kind of practitioner, imbibing them with certain masculine traits, such as strength, patience, sacrifice, and passion, all shaped by perseverance and practice.

The men working at the *karkhana* are socialised into becoming experts. This includes moulding them into certain body postures (that change with the tool in hand), and certain ways of using language, routines, discipline, and bodily strength. While producing the craft, a craftsman imbibes the raw material with the masculine characteristics of sturdiness and strength, while at the same time, the raw material constantly produces a stronger and more seasoned craftsman. Through this process, the walnut wood and its craftsman are constantly engaged in the process of making each other.[13]

Training to be an accomplished practitioner or a craftsman is mediated by certain materials such as tools, raw materials, and a *jhazeer* (a hookah), the materiality of which is also gendered. Tools for carving, cutting, and polishing wood evoke a masculine image of a man's hand holding and using them even in the non-artisanal world of work. Craftsmen in *karkhanas* rely on the *jhazeer*, from which they smoke tobacco from time to time to focus their creative energy. And while they work, the craftsmen sing songs, share political ideologies, and speak with each other freely. Before the raw material walnut wood reaches a *karkhana*, it passes through different forms and processes that can be conceived as masculine. Walnut wood comes from forests through a process of auctioning, passing through a clandestinely operating wood mafia, amid corrupt practices of taxes and transportation bribes. It reaches the wood market in the city where men work on mechanised equipment to see large and heavy logs of wood. It is from here that craftsmen buy their raw materials. Before it is used, the raw material must also be seasoned for several months to make it sturdy. A novice in the process also cultivates a set of personal values and dispositions, as well as embodying personal qualities necessary for an accomplished craftsman (Jones & Yarrow 2014; Marchand 2008; Venkatesan 2010). Hence, what the training instils is not only the technical skills of crafts but also prolonged learning in becoming a craft practitioner and a master, or *ustad*. What a walnut-wood carving craftsman embodies are the values of practice, strength, hard work, discipline, endurance, and sacrifice. The artisanal community sees these virtues as the qualities of all good craftsmen. Those who possess these skills are able to protect the craft (in particular, from being degraded in the wake of capitalism) and to sustain their families.

This masculinity imbedded in the practice of wood carving resonates with that embodied by military training. The armed personnel undergo rigorous training in combating resistance in order to protect the nation. While describing the making of a serviceman, Mazumder (2003) explains that the discipline of military life instils concepts of time, punctuality, cleanliness, dress code, and healthy diet into the recruits (p. 38). These traits are drilled into them day in and day out and are not easily forgotten. The rigorous routine echoes that of a young apprentice who learns to practice the craft from his master. Thus, it is this interspersing of traits (of endurance and sturdiness) as well as the undertones of masculinity of the walnut wood that invoke interest and desire towards wood carving objects amongst the armed personnel. I suggest that it is this similarity that has shaped the material culture of conflict in Kashmir.

## Conclusion

The military *kaam* in Kashmir embodies a material culture of conflict that developed because of army deployment in the wake of the insurgency in Kashmir. The existence of military *kaam* reflects the fact that craftsmen could not sell their crafts due to the rising conflict and concomitant demise of tourism in the valley. The craftsmen began to depict conflict in their work for the people who are the reason behind much of their agony and who represent the much-despised Indian nation state. On the surface, military *kaam* reveals a symbiotic relationship between craftsmen and army men. However, in the face of a quotidian conflict, it is a battle for existence and survival for craftsmen to engage with and produce for them. Their craft serves as a bridge that connects two groups that are at political odds with each other.

## Notes

1 *Kaam* means work.
2 The ethnography was conducted primarily in the *karkhana* of *Ustad* (master) Ghulam Qadir Sheikh in the Safa Kadal area of downtown Srinagar. The *karkhana* specialises in producing furniture. The *karkhana* has a vast clientele from the armed forces, mostly high-ranking officers, who visit the *karkhana* for both their domestic and official orders. As a part of my ethnography, I actively participated in sale of finished objects at the *karkhana* especially to the Urdu/Hindi-speaking customers.
3 For more on *karkhana*, their meaning, history, and transformation in eighteenth and nineteenth centuries, see Verma (1994) and Roy (1999).
4 *Chinar* or Platanus Orientalis is a deciduous tree that grows in Kashmir. The *chinar* motif is commonly used by craftspeople in Kashmir to adorn their craft. Within the walnut-wood carving repertoire, the *chinar* motif adorns objects such as dining tables, jewellery boxes, and chairs. *Chinar* is also a shape in which things like wall-hangings or key chains are made. Apart from walnut-wood carving, *chinar* commonly adorns other objects, such as a pashmina shawl, or papier mache artefacts.
5 The following works trace the genealogy of conflict in Kashmir: Snedden (2012), Puri (1993), Noorani (2013), Bazaz (1954), Rai (2004), and Zutshi (2003).
6 The locals in Kashmir inclusively use the term 'army' colloquially. It includes all the defence and military organisations like CRPF, BSF, and the Indian Army, that have been sending their forces for counter insurgency purposes. Throughout this chapter, I have used the terms armed personnel and army men to refer to the deployed officers of the Indian army and CRPF in the city of Srinagar.
7 These workshops were started by practicing walnut-wood carving craftsmen who saw an opportunity in army's interest and as a result shifted their focus, either entirely or partially, on military *kaam*. This means that there are *karkhanas* that produce craft objects only for the army as well as those that cater to both military and non-military demand.
8 The craftsmen in Saharanpur, western Uttar-Pradesh, traditionally use sheesham wood. However, due to dearth of sheesham wood and protection provided to this timber under forest laws, the industry has shifted to a cheaper alternative of using mango wood. The advantage with mango wood is that it can be coloured and hence can be easily faked as walnut wood by darkening its shade. There are networks between traders in Srinagar and Saharanpur who facilitate the transport of craft objects from Saharanpur to Kashmir where it is sold as walnut-wood carving souvenirs to tourists as well as army clients.
9 The exploitative channel between craftsmen and traders results in reduced profit margins and delay in payments for the craftsmen.
10 Pseudonym used.
11 Pseudonym used.
12 Ghulam Qadir displayed things he produced in the shop attached to the *karkhana*. As a part of my ethnographic study, I assisted Ghulam Qadir in the shop and would often attend to Hindi/Urdu-speaking customers.
13 See Naji (2009) on how the things that people make, make people.

## References

Al-Khalil, S 1991, *The monument: art, vulgarity and responsibility in Iraq*, Andre Deutsch, London.

Auslander, L & Zahra, T 2018, 'The things they carried: war, mobility and material culture,' in L Auslander & T Zahra (eds.), *Objects of war: the material culture of conflict and displacement*, Cornell University Press, Ithaca, NY, pp. 1–22.

Batool, E, Butt I, Mushtaq, S, Rashid, M, & Rather, N 2016, *Do you remember Kunan Poshpora?* Zubaan, New Delhi.

Bazaz P 1954, *The history of the struggle for freedom in Kashmir: culture and political, from the earliest time to present day*, Pamposh Publications, New Delhi.
Bhan, M 2014, 'Morality and martyrdom: dams, "dharma" and the cultural politics of work in Indian occupied Kashmir,' *Biography*, vol. 37, no. 1, pp. 191–224.
Cork, R 1994, *A* bitter *truth: avant-garde art and the great war*, Yale University Press, New Haven, CT.
Jones, S & Yarrow, T 2014, 'Stone is stone: engagement and detachment in the craft of conservation masonry,' *Journal of the Royal Anthropological Institute*, vol. 20, no. 2, pp. 256–75.
Kabir, AJ 2009, *Territory of desire: representing the valley of Kashmir*, Permanent Black, Ranikhet.
King, A 1998, *Memorials of the great war in Britain: the symbolism and politics of remembrance*, Berg, Oxford.
Marchand, T 2008, 'Muscles, morals and mind: craft apprenticeship and the formation of person,' *British Journal of Educational Studies*, vol. 56, no. 3, pp. 245–71.
Mathur S 2016, *The human toll of Kashmir conflict: grief and courage in the South Asian borderland*, Palgrave Macmillan, New York.
Mazumder, R 2003, *The Indian army and the making of Punjab*, Permanent Black, New Delhi.
Naji, M 2009, 'Gender and materiality in the making: the manufacture of Sirwan femininities through weaving in Southern Morocco,' *Journal of Material Culture*, vol. 14, no. 1, pp. 47–73.
Noorani AG 2013, *The Kashmir disputes 1947–2012,* 2 vols., Tulika Books, New Delhi.
Puri B 1993, Kashmir *towards insurgency*, Orient Longman, New Delhi.
Rai M 2004, *Hindu rulers, Muslim subjects: Islam, rights, and the history of Kashmir*, Permanent Black, New Delhi.
Rai M 2018, 'Kashmir: from princely state to insurgency,' in *Oxford Research Encyclopaedia of Asian History,* Oxford University Press, Oxford, https://doi.org/10.1093/acrefore/9780190277727.013.184
Roy T 1999, *Traditional industry in the economy of colonial India*, Cambridge University Press, Cambridge.
Saunders, N 2000, 'Bodies of metal, shells of memory: "trench art" and the great war re-cycled,' *Journal of Material Culture*, vol. 5, no. 1, pp. 43–67.
Saunders, N 2002, 'Memory and conflict,' in V Buchli (ed.), *The material culture reader*, Berg, Oxford, pp. 175–7.
Snedden C 2012, *Kashmir: the unwritten history*, Harper Collins, Noida.
Venkatesan, S 2010, 'Learning to weave; weaving to learn…what?' *Journal of the Royal Anthropological Institute*, vol. 16, no. 1, pp. S158–75.
Verma T 1994, *Karkhanas: under the Mughals from Akbar to Aurangzeb*, Pragati Publications, New Delhi.
Zutshi C 2003, *Languages of belonging: Islam, regional identity, and the making of Kashmir*, Permanent Black, New Delhi.

# 8 The *Tawa'if* in Colonial India

## Changing Livelihoods and Emerging Technologies (1790s–1920s)

*Shweta Sachdeva Jha*

The *tawa'if* were the most elite women performers who excelled in the arts of Urdu poetry, as well as musical genres such as *Thumri, Khyal, Dadra, Tappa, Ghazal*, and *Kathak* dance. They performed in princely courts as well as their own salons, or *kotha*s. These performers experienced a rapid decline in their status and fortunes in the aftermath of the Rebellion of 1857 (Oldenburg 1990). In the last two decades, various scholars of music (Macziewski 2006; Morcom 2014) and dance studies (Chakravorty 2008; Walker 2014) have tried to restore the position of the *tawa'if* and their contribution to the history of the arts. Continuing their work, I follow a socio-historical trajectory that focuses on the musical and poetic training practised by women to become accomplished *tawa'if* in the courtly cultures of Awadh and Hyderabad as labour.[1] In particular, I approach the history of livelihoods in relation to changes in the socio-political sphere of the successor states, patterns of patronage, the rising power of the British East India Company (EIC), and the arrival of gramophone companies, helping us to trace shifts in sites of performance in colonial India. I highlight the new strategies of self-fashioning the *tawa'if* employed to cope with these changes. Using a few life-histories, I also chart the ways in which the arts of poetry, music, and dance diverged in the cultural economy of the emerging nation-state.

### Transformations of Labour and Value for the *Tawa'if*

It is well documented that since the seventeenth century, a vast number of itinerant groups of female performers travelled to courts and cities in search of patronage (Trivedi 2002). By 1800, *tawa'if* was a common term for a 'unitary meta-community for elite female performing artists' (Schofield 2012, p. 152). Etymologically, the Urdu word *tawa'if* has its origins in the Arabic *tavaf,* which means 'moving round the Mecca' (Platts 1884, p. 754). Socially, the term referred to women performers who began to settle in the successor states of Awadh, Jaipur, and Hyderabad in the late eighteenth century. The famous chronicler of Lucknow, Abdul Halim Sharar (1975) recounted the presence of *deredar tawa'if* (those who set up their camps, or *dera*) near the camps of the royal armies, as they moved from Faizabad to Lucknow, the capital city of Awadh (Cole 1988). In the cities, the *kotha* (salon) was an establishment with several women and men who worked as

DOI: 10.4324/9781351031028-9

singers, poets, cooks, musicians, dancers, pimps, and *ustads* (teachers). The lowest among the women in the *kotha* were prostitutes (*khangi, randi, kasbi)* who mainly offered sexual services and were not performers. Young women with potential for artistic talents as poets, singers, and dancers acquired training and performed for elite and wealthy men with whom they also had sexual relationships (Oldenburg 1990). Visiting the *tawa'if* was a part of the cultural education of young men from royal and wealthy families. Aspiring courtiers became connoisseurs of poetry and music through their interactions with the *tawa'if* who taught them the finer aspects of refinement (*tahzib*) and shaped their musical and poetic tastes (Sharar 1975). To become performers, young girls trained for hours in music, dance, and poetry under the tutelage of *ustads* (male teachers).

The nature of skills and the labour involved changed with shifts in patronage. From princely courts as institutions of patronage to gramophone companies, the *tawa'if* adapted to new technologies and audiences. Despite these complex social processes, the *tawa'if* continued to undergo arduous training, and the effort they put in provided them with a sense of dignity and pride. Oldenburg (1990), for example, recalls how the descendants of erstwhile *tawa'if* in 1970s Lucknow strongly asserted their training and role as custodians of culture and refinement. Graeber (2001, p. 12) defines value as the 'way in which actions become meaningful to the actor by being incorporated in some larger, social totality—even if in many cases the totality in question exists primarily in the actor's imagination.' The *tawa'if* valued themselves as artists despite the cataclysmic changes of the Rebellion of 1857, and subsequent struggles for dignified livelihoods, including into the twenty-first century. This chapter traces this history of change in labour and value till the 1930s when the new technology of cinema completely transformed the experience of music, dance, and poetry for its audience.

## **Tawa'if** ***and Courtly Culture***

The *tawa'if* Mah Laqa Bai 'Chanda' (c.1767–c.1824) of Hyderabad was a talented poet, singer, and dancer. Her training included learning multiple languages (Arabic, Persian, and Urdu), as well as instruction in poetic composition, archery, singing, and dancing. She was a *sahib-e-divan* ('possessor of a complete volume of poetry') poet, which is a mark of immense talent and prestige. As a performer, she began her career in the court of Nizam Asaf Jah II (r. 1761–1803) and was honoured with the title Mah Laqa Bai ('with an angelic face like the moon') in 1815 in the court of Nizam Sikandar Jah Asaf Jah III (r. 1803–1829). Chanda performed in six courts during her career and, in addition to the Nizams, her patrons included Nawab Aristu Jan (1732–1804), Nawab Mir Alam (1752–1808), and Raja Chandu Lal (1761–1845). All these patrons were powerful ministers who held separate court establishments in imitation of the cosmopolitan court of the Nizam (Leonard 1971). The Nizamat had an exclusive department, called the *Daftar-i-Arbab-i-Nishat* (Office of Masters of Pleasure), which employed both male and female performers like Chanda (Raj 1987; Sachdeva 2008). Any disputes regarding these performers came under the jurisdiction of the *Kanchan Kachehri* (The Kanchan Court). As a *tawa'if,* Mah Laqa Bai received different salaries from each of the courts and gifts in the form of lands, while being exempt from paying taxes (Kugle 2010). Princely courts such as Hyderabad, Awadh, and Jaipur were modern institutions of patronage who had exclusive departments to deal with payments and commissions to performers and artists (Bakhle 2005; Sachdeva 2008). The *gunijankhana* (house of melody) in Jaipur and the *kalawant karkhana* (house of talented artists) in Baroda offered employment to musicians and dancers and were similar to the *Daftar-i-Arbab-i-Nishat* (Erdman 1985; Bakhle 2005; Sachdeva 2008).

However, apart from princely states, an astute *tawa'if* had to search for new forms of patronage as times changed. At a performance held at the court of Mir Alam Bahadur on 18 October 1799, Chanda gifted a handmade copy of her *divan* to a newly appointed British East India Resident, John Malcolm (Dalrymple 2002). Gifting the *divan* was a means for Chanda to seek patronage as well as a tool of political diplomacy, showing her allegiance to the British, a rising power centre in the Deccan (Jha 2015).

After her death at the age of 58, Chanda's properties were auctioned and the wealth accrued was deposited back to the Nizamat according to the norms of the State. As a courtesan, Chanda was a patron as well as a performer. She had employed almost 300 attendants, including slave girls (*kaniz*) and (*khanazad*) male servants (Jha 2015). Among her employees were artists, calligraphers, and chroniclers, such as Ghulam Hussain 'Jauhar,' who she commissioned to write a history of the State of Hyderabad. He dedicated the chronicle *Tarikh -i- Dilafruz* (History of the Enlightened Heart) written between 1814 and 1819 to her (Jha 2015). Chanda supported the festivities and celebrations of *urs* (annual celebrations) near Hazrat Ali's shrine in Hyderabad and provided pilgrims with food and accommodation during the *khat mela.* She supported the building of *ashurkhana* (house of mourning) during Muharram. Besides a grand *haveli* (palatial house) where she lived, she also had a *baoli* (stepwell) and a grand mausoleum constructed for her mother. After her death, Chandra was buried there. She had not married and was not known to have any children. However, the Nizam's office continued to pay her employees a fixed pension till the death of Nizam Asaf Jah III in 1829 (Azmi 1998; Jha 2015). This brief life-history of Chanda shows how her status and work as a performer are positioned within a wider web of networks with chroniclers, poets, artisans, and performers. The architectural traces she left behind reveal her desire to be valued as a courtesan and an elite patron (Jha 2015).

## *Tawa'if* and Modern Institutions of Patronage: The *Parikhana*

In the successor state of Awadh (1722–1856), the last nawab, Wajid Ali Shah (r. 1847–1856) was a poet, performer, and a patron of extensive troupes of performers. He maintained a *parikhana* (house of fairies) which included female performers of different talents. Salaries were fixed according to their performative abilities and musicians were employed for choreographing pieces and providing music and dance training. The performances were arranged during festivals and for the private entertainment of the Nawab and his friends. Sometimes the Nawab also participated and performed in these choreographed events (Jones 2014; Sachdeva 2008).

Although a patron of the arts, Wajid Ali Shah was maligned by the British EIC as a debauched, extravagant, and inefficient ruler (Fisher 1998; Jones 2014). He was forced to go into exile with the implementation of the Doctrine of Lapse by the Governor General Dalhousie (1848–1856) and the annexation of Awadh. The Rebellion of 1857 against the British EIC marked a historic movement, resulting in solidarities across regional and religious communities, castes, soldiers, and women, such as the *tawa'if* (Singh 2007; Dewan 2019). It shook the foundations of the EIC and, in the following months, led to stringent legal and military policies as Queen Victoria declared India a colony of the British Empire in 1858.

In the aftermath of the Rebellion of 1857, the *tawa'if* were heavily penalised for their support of the rebels (Dewan 2019; Oldenburg 1990). They lost social and economic status substantially with the annexation and subsequent policies such as the Contagious Diseases Acts of 1868, which penalised them as prostitutes and as the cause of the high incidents of venereal disease among Company soldiers (Oldenburg 1990). Erica Wald (2009) reveals that 'the superintending surgeons not only created an artificial social and sexual cleavage in colonial society in India, but also fundamentally altered the ways in which various groups of Indian women were viewed' (p. 23). The anti-Nautch movement led by European missionaries and the moral critique of *nautch* (literally 'dance,' specifically, performances by *tawa'if*) by Indian social reformers made the *tawa'if* prominent subjects in debates on sexuality and obscenity (Gupta 2001; Hubel 2005). Colonial legislation and the accompanying social and moral criticism had a drastic effect on their livelihoods. The erstwhile *kotha* with its widely variegated and hierarchical nature of livelihoods became increasingly synonymous with a brothel (Dewan 2019). Due to oppressive laws and moral disapproval, most *tawa'if* found it difficult to survive. Census reports clearly show large-scale migration out of Lucknow, the erstwhile political and cultural centre of Awadh (Cole 1988; Sachdeva 2008). A few women found ways to adapt to this transformation to become *ganewali*s, or professional singers. This transition to the *ganewali* is best illustrated through the life-history of Malka Jan 'Banaraswali' (c. 1857–1906).

## From Poetry to Songbooks: Erased Voices

When Wajid Ali Shah moved to Matiya Burj in 1857, he arrived with retainers, servants, family, and a large-scale migration of male and female performers (Das Gupta 2005; Williams 2017). Soon, upwardly mobile groups of clerks (*babus*) who worked under British EIC officials and wealthy landowners became interested in the talents of the *tawa'if*. The fortunes of many itinerant performers had dwindled, and a larger number of the women were forced into prostitution. However, some had left Lucknow for other cities and continued to perform under popular professional names such as 'Malka' and 'Umrao' (Sachdeva 2008).

Adeline Victoria Hemming, also called Biki, was a 15-year-old girl born of a British father and his native concubine Rukmani, when she married Robert William

Yeoward, a 20-year-old man of Armenian descent in Azamgarh (Sachdeva 2008; Sampath 2012). They had a daughter on 26 June 1873 whom they named Angelina. The couple legally separated in the year 1879 and Adeline moved to Banaras with her mother. There, she converted to Islam and adopted the name Malka Jan while her daughter became Gauhar Jan (c. 1873–1930). To become 'Badi Malka,' Adeline spent eight years training in music, dance and poetry, and was known as *Tawa'if* Malka Jan Banaraswali, or Memsahib *Tawa'if* Banarasi (Jha 2009; Sampath 2012). Gauhar Jan was employed as a performer in Wajid Ali Shah's entourage and lived in Bow Bazar, Calcutta in 1883. Soon wealth and popularity helped her to buy a house on Chitpore Road (Sampath 2012). Her contemporaries included Malka Jan of Agra, Malka Jan of Mulk Pukharaj, and Malka Jan of Chulbuli. Male musicians traced their artistic lineage from a musical household (*gharana*) led by a teacher (*ustad*) in a town or city, and for the *tawa'if,* the name of the town or city became a marker of their identity (Neuman 1980). These regional markers point towards new patrons in cities and towns that included local elites such as landowners, nawabs, clerks, and authors.

For writers like Mirza Muhammad Hadi 'Ruswa' who wrote the famous novel Umrao Jan 'Ada' (1899), the *tawa'if* became a muse. Literary representations of the *tawa'if* abound in Urdu fiction such as Sarshar's Fasana-e-Azad (1907), Sayyid Muhammad Hasan Shah's lost novel, *Nashtar* (1790) which was found and translated into English by Qurratulain Hyder (1993) and many other stories (Pietrangelo 2004). The publication of Ruswa's Junun-e-Intizar (1899) created a furore among his contemporaries because it claimed to be *Tawa'if* Umrao's response to his earlier novel. Autobiographical writing by *tawa'if* other than the debatable *Junun-e-Intizar* remains largely unknown, though autobiographical traces exist in the form of buildings commissioned by the *tawa'if* and the poetry they wrote (Jha 2015).

The main reason for the erasure of *tawa'if* as writers from literary histories of Urdu lies in the literary and cultural restructuring of the Urdu poetic sphere after the Rebellion (Sachdeva 2008, Jha 2022). Poets and scholars of poetry sanitised and 'reformed' erstwhile Urdu poetic practices to mould taste and readership for a 'modern' style of poetry, paralleling the sanitisation of the performing arts (Pritchett 2003). Critical texts, such as Muhammad Hussain 'Azad's Ab-i-Hayat (1880) and Altaf Hali's Muqaddama-i-She'r-o-Sha'iri (1883) played a central role in this re-shaping of the Urdu poetic sphere. These texts established Mirza Asadullah Baig Khan 'Ghalib' (c. 1797–1869), Mir Taqi 'Mir' (1723–1810) and others as canonical poets and instead of love, wine, women, and entertainment, poetry was to be a means to inspire (Pritchett 2003).

However, this restructuring of the Urdu print sphere did not completely replace earlier practices of poetry, which continued to be a heterogenous sphere. Owners of vernacular printing presses printed songbooks, pamphlets, satires, and detective fiction for the reading pleasure of a widening public as much as official reports and newspapers (Oesterheld 2004; Orsini 2009). Cheap and varied in tastes, these printed texts included *tazkiras* (biographical dictionaries) on women's poetry and songbooks by women singers (Petievich 2005). Ranj's *Baharistan-i-Naz* (Garden of Grace 1864) had multiple editions in 1869 and 1882; Durgaprasad Nadir's

*Gulshan-i-Naz* (Rose Garden of Grace 1876) and its sequel Chaman Andaz (1878) are a few examples of *tazkiras* only on women. These *tazkiras* offer an alternate history to the more canonical one established by Azad and reveal the contested world of Urdu poetry (Jha 2022).

These texts carried brief poems by the *tawa'if* and show them to be active in poetic circles in the towns of Tonk, Kanpur, Delhi, Hyderabad, Lucknow, Calcutta, and Murshidabad. Songbooks by the *tawa'if* were being printed from 1864 (Sachdeva 2008; Williams 2017); these included Badi Malka Jan's songbook, Diwan-i-Malka Jan (1886). Saksena (1941) wrote that her songs 'bear testimony to her great knowledge of music, and her proficiency of Hindi language' (p. 295). Malka Jan's contemporaries, the *tawa'if* sisters Zohra and Mushtari, also had songbooks printed from Lucknow (Sitapuri 1962). *Tarana-i-Khayal* (Song of Khayal) also known as *Diwan-i-Mushtari* (Diwan of Mushtari) contained about 100 *ghazals* (Sitapuri 1962) and Malka's daughter Gauhar Jan also published her poetry under the pen name *Hamdam* (Lover; Bari 'Asi' 1929). These songbooks helped the *tawa'if* claim their identity as poets and writers while offering the readers an affordable way to be close to these artists albeit in a literary setting (Jha 2022). However, reformers in literature were busy crafting nationalist histories of music, dance, and poetry. The *tawa'if* had to be kept out of these sanitised histories of poetry and performance (Sachdeva 2008). Malka Jan knew the times were changing and the newly arrived gramophone companies could play a significant role as patrons.

## The Queen of Gramophone Recording and Changing Livelihoods in the Early Twentieth Century

As a young girl when Gauhar Jan arrived in Calcutta with her mother in the 1880s, Malka Jan made sure that her daughter acquired the best musical and dance training under famous *ustads*. Gauhar Jan learned multiple genres such as *khyal*, *thumri*, *kajri*, and *tappa* as well as *bhajans* (devotional songs). She gave her first performance at the age of 12 in the court of Darbhanga, one of the powerful estates in the state of Bihar (Jha 2009; Sampath 2012).

The Gramophone and Typewriter Limited (GTL) was set up in 1898 in England and its first known disc recordings of Indian artists were made in London in 1899. Within three years, the GTL opened a branch in Calcutta, initiating an era of gramophone music in India. Initially, the songs were recorded in India, but the records were pressed in Europe. By 1908, the GTL had established its own factory in Sealdah, Calcutta, to press records (Kinnear 2000). Tours, also called expeditions by the Company, were made to the colonies to scout for native talent and established the GTL's success worldwide. Part of the imperialist agenda of the British Empire, these companies soon secured a presence in colonies like Egypt and India (Farrell 1997; Kinnear 2000).

Most of the recordings of GTL between 1902 and 1920 were recorded by the *tawa'if* thus helping the GTL become a successful venture (Das Gupta 2005, pp. 465–7). During his tour to India, FW Gaisberg, the representative of the GTL attended a private musical gathering of a famous singer of the time, Gauhar Jan. He recalled that she was a celebrity who could sing in 20 languages and dialects (Gaisberg 1942). She charged a heavy sum of INR 300 for one evening and rode in a fine carriage on the *Maidan* at sundown. Engaging in a grand public display of power and stature, she knew her own 'market value' (Gaisberg 1942, p. 56). The 600 records she made for the GTL laid a 'firm foundation' for the new enterprise (Gaisberg 1942, p. 57).

In the early decades of the twentieth century, *tawa'if* adapted to sound recording in search of new livelihoods. Discographies of the GTL show recordings by women singers from Hyderabad, Bombay, Gwalior, Delhi, Patna, Calcutta, Panipat, Agra, Lucknow, Ambala, Meerut, Jhajar, Patiala, Allahabad, and Multan (Kinnear 2000). The *tawa'if* far outnumbered male singers, who were reluctant to record their music (McNeil 2018). Perhaps, the men were not as adept for this new technology and felt less pressure to adapt since their status was reaffirmed through their *gharana*. For example, the singer Hafiz Ali Khan recalled that:

> Once I was nearly caught by the record company people. Yes, several of them came together to Gwalior and persuaded the Maharaja to make a record for them. I was in a terrible quandary. I could not refuse my gracious patron. Very tactfully I explained my feelings to him adding that when my records would be played in pan shops etc. and jeered at by people to whom my classical music is something to laugh at, those records would bear the name of Hafiz Ali Khan of Gwalior and the name of his Darbar would be subjected to the same indignities as my name and music. This last aspect appealed to the Maharaja and he stopped importuning me and I was able to get rid of the record company people.
>
> (McNeil 2018, p. 16)

Male musicians could sharply delineate their exclusivity, but women could not afford to do that given the many ways their status and livelihoods were being undermined at the time. Each record carried the name of the artist. For Hafiz Khan, it was a cause for anxiety, whereas for Gauhar Jan, it was a means to carve out a space in the modern soundscape.

In this modern world of musical practice, control and ownership, the *tawa'if* clearly worked to understand industrial methods of music making and production. These meant business contracts and cash payments instead of gifts or lands as in the cultural economy in which Chanda existed. Initially, gramophone companies tried to issue exclusive contracts for women singers, and many signed these contracts. However, celebrity singers like Gauhar Jan did not sign exclusive contracts, insisting on cash payments for each performance and thus retained their independence (Kinnear 2000). The need to negotiate payments and performance marked a crucial change in the production and circulation of music. Unlike Gauhar Jan, many *tawa'if* singers may not have received adequate payments and were bound by contracts. However, if the new technology of musical production transformed the nature of work for *tawa'if*, it also 'reconfigured the modes of listening to music' and 'introduced issues of individual ownership over collective traditional material, and transmission of knowledge' (McNeil 2018, p. 16). A gramophone queen and a courtesan, Gauhar Jan died in 1930 as an employee at the court of Mysore. Cinema was to change the experience of music and dance in the 1930s when women from non-performing backgrounds began to replace erstwhile performers as singers and poets pushing the *tawa'if* towards illicit worlds of prostitution and penury (Morcom 2014).

## Conclusion

Labour and value can offer a nuanced way to understand the position of women performers in cultural economies and the complex process of social change. The *tawa'if* were talented artists who depended on patronage of wealthy and powerful courtiers. After the Rebellion of 1857, they became victims of social and political discrimination by the colonial state as well as the moral critique of social and cultural reformers. However, the *tawa'if* fought back, albeit in different (and less prestigious) circuits; they continued their work of offering music and poetry as means of pleasure. Part of extensive networks of *gharanas* and erstwhile custodians of *tahzib*, they moulded themselves to cultivate a new self-image and sense of dignity. Their transformation from courtesans to recording artists marks a crucial change in the production and consumption of music. Gramophone recordings took their music beyond salons to households. Subsequently, new ideas of femininity and performance and new creative economies were scripted by marginalising women from performing backgrounds as the stage and school replaced the salon and the court in the new nation-space (Soneji 2012).

## Note

1 See Mason (2013) on a theorisation of music as labour, and on the former *tawa'if*, see Morcom (2017).

## References

Asi, AB 1929, *Tazkirat-al-khavatin*, Naval Kishore Press, Lucknow.

Azad, MH, & *Ab-i-Hayat* 1880, translated and edited by Frances W Pritchett and Shamsur Rahman Faruqi, Oxford University Press (Delhi), 2001

Azmi, R 1998, *Mah laqa: halat-i-zindagi: mah-i-diwan*, Urdu Academy, Hyderabad.

Bakhle, J 2005, *Two men and music: nationalism and the making of an Indian national tradition*, Oxford University Press, New York.

Chakravorty, P 2008, *Bells of change: kathak dance, women and modernity in India*, Seagull Books, Kolkata.

Cole, J 1988, *Roots of North Indian Shiism in Iran and Iraq: religion and state in Awadh 1722–1859*, University of California Press, Los Angeles.

Das Gupta, A 2005, 'Women and music: the case of North India,' in B Ray (ed.), *The history of Indian philosophy, science and culture*, vol. 8, Government of India, Sage Publications, New Delhi, pp. 458–84.

Dewan, S 2019, *Tawa'ifnama*, Context Books, New Delhi.

Erdman, JL 1985, *Patrons and performers in Rajasthan: the subtle tradition*, Chanakya Publications, New Delhi.

Farrell, G 1997, *Indian music and the West*, Clarendon Press, Oxford.

Fisher, MH 1998, 'Women and feminine in the court and high culture of Awadh, 1772–1856,' in GR Hambly (ed.), *Women in the medieval Islamic world: power, patronage and piety*, St Martin's Press, New York, pp. 489–520.

Gaisberg, FW 1942, *The music goes round: an autobiography*, The Macmillan Company, New York.

Graeber, D 2001, *Toward an anthropological theory of value: the false coin of our own dreams*, Palgrave Macmillan, New York.

Gupta, C 2001, *Sexuality, obscenity, community: women, Muslims and the Hindu public in colonial India*, Permanent Black, New Delhi.

Hali, AH, 1895, *Musaddas-i-Hali*, Munshi Naval Kishore Press, Lucknow.

Hubel, T 2005, 'The high cost of dancing: when the Indian women's movement went after the devadasis,' in L Lengel (ed.), *Intercultural communication and creative practice: music, dance and women's cultural identity*, Praeger Publishers, Westport, CT, pp. 121–40.

Jan, M 1886, *Diwan-i-Malka Jan*, Ripon Press, Calcutta.

Jha, SS 2009, 'Eurasian women as *tawa'if* singers and recording artists: entertainment and identity-making in colonial India,' *African and Asian Studies*, vol. 8 no. 3, pp. 268–87.

Jha, SS 2015, 'Tawa'if as poet and patron: rethinking women's self-representation,' in SL Hurley & A Malhotra (eds.), *Speaking of the self: gender, performance and autobiography in South Asia*, Duke University Press, Durham, NC, pp. 141–64.

Jha, SS 2022, 'Situating the *tawā'if* as a poet: nostalgia, Urdu literary cultures and vernacular modernity,' in I Bhaskar & R Allen (eds.), *Bollywood Islamicate histories*, Intellect Books, London, pp. 106–31.

Jones, R 2014, *The last king in India: Wajid Ali Shah 1822–1887*, Hurst and Company, London.

Kinnear, M 2000, *The Gramophone Company's Indian recordings 1908–1910,* Bajakhana, Victoria.

Kugle, S 2010, 'Mah Laqa Bai and gender: the language, poetry and performance of a courtesan in Hyderabad,' *Comparative Studies of South Asia, Africa and the Middle East*, vol. 30, no. 3, pp. 365–85.

Leonard, K 1971, 'The Hyderabad political system and its participants,' *The Journal of Asian Studies*, vol. 30, no. 3, pp. 569–82.

Macziewski, A 2006, 'Tawa'if, tourism and tales: the problematics of twenty-first century musical patronage for North India's courtesans,' in M Feldmann & B Gordon (eds.), *The courtesan's arts: cross-cultural perspectives*, Oxford University Press, Oxford, pp. 332–68.

Mason, K 2013, 'Musicians and the politics of dignity in South India,' in P Bohlman (ed.), *The Cambridge history of world music*, Cambridge University Press, Cambridge, pp. 441–72.

McNeil, A 2018, 'Hereditary musicians, Hindustani music and the public sphere in late nineteenth century Calcutta,' *South Asia*, vol. 41, no. 2, pp. 297–314.

Morcom, A 2014, *Courtesans, bar girl and dancing boys: the illicit worlds of Indian dance*, Hachette India, NewDelhi.

Morcom, A 2017, '"The cure is worse than the disease": Mumbai dance bars, and new forms of justice in the history of female public performers in India,' *Cultural and Social History*, vol. 14, no. 4, pp. 499–512.

Nadir, D 1876, *Gulshan-i-naz*, no publisher, New Delhi.
Nadir, D 1878, *Tazkirat-al nisa nadiri*, no publisher, New Delhi.
Neuman, D 1980, *The life of music in North India: the organisation of an artistic tradition*, Manohar, New Delhi.
Oesterheld, C 2004, 'Entertainment and reform: Urdu narrative genres in the nineteenth century,' in S Blackburn & V Dalmia (eds.), *India's literary history: essays on the nineteenth century*, Permanent Black, New Delhi, pp. 167–212.
Oldenburg, V 1990, 'Lifestyle as resistance: the case of the courtesans of Lucknow, India,' *Feminist Studies*, vol. 16, no. 2 (Summer), pp. 259–87.
Orsini, F 2009, *Print and pleasure: popular literature and entertaining fictions in colonial North India*, Permanent Black, New Delhi.
Petievich, C 2005, 'Feminine authorship and Urdu poetic tradition: *Baharistan-i-naz* vs *tazkira-i-Rekhti*,' in K Hansen & D Lelyveld (eds.), *A wilderness of possibilities: Urdu studies in transnational perspective*, Oxford University Press, New Delhi, pp. 223–50.
Pietrangelo, V 2004, 'Urdu literature and women,' *The Annual of Urdu Studies*, vol. 19, pp. 151–72.
Platts, JT 1884, *A dictionary of Urdu, classical Hindi and English*, W H Allen & Co, London.
Pritchett, FW 2003, 'A long history of Urdu literary culture, part 2,' in S Pollock (ed.), *Literary cultures in history: reconstructions from South Asia*, University of California Press, Berkeley, pp. 864–911.
Raj, S 1987, *Medievalism to modernism: socio-economic and cultural history of Hyderabad 1869–1911*, Popular Prakashan, Bombay.
Ranj, MF 1864, *Baharistan-i-naz*, no publisher, Meerut.
Ranj, MF 1882, *Baharistan-i-naz*, no publisher, Meerut.
Ruswa, MH 1971[1899], *Umrao Jan 'Ada*,' 2nd edn, Maktaba Jamiya Limited, New Delhi.
Ruswa, MH 2015[1899], *Junun-i-intezar*, trans. K Shandilya & T Shahid, Zubaan Books, New Delhi.
Sachdeva, S 2008, 'In search of the *tawa'if* in history: courtesans, *nautch* girls and celebrity entertainers in India (1720s–1920s),' PhD thesis, University of London.
Saksena, RB 1941, *European and Indo-European poets of Urdu and Persian*, Naval Kishore Press, Lucknow.
Sampath, V 2012, *My name is Gauhar Jaan!: the life and times of a musician*, Rupa Publishers, New Delhi.
Sarshar, RN 1907, *Fasana-i-Azad*, 2 vols., Naval Kishore Press, Lucknow.
Schofield, KB 2012, 'The courtesan tale: female musicians and dancers in Mughal historical chronicles, c. 1556–1748,' *Gender and History*, vol. 24, no.1 (April), pp. 150–71.
Shah, SMH 1993[1790], *Nashtar*, trans. Qurratulain Hyder, New Currents, New Delhi.
Sharar, AH 1975, *The last phase of an oriental culture*, trans. ES Harcourt & F Hussain, Westview, Boulder, CO.
Singh, L 2007, 'Courtesans and the 1857 revolt: role of Azeezun in Kanpur,' *Indian Historical Review*, vol. 34, no. 2, pp. 58–78.
Sitapuri, N 1962, *Ghalib nam 'auram*, Idarah-farogh-i-Urdu, Lucknow.
Soneji, D 2012, *Unfinished gestures: devadasis, memory, and modernity in South Asia*, University of Chicago Press, Chicago, IL.
Trivedi, M 2002, 'Female performing artistes in North India: a survey,' in AJ Qaisar & SP Verma (eds.), *Art and culture: painting and perspective*, Abhinav Publications, New Delhi, pp. 153–65.

Wald, E 2009, 'From begums and bibis to abandoned females and idle women: sexual relationships, venereal disease and the redefinition of prostitution in early nineteenth-century India,' *Indian Economic and Social History Review*, vol. 46, no. 1, pp. 5–25.
Walker, ME 2014, *India's kathak dance in historical perspective*, Ashgate, Surrey.
Williams, R 2017, 'Songs between cities: listening to courtesans in colonial North India,' *Journal of the Royal Asiatic Society*, vol. 27, no. 4, pp. 591–610.

# 9 Remaking Labouring Lives through Crisis

## Artisan Weaponsmiths in Colonial North India

*Amanda Lanzillo*

In 1878, the Indian Arms Act made it illegal for Indians to manufacture 'firearms, bayonets, swords, daggers [and] spears,' without a government license, presenting a moment of crisis for India's artisanal weaponsmiths (Home Department United Provinces 1910, p. 4). In practice, the Act made it nearly impossible to independently manufacture guns within British India and placed significant limitations on the manufacture of swords, knives, and daggers (Home Department United Provinces 1910, p. 16). Moreover, because the Act created a strict licensing system that prevented most Indians from buying and carrying weapons, artisan weaponsmiths who attempted to continue their trade saw decreased demand for their wares.

Colonial reports from the following three decades emphasise the collapse of regional centres of artisan weaponsmithing, often attributing this decline to the Act (Dobbs 1908, pp. 17–8; Worsley 1908, p. 4). But even before 1878, Indian weaponsmiths were challenged by severe economic pressures. Facing competition from London- and Birmingham-manufactured guns, as well as other foreign weapons from the early nineteenth century, by 1878, Indian weaponsmiths had already seen a precipitous decline in demand.

This chapter focuses on and compares the experience of weaponsmiths in Rohilkhand, in the present-day Indian state of Uttar Pradesh, and in Punjab between Sialkot and Gujranwala, in present-day Pakistani Punjab. It analyses how these craftworkers negotiated colonial regulatory and economic pressures of the late nineteenth century. Although colonial reports portrayed Indian weaponsmithing and aligned industries as dead or in severe decline after 1878, artisans sought to adapt their trade (Dobbs 1908; Fisher 1883; Hoey 1880). While many transitioned to other forms of metalsmithing and craftwork, they also attempted to preserve social identities as weaponsmiths. Weaponsmiths faced a limited range of choices, but with these limitations, their decisions frequently reflect efforts to preserve community and family identities as producers of firearms, swords, or blades.

Motivating this analysis are broader questions of how craftworkers organised and conceptualised their own labouring lives in the wake of momentous political, economic, or social breaks. The chapter builds off Nita Kumar's (1988) argument that the social worlds of artisan communities in North India are characterised by efforts of 'self-definition' in contexts of frequent 'economic stringency' (p. 12). What, this chapter asks, does the self-definition of a social and labouring world

DOI: 10.4324/9781351031028-10

look like within a trade that was radically challenged within the colonial political economy? Moreover, how do we locate artisan self-definition in a colonial-era trade that was never a target of *swadeshi* efforts nor conceptualised as a Gandhian cottage industry? (Menon 2020). By the 1920s, weaponry was positioned in a very different corner of the South Asian moral economy than other artisan-manufactured goods, as nationalists who reasserted swadeshi in the post-World War I era often also advocated non-violence (Goswami 2004; McGowan 2009). Nonetheless, the histories of weaponsmiths are histories of craftsmanship, and they offer broader insights into how artisans negotiated economic marginalisation while asserting community identity and status.

Ultimately, even as their trade was rendered marginal by colonial regulatory and economic pressures, some prominent weaponsmiths sought not only to sustain livelihoods but to also assert status and prestige for their community or family. At the same time, weaponsmiths with less economic and social capital often had few choices beyond state-run armaments factories, where they were readily hired for their skills, but where they also experienced the gradual marginalisation of forms of community knowledge and training.

## Material Adaptation: Weaponsmiths in Pre- and Early Colonial North India

When British administrators described the decline of weaponsmithing as a trade in the late nineteenth and early twentieth centuries, they argued that Indian weaponsmiths had proved unable to keep up with European material and technological changes (Dobbs 1908, pp. 18–9). In contrast, prior to the nineteenth century, North Indian weaponsmiths were often praised, in both Indian and European records, for their creativity and ability to incorporate new models and technologies of work, including those imported from abroad. For instance, descriptions of *firangi* (European-style) weaponry were common in Persian-language compendia of crafts produced in the seventeenth- and eighteenth-century Mughal empire and other regional polities. These texts were primarily descriptive, profiling the types of work done in a region, especially within royal workshops. However, they may have served a prescriptive role for craftworkers because many were extracted and circulated among merchants. Extracted compendia of crafts texts served as guides to the type of work merchants could commission from craftworkers. One Mughal-era *Majmuʿat al-sanaiʿ* (Compendium of Crafts) was first written around 1620 but extracted throughout the eighteenth and early nineteenth century (*Majmuʿat al-sanaiʿ* 1780). Among the many trades it profiled was sword- and blade-smithing. It compared the properties and processes of making various 'blades, arrows, and spears, which, if an enemy is struck by them, he cannot recover from his wounds' (*Majmuʿat al-sanaiʿ* 1780, f. 21b). These included 'a firangi blade that is as thin as a piece of paper,' as well as *mehrabi*s (arched blades), and *shamshir*s (longer curved swords) (*Majmuʿat al-sanaiʿ* 1780, ff. 21b–23a).

The emphasis on material and technological adaptation, and especially on fluidity between styles of weaponsmithing, both firangi and Hindustani, suggests an artisan weaponsmithing market that was competitive, and weaponsmiths who frequently learned new practices. Similarly, despite later arguments that Indian gunsmiths failed to adopt European innovations, until the early nineteenth century, European observers sometimes admired the creativity, and technological adaptability of Indian gunsmiths (Khan 2004, pp. 36–8). In a memoir of his travels in India in 1817, George Augustus FitzClarence, the illegitimate son of King William IV, praised the firearms and artillery manufactured in India, even as he maintained that European 'ascendency in war … over the eastern nations' was due to superior western weaponry (FitzClarence 1819, pp. 254–6). He noted, for instance, the quality of flintlocks, 'an introduction of the Europeans,' manufactured in Lahore. He suggested that while the Indian 'art of war' had stagnated, craftsmen who manufactured weapons, whether guns, blades, or artillery, had adapted new technologies and styles (FitzClarence 1819, p. 256).

Taken together, these descriptions suggest not only that weaponsmiths incorporated new technologies into their work, but also that elite observers, whether Indian or European, often saw North Indian weaponsmiths as adaptive craftworkers. As we shall see, what changed in the second half of the nineteenth century was not, primarily, the technological competencies of weaponsmithing communities. Instead, new regulatory pressures on Indian weaponsmiths, along with imperial economic support for the London and Birmingham weapons industries, limited the access of Indian producers to the regional market. We turn now to the geographies of weaponsmithing in colonial North India, asking how North Indian centres of trade were reshaped by colonial regulatory and economic policies throughout the nineteenth century.

## Geographies and Communities of Artisan Weaponsmithing in Colonial India

Colonial economic pressures on artisan weaponsmiths in North India were first felt most keenly by gunsmiths. As Priya Satia has recently shown, from the late eighteenth century, the British fire-arms industry grew exponentially through a series of state policies. Major East India Company (EIC) and other imperial contracts were given to gunmakers first in London and later in Birmingham (Satia 2018, pp. 146–82). The massive number of guns ordered by the EIC, the Royal Ordinance, British slave traders, and others allowed British gunsmiths, first in London and later in Birmingham, to rapidly scale up their manufacturing processes. By the late 1850s, there were mechanised gun factories in both London and Birmingham, both of which had been opened with the financial support of the British state (Goodman 1865, pp. 499–500).

The dominance of imported weapons reshaped the artisan industries of North Indian cities that had historically been associated with weaponsmithing. Rohilkhand, located in what was the North-Western Provinces until 1902, and the United Provinces thereafter, was among the regions most renowned for this craft. From at least the early eighteenth century, the artisans of its cities developed distinctive metalsmithing traditions, with weaponsmithing one part of a larger regional association with metalwork. Tirthankar Roy (1996, p. 368) has shown that Moradabad, one of the largest cities in Rohilkhand, emerged as a prominent centre of brass work by the eighteenth century, in part due to the expertise of its workers in brass-casting firearms. Still known today as a 'brass city,' Moradabad was often used in colonial industrial reports to illustrate the best and most successful practices of Indian metalsmithing, long after it had ceased to be a centre for the production of weapons (Dampier 1899). Other cities in the region, including Shahjahanpur, Bareilly, and Bijnor, were likewise noted for weaponsmithing traditions in the early nineteenth century (Fisher 1883, p. 130).

In early nineteenth-century Rohilkhand, the weaponsmithing industry included craftworkers who specialised in firearms, swords, or blades, as well as an array of aligned trades. These included *kathigar*s, who made scabbards and sheaths for swords, *saiqalgar*s, who specialised in polishing, and *minasaze*s, who engaged in engraving for guns and blades, as well as craftsmen who specialised in making blade handles from bone, ivory, or horn (Crooke 1869, p. 257; Hoey 1880, p. 184). The importation of European weaponry, along with restrictions that limited which Indians were allowed to carry arms, impacted the livelihoods not only of gunsmiths, bladesmiths, or swordsmiths but also of craftworkers in these aligned trades.

The impact of pre-1878 economic and regulatory pressures on both weaponsmiths and craftworkers in connected trades is even clearer in a second major Indian centre of weaponsmithing, the north-central region of undivided Punjab. Like Rohilkhand, Punjab – particularly between the cities of Sialkot and Gujranwala – was home to several cities and towns that hosted successful weaponsmithing communities by the early eighteenth century. Sialkot and the small neighbouring towns of Kotli Loharan were especially renowned for the aligned trade of damascening, or inlaying metals, which was practiced most prominently on knives, swords, guns, and other arms manufactured in the area (Khan 2014, pp. 32–5).

Punjabi weaponsmiths and aligned workers faced similar economic pressures to their counterparts in Rohilkhand, as well as a concerted period of colonial disarmament between 1849 and 1856 (Worsley 1908, p. 6). Punjab was one of the last major regions to be incorporated into British India, annexed after a series of costly wars between the EIC and the Sikh Empire. Beginning in 1849, in the wake of the Anglo-Sikh Wars, the colonial administration sought to disarm Punjabis. While disarmament policies were not unique to Punjab, post-1849 efforts, there were more concerted and widespread than elsewhere in British India. Moreover, even before the consolidation of the idea of Punjabis as the embodiment of what colonial writing termed a 'martial' identity on the subcontinent later in the nineteenth century, British administrators viewed inhabitants of the region as both skilled and dangerous with weaponry (Condos 2017, pp. 75–6, 107–8). These administrators sought to confiscate weaponry in the region and prevent the sale of new weapons to Punjabi subjects.

Both regional disarmament and the growth of weapons imports forced weaponsmiths and members of aligned trades to adapt their practices in mid-nineteenth-century Punjab. For those engaged in *koftgari* (damascening) in Kotli Loharan and Sialkot, it initially meant simply applying this skill to items other than locally manufactured weaponry. But the decrease in demand for weapons also decreased the demand for elaborate damascening, with a European report in 1907 describing it as only of interest to the 'tourist and curio collector,' who rarely valued high-cost damascened items (Worsley 1908, p. 7). As a result, many of the craftworkers instead sought employment in other metalsmithing fields. By the 1910s – and especially during the First World War – Sialkot became a prominent centre for the manufacture of surgical tools (Abbott 1921, p. viii). The more reliable pay of surgical tool factories attracted some *koftagari* workers, but the funnelling of workers into these factories meant that they were sometimes unable to pass on their skill in *koftagari* to the following generations (Khan 2014, p. 35) (Figure 9.1).

*Figure 9.1* A sketch of koftgari and inlaid weapons and armour, primarily produced in Sialkot and surrounding regions. The weapons were displayed at the Lahore Exhibition of 1864, and the sketch was printed in B.H. Baden Powell, Handbook of the Manufactures and Arts of the Punjab, published in 1872.

Although weaponsmiths in both Rohilkhand and Punjab faced significant challenges to their trades well before 1878, colonial administrators portrayed the Arms Act of 1878 as a death knell, especially for gunsmiths. This reflected state recognition of the economic impact of the Act, as well as an incorporation of the Act into a broader colonial narrative of the technological and material decline of Indian weaponsmiths. Under the new licensing policies, it was nearly impossible to legally manufacture guns within British India, with no Indian gunsmiths being issued licenses by British authorities in either region between 1878 and 1907. However, small numbers of swordsmiths and bladesmiths were issued licenses. In the city of Bareilly, in Rohilkhand, there were two licensed swordsmiths in 1907, though none were left in Moradabad (Dobbs 1908, p. 17). The declining fortunes of swordsmiths were attributed both to the licensing regime and falling demand, as the Act prevented Indians from purchasing weapons without licensees. A 1907 regional report on iron and steel work noted that the two remaining swordsmiths of Bareilly largely engaged in repairs, rather than manufacture (Dobbs 1908, p. 17).

Conversely, in Sialkot in 1907, over 50 shops or individuals were licensed and engaged in 'making swords and lance points,' though many were reported to be struggling or engaged primarily in repair (Worsley 1908, p. 4). Still, this was a stunning difference from Bareilly and Moradabad, attributable partially to the fact that in Punjab, Sikhs were given a religious exemption from licensing laws to carry the *kirpan*, a sword or blade that had been categorised as a religious duty by the tenth Sikh Guru (Home Department United Provinces 1910, p. 2). The Sikh population in Punjab, along with other communities that had been given exemptions to the Arms Act of 1878, drove demand for the manufacture and repair of swords. As a result, some swordsmiths were able to continue their trade, even if they struggled to sustain profits and were sometimes forced to incorporate other metalsmithing fields into their workshops.

In both Punjab and the North-Western Provinces, weaponsmiths made a wide variety of decisions when facing the economic pressures that accompanied the Arms Act of 1878 and the other crises for their trade in the late nineteenth century. It is impossible to capture the full range of weaponsmith responses to these moments of radical change. Nevertheless, certain choices seem to have been particularly common. Among the most significant was migration to quasi-autonomous Indian princely states. These states were not immediately subject to the Arms Act of 1878, and they rapidly became the important sites of weaponsmithing on the subcontinent. Other weaponsmiths sought employment in regional British Indian ordnance factories, manufacturing arms for the state in an increasingly industrialised system. Still, others transitioned to aligned fields, primarily within metalsmithing, using their familial connections to weaponsmithing to assert distinct forms of artisanal expertise. We turn now to this variety of choices, analysing the degree to which they reflect forms of community self-definition among craftworkers.

## Migration: Weaponsmiths in Princely Rampur

In 1907, an unnamed gunsmith from the North Indian city of Rampur was interviewed by a member of the provincial industrial survey, who was collecting details on the region's iron and steel production. According to the interviewer, the gunmaker's process included making a 'strip of iron half an inch thick and half an inch broad,' which he twisted around a rod and forged into a single piece. He subsequently bored out the tube with oil and resin (Dobbs 1908, p. 18). The interviewer provided details about the gunsmith's process to argue that Indian weaponsmithing was labour-intensive, and slow to incorporate new technologies. 'In the absence of modern tools, the method of work is somewhat primitive,' he wrote, noting that the initial forging and boring of the tube often required four men to labour for weeks (Dobbs 1908, p. 18). Despite lamenting these supposedly technology-poor methods, he admitted that Rampuri gunsmiths produced quality goods. He marvelled that local gunsmiths could create copies of 'good European firearms … indistinguishable from the original' (Dobbs 1908, p. 19).

What underscored the interviewer's understanding of gunsmithing in Rampur as work-intensive and technology-poor, but skilful, was the fact that the state was one of the few areas in the Rohilkhand where the trade was still practiced. Rampur was a princely state, with quasi-autonomous local leadership, and not bound by the Arms Act of 1878. As the only post-1857 princely state within Rohilkhand, and one of the few in the populous North-Western Provinces, Rampur rapidly became a prominent site of weaponsmithing in North India. It drew in artisan migrants from Moradabad, Bareilly, and the other major metalworking and weaponsmithing cities of Rohilkhand, who jostled for state patronage, contributing to a competitive space of artisan weaponsmithing (Khurshid 2001, pp. 21–2, 28–31). Rampur's *banduqi chowk* (guns *chowk*), already a prominent centre for the manufacture and sale of arms from the mid-nineteenth century, expanded rapidly as migrants set up workshops.

Colonial administrators were well aware – and concerned – that Rampur served this role. It was surrounded by British Indian territory, and Rampuri elites maintained economic interests and prestige in major British Indian cities and town such as Moradabad. As a result, from 1878, colonial officers deputed to Rampur pressured the state's ruling Nawab to adopt at least some elements of the British Indian Arms Act of 1878. In response, in 1896, the Nawab created his own licensing system for local gunsmiths, although he continued to permit the manufacture of most blades, swords, and knives (Internal Branch 1932). Gunsmiths who sought to continue their trade were forced to compete for the small number of positions within the state's official workshop. This state workshop was where, in 1907, the unnamed gunsmith was interviewed by the colonial industrial survey.

Although Rampur was renowned for the high quality of the firearms produced in its state workshop, most gunsmiths who migrated there were unable to secure work making firearms (Official Report of the Calcutta International Exhibition 1885, p. 188). Instead, from the early twentieth century, gunsmiths in Rampur made yet another transition, with many turning to other forms of weaponsmithing, as well as other forms of metalsmithing. In the *banduqi chowk* gun market, craftworkers adapted their workshops, and the area soon became known not for guns, but as one of the sites to purchase the Rampuri *chaku*, a long, rough-edged knife. Today, the city's famous knife, often simply called a 'Rampuri,' is most well-known from

Bollywood mobster films, as it became a chosen weapon of filmic villains in the 1960s, 1970s, and 1980s (Ramachandran 2007).

The history of the Rampuri *chaku* reflects a broader narrative of craftworker adaptation, as weaponsmiths flocked to the city and then found other forms of their trade – especially gunsmithing – limited by a state licensing regime. The state's proximity to other cities in Rohilkhand meant that although consumers from British India were officially prohibited from transporting weaponry from princely states, many came to Rampur to purchase weapons anyway, seeking to use it as a loophole in the colonial licensing regime. The *chaku* became synonymous with Rampur because the city drew in weaponsmiths from across Rohilkhand, who made it the centre of a dynamic industry even after the Nawab adopted limitations on the trade.

## Alternative Sites of Employment for Artisan Weaponsmiths

Migration to a princely state – whether Rampur, another state in the North-Western provinces, one of the several states in Punjab, or somewhere further afield – was not a choice open to all artisan weaponsmiths in the wake of 1878. Migration to a princely state required a level of economic capital, or local connections, often in the form of kinship or community ties (Roy & Haynes 2013, pp. 50–3). Weaponsmiths needed funds to establish themselves in a new locale, and they risked facing diminished martial prospects for their children if they left a city where they were well established (Chambers 2020, pp. 42–3; Roy & Haynes 2013, p. 5).

For poorer weaponsmiths, or those without the social capital to migrate, an alternative was to seek work in the colonial state's armament factories. This decision likewise usually required a weaponsmith to uproot himself and migrate, but because these factories had a high level of demand for labour, weaponsmiths could start earning almost immediately upon their arrival. For instance, a 1908 report on iron and steel production in central Indian claimed that work in state armaments factories was one of the best-renumerated options for metalsmiths in the region (Begbie 1908, p. 57). Even if this was overstated, it reflected the fact that labour in armaments factories offered a form of economic security to artisans whose trade was in crisis.

The other choice pursued by some weaponsmiths who could no longer sustain livelihoods in that trade was to transition to other forms of artisan metalwork. Historical centres of weaponsmithing in North India became, over the course of the nineteenth century, more closely associated with other forms of metalsmithing, such as the production of cutlery, surgical tools, scissors, or decorative metalwares. From the final decade of the nineteenth century, new Indian capitalist classes in cities such as Moradabad and Sialkot embraced the cities' association with metalworking traditions and the skill of artisan families to develop their own industrial interests. Some members of successful former weaponsmithing families maintained their own workshops for decorative metalwork, but many others were forced to seek employment in new workshops and factories owned by regional merchants. In Sialkot, many found work in the city's emerging surgical tools industry (Abbott 1921, p. viii). In Moradabad, many transitioned into the city's famed – and increasingly industrialised – brass and copper industries (Dampier 1899, pp. 35–6).

But transitioning to colonial armament factories and other forms of metalwork posed social and professional challenges for many artisan weaponsmiths. The industrialisation of metalwork in either state-run or privately owned factories meant that communities were unable to sustain practices of apprenticeship and training, which together with labour specialisation led to a loss of skills. Moreover, artisans who left weaponsmithing for other forms of metalwork sometimes experienced a loss of social status.

Indeed, when weaponsmiths chose to migrate or transition fields, they likely considered not only economic pressures but also family and kinship ties, social hierarchies, and marriage prospects. In both Rohilkhand and Punjab, weaponsmithing communities were predominantly – though never exclusively – Muslim (Abbott 1921, p. xiii; Rose 1911, pp. 234–6). While regional social hierarchies among Muslims had long histories, they were strengthened and reified through colonial efforts to categorise communities. Weaponsmithing was a laborious craft, and many workers in the trade were historically from marginalised Muslim communities. But because it was also associated with war and military work, workers were sometimes able to claim forms of social respectability that eluded other metalsmiths and Muslim craftworkers more generally.

In a period when a range of Muslim craftworkers sought to claim *ashraf,* or Muslim genteel identity through census and other colonial categorisation projects, the claims of weaponsmiths were sometimes taken more seriously than their counterparts in other trades. For instance, some metalsmiths in late nineteenth-century North India sought to register themselves in colonial records as 'Mughal,' meaning descended from migrants from Central Asia, a category associated with the North Indian *ashraf.* For the most part, colonial record keepers, along with the metalsmiths' elite Muslim contemporaries, rejected these claims, arguing that the metalsmiths were instead the descendants of Hindu converts. But weaponsmiths were more readily accorded Mughal status – or other ancestries that implied high social status – than other Muslim craftworkers, both by ethnographers and local Muslim communities (Amin 1941, p. 44).

## Weaponsmiths and Social Identity: The Case of Bulaqi

The experiences of a weaponsmith identified as Bulaqi *Banduq-saz* (Bulaqi the gunmaker) in Rampuri records are indicative of the ways in which weaponsmiths adapted their trades while attempting to preserve and present social identities as weaponsmiths. From a family of Rohilkhandi weaponsmiths who had settled in Rampur, Bulaqi was selected as a gunsmith for the Nawab's workshop in 1889 (Fihrist-i Mulāzmīn 1904, pp. 22–3; Khurshid 2001, pp. 21–2). In the 1890s, Bulaqi used his funds and prestige from state employment to open an independent workshop in the *banduqi chowk.* There, he relied on his reputation as a state-employed weaponsmith to secure apprentices. But because of the new regulations on independent weaponsmithing in the city, in his independent workshop, he largely focused on decorative metalwork, along with some blades. Apprentices in his workshop often focused on making ornate *pandans* – boxes for holding betel leaf – and hookahs (Abel 1911, p. 35).

Although the workshop primarily engaged in decorative metalsmithing, for the sons of weaponsmiths who trained under Bulaqi, his status as a state weaponsmith meant that they could also maintain the trade as part of their social identity. Sometimes also recorded as Bulaqi Ustad (Bulaqi the teacher) the state gunmaker's association with weaponsmithing brought both economic opportunity and social status for his students, who were recorded in state histories as weaponsmiths, even if they made few if any weapons (Khurshid 2001, p. 22). The experience of Bulaqi and his students reflects the importance weaponsmiths placed on maintaining the trade as a social identity, as well as the degree to which prominent craftworkers could sometimes lend legitimacy and status to apprentices.

## Community Self-Redefinition and Colonial Crises

Weaponsmiths in late nineteenth- and early twentieth-century North India faced challenges to their livelihoods, sparked by both state regulations and colonial economic policies. In their efforts to secure work and income, these craftworkers engaged in community redefinition. Many migrated or shifted to alternative trades, even as they simultaneously sought to preserve their identities as weaponsmiths. Regional social hierarchies – often based on Muslim claims of ancestral descent but entrenched through colonial ethnographic projects – meant that craftworkers sometimes experienced increased social marginalisation if they left weaponsmithing.

Within a limited range of choices, it was craftworkers with the most economic and social capital who were to continue to assert their status and positionality as manufacturers of weapons. Weaponsmiths without these benefits were often funnelled into either colonial armament factories or industrialised workshops in alternative metalworking trades. Even as they sought to assert community claims to a tradition of weaponsmithing, they were limited in their ability to pass on the trade and its associated skillsets to subsequent generations. Despite these radical breaks and realignments among weaponsmiths, as we saw in the case of Bulaqi and his apprentices, some weaponsmiths did use bonds of education and community to maintain a social identity as weapons manufacturers even as they transitioned primarily to work in other trades.

Weaponsmiths were rarely positioned within the economic projects that accompanied the Swadeshi movement or Gandhian interest in craftwork. But their experiences nonetheless help us understand how artisans responded to crises sparked by colonial economic and regulatory policies. The extreme nature of the marginalisation of their trade sheds light on how artisans negotiate limited sets of choices and maintain livelihoods and social identities in the context of radical challenges to their livelihoods.

## References

### *Primary Sources*

Abbott, ER 1921, *Annual report of the Department of Industries in the Punjab for the year ending* 31 March 1921, Punjab Government Press, Lahore.

Abel, WC 1911, *Gazetteer of the Rampur State*, Government Press of the United Provinces, Allahabad.

Amin, MA 1941, *Islah-i Watan*, Murtaza Barqi Press, Rampur.

Begbie, LF 1908, *A monograph on the iron and steel industry in the Central Provinces*, Secretariat Press, Nagpur.

Crooke, W 1869, *Tribes and castes of the North-Western Provinces and Oudh*, vol. 4, Government Printing, Calcutta.

Dampier, GR 1899, *Monograph on the brass and copper wares of the North-Western Provinces and Oudh*, Government Press, Allahabad.

Dobbs, WEJ 1908, *Monograph on iron and steel work of the United Provinces of Agra and Oudh*, Government Press, Allahabad.

*Fihrist-i Mulāzmīn Riyāsat-i Rāmpūr* 1904, Government Press, Rampur.

Fisher, FH 1883, *Statistical, descriptive and historical account of the North-Western Provinces of India*, vol. IX, Government Press, Allahabad.

FitzClarence, GA 1819, *Journal of a route across India, through Egypt, to England, in the latter end of the year 1817, and the beginning of 1818*, John Murray, London.

Goodman, JD 1865, 'On the progress of the small arms manufacture,' *Journal of the Statistical Society of London*, vol. 28, no. 4, pp. 494–506.

Hoey, W 1880, *A monograph on the trade and manufactures in northern India*, American Methodist Mission Press, Lucknow.

Home Department United Provinces 1910, *The Indian Arms Act 1878 and the Indian Arms Rules 1909*, India Office Records (IOR), British Library, London.

Internal Branch 1932, 'Question of paramountcy in connection with the restrictions on the manufacture and importation of arms and ammunition,' File 353, India Office Records (IOR), British Library, London.

Majmuʿat al-sanaiʿ 1780, *IO Islamic 2363*, British Library, London.

*Official Report of the Calcutta International Exhibition, 1883-4*, vol. 1, 1885, Bengal Secretariat Press, Calcutta.

Rose, HA 1911, *A glossary of the tribes and castes in the Punjab and North-West Frontier Province*, vol. ii, Civil and Military Gazette Press, Lahore.

Worsley, G 1908, *Monograph on the iron and steel industries in the Punjab*, Civil and Military Gazette Press, Lahore.

### *Secondary Literature*

Chambers, T 2020, *Networks, labour and migration among Indian Muslim artisans*, UCL Press, London.

Condos, M 2017, *The insecurity state: Punjab and the making of colonial power in British India*, Cambridge University Press, Cambridge.

Goswami, M 2004, 'From *swadeshi* to *swaraj*: nation, economy, territory in colonial South Asia, 1870–1907,' *Comparative Studies in Society and History*, vol. 40, no. 4, pp. 609–36.

Khan, A 2014, 'Power in the field,' in SK Chaudhuri & SS Chaduri (eds.), *Fieldwork in South Asia: memories, moments, and experiences*, Sage Press, New Delhi, pp. 31–69.

Khan, IA 2004, *Gunpowder and firearms: warfare in medieval India*, Oxford University Press, New Delhi.

Khurshid, IH 2001, *Tazkirah-yi hunarmandān-i Rāmpūr*, Raza Library Press, Rampur.

Kumar, N 1998, *The artisans of Banaras: popular culture and identity, 1880–1986*, Princeton University Press, Princeton, NJ.

McGowan, A 2009, *Crafting the nation in colonial India*, Palgrave, New York.

Menon, N 2020, 'Gandhi's spinning wheel: the charkha and its regenerative effects,' *Journal of the History of Ideas*, vol. 81, no. 4, pp. 643–62.

Ramachandran, A 2007, 'Rampuri chaku losing its legendary edge,' *Economic Times*, 16 April.

Roy, T 1996, 'Home market and the artisans in colonial India: a study of bass-ware,' *Modern Asian Studies*, vol. 30, no. 2, pp. 357–85.

Roy, T & Haynes, D 2013, 'Mobile artisans,' in J Chatterji & D Washbrook (eds.), *Routledge handbook of the South Asian diaspora*, Routledge, London, pp. 43–52.

Satia, P 2018, *Empire of guns: the violent making of the industrial revolution*, Penguin, New York.

# 10 Court Music Outside the Court

## Defining the 'Professional' Musician in Nineteenth-Century Bengal

*Richard David Williams*

How did the social position of professional Hindustani musicians change over the nineteenth century? The fall of the Mughal Empire in 1857, along with the devastation of imperial Delhi and *nawabi* Lucknow, is recognised as a major turning point in the history of courtly patronage. Established centres like the Emperor's court were destroyed, while leading musical patrons, like the Nawab of Awadh, were sent into exile. At the same time, other courts – like Rampur, Jaipur, and Hyderabad – became increasingly sought-after centres for Hindustani musicians. As performing artists moved, taking their families and students with them, they adapted their forms of social organisation, repertoires, and modes of teaching.

It is tempting to take these political developments – the end of the Mughals and the consolidation of the British Raj – as initiating the modern era of Hindustani music. Musical histories that dwell on the end of the nineteenth century are often built on the premise that performing artists were navigating a 'colonial modernity,' having passed through a historical rupture: modernisation appears economically coded and assumes that musicians stepped outside of a static system of feudal patronage, into a new urban marketplace engineered by upwardly mobile, middle-class patrons who invested themselves in institutions (schools, concert halls, proscenium theatres), technologies (including notation and gramophone recording) and reformist agendas (revolving around nation, women and morality – especially concerning courtesans) (e.g. Bakhle 2005, pp. 62–82; McNeil 2018; Sachdeva 2008; Subramanian 2000).

However, it would be misleading to think in terms of a teleological transition from elite patronage to a commercialised market. Looking ahead in time, long-established systems of feudal patronage continued into the twentieth century (Morcom 2014; Qureshi 2002), and many aristocratic and *zamindari* (landed gentry) patrons were only seriously diminished as late as the 1950s, such as the UP Zamindari Abolition and Reforms Act, 1951, or the abolition of the privy purses in 1971 (Ikegame 2013; Metcalf 1967; Erdman 1985). Before 1857, musicians had already been adjusting to a changing cultural and economic landscape. Migrating between centres was hardly a nineteenth-century development; many celebrated lineages of hereditary musicians had moved between patrons as they navigated the political upheavals of the eighteenth century and, to some extent, it had always been conventional for court musicians to work along circuits between patrons.

DOI: 10.4324/9781351031028-11

Such was the case for other early-modern classes of mobile courtly retainer, including artists and poets (De Bruijn & Busch 2014). Politically significant patrons were themselves not fixed to a single location and could be relocated between different, geographically remote, administrative posts under the Mughal *mansabdari* system (Roy 2013). Biographical anthologies (*tazkira*), such as the late-eighteenth-century *Hayy al-Arwah*, documented the flows of musicians between different centres across the subcontinent (Schofield 2021; Williams 2023, pp. 32–3). However, while it was conventional to travel to earn a livelihood, the nature of the relationship between patrons and musicians was changing from the early nineteenth century onwards. While professional musicians might have hoped for learned patrons trained in the arts of listening, they were increasingly expected to take on these patrons as students of performance (Scarimbolo 2014). This required a different kind of client relationship; a policy on the kinds of repertoire that the musician would impart to a non-hereditary, socially superior disciple; and demanded that professional artists both market themselves as teachers and distinguish themselves from amateur – or at least non-hereditary – musicians.

While it is clear that many musicians were (and in some contexts still are) considered service providers, employed by their patrons for their technical expertise or hereditary obligations (McNeil 2007; Qureshi 2002), does this accurately reflect the status of the individuals who fashioned themselves as artists and masters of their craft? While historians such as Janaki Bakhle (2005) have suggested that musicians were low-status servants in royal courts, the archives indicate a more complex picture. Some musicians were low status, but others occupied liminal positions, being treated as celebrities or the respected teachers of princely clients (Brown 2007). With the rise of 'amateur' musicians from non-hereditary and often upper-class family backgrounds, how did 'professional' musicians define and demarcate their expectations and obligations? This essay considers the longer history of middle-class, non-hereditary performers, and how the labour of musicianship cultivated forms of intimacy, especially in the context of teaching. Examining the relationship between one Muslim musician and his Brahmin disciple, I consider the emotional implications of musicians living and working in their clients' homes, not only as performers and teachers but also as the spiritual advisers of their client-disciples.

## Anxiety and Reputation

A number of Hindustani musicians documented their experience of working in the late nineteenth century, including Alladiya Khan (1855–1946), who recorded his memoirs through his son. Amlan Das Gupta and Urmila Bhirdikar have considered how these memoirs speak to wide-ranging transformations in musical society, including changes in performance practices, modes of musical training, and repertoire (Khan 2012, pp. 1–33). Professional musicians had plenty to be anxious about; Alladiya Khan routinely travelled in search of a patron, and while some were renowned for their lavish generosity (Khan 2012, pp. 62–3), remuneration, or even the chance to perform, was never guaranteed (Khan 2012, pp. 50–1). Alladiya

Khan's reminiscences of rivalries and amicable competitiveness indicate a deeply felt need to garner respect among one's peers within the profession. He was also conscious of protecting the integrity of his family's repertoire: 'Singers of my family never learnt from people whose musical lineage was uncertain, and learnt only within the family tradition' (Khan 2012, p. 43).

This apparently conservative remark gestures to a larger set of considerations around musical pedigree and embodied repertoires. Alladiya Khan took note of how Behram Khan trained students from non-musical families, which made hereditary professionals re-think technical standards (Khan 2012, p. 69). The memoir also scathingly comments on the reputations of Haddu and Hassu Khan, who are called *suni shagirds* (Khan 2012, pp. 17, 72), 'disciples by listening', suggesting that they had not been formally trained but had learned by (over-)hearing other performers and imitating them.[1] Alladiya Khan claimed that such musicians were called *rang bhariye*, that is full of colour or verve, but technically deficient (Khan 2012, p. 72).

Questions about who was learning what, from whom, and how, had already been raised in the 1860s, when Alladiya Khan was a child. Muhammad Mardan Ali Khan laid out his opinions on the matter in his music treatise, the *Ghunca-yi Rag* (Khan 1863), as in his discussion of dancers:

> In dance, the *gharana* of Miyan Abdullah and Pragas is the most celebrated of its time. Talk of them is in every city…Those *tawa'if* who have taken instruction from them, are also brilliant – they are described as beautiful and even as prodigies.
>
> (Khan 1863, p. 124; c.f. Williams 2017, p. 598)

This is perhaps the earliest known reference to a performing arts *gharana* (a musical household, associated with a particular lineage and style); intriguingly, this category appears in a section that also comments on prodigies, or *le-bhagu*, a term which implies picking up some ideas and running off with them. Allyn Miner (2015) considers the *Ghunca-yi Rag*'s author amid a set of sitar enthusiasts who wrote manuals over the 1860s–1870s and were contemplating how best to learn and perform, given the multiple options available in the musical market. Mardan Ali was wary of teachers who were dependent on music for an income but gave their students inaccurate techniques and misleading information and had gathered his own impressions having listened to hereditary, non-hereditary, and self-taught performers (Miner 2015). These value judgements about proficiency anticipate later hierarchies of competence that developed among professional musicians, including the rubric of *asli*, *naqli*, and *fasli* (authentic, counterfeit, and seasonal) performers (Katz 2017, p. 83).

## Amateur Musicians in Calcutta

While musicians from Hindustan had been following eastbound circuits to find work at Bengali courts across the early modern period, their numbers increased dramatically in the final years of the 1850s, following the 1856 Annexation of Awadh and the exile of the celebrated musicologist and patron Nawab Wajid Ali Shah (1822–1887). Wajid Ali Shah's court-in-exile at Matiyaburj provided a platform for a collective of singers, instrumentalists, and dance choreographers, who found enthusiastic audiences and subsidiary patrons among Calcutta's *bhadralok* gentry from the 1860s onwards (Williams 2023).[2]

These musicians proved influential in the development of new institutional forms of engaging with music, especially the Bengal Music School (est. 1871), spearheaded by Sourindro Mohan Tagore (1840–1914) (Capwell 1991), and the Bhawanipur Sangit Sammilani, coordinated by Kesabcandra Mitra (1822–1901) and Jadab Krishna Basu (1848–1926) (Williams 2023, pp. 164–84). However, Hindustani musicians arguably had a more pervasive impact through more intimate gatherings in *bhadralok* (Bengali 'genteel') households across the city, as well as in their new patrons' rural *zamindari* homesteads (Chatterjee 1996, pp. 206–11). These domestic spaces facilitated a network of musical gatherings that were courtly in tone and appealed to elite Mughal sensibilities. Although these gatherings, variously termed *mehfil*, *sabha*, *majlis*, *baithakkhana*, and *jalsa*, were not public, staged events like the concerts of the Bengal Music School, they were not wholly private; participants frequented each other's residences and documented who was attending the music parties with relish. Over time, Bengali authors developed a literary tradition of listing the names of musicians, students, and patrons, and recounting specific gatherings of celebrity artists.[3]

An early instance of this literature is one nuanced text, *Samaj-kucitra* ('The evils of our society'; Nisacar 1865), by an anonymous author who wrote under the pen name Nisacar (literally a 'nocturnal creature' though on the cover translated as 'a midnight traveller'). This text has much in common with other works of Bengali satirical-sketch (*naksa*) literature (Harder 2004). Nisacar's Calcutta was the city of playboy *babu*s and reverberated with a soundscape of excess, music being treated in the same breath as intoxicants: '*tanpura*, *sarangi*, flute, *bina*, and *mridang* play unremittingly. "Spirits," hashish, and ganja do the rounds non-stop' (Nisacar 1865, p. 29). *Samaj-kucitra* abounds with irony and parody but also inventoried Hindustani musicians and their Bengali students:

> Sigh! Such is the misfortune of Bengal's musicology (*sangita-sastra*)! Such charming and admired musical knowledge has been forsaken in this land. Long ago, many superior *kalawant*s [artistes] descended in the western quarter. The *babu*s of Calcutta know their names, so that modern troupes remember them, and some ancient name gets invoked for a day. Tansen, Gopal Nayak, Bayju Baura, Amir Khusrau, Hasnu Khan, Shah-Saheb, (Bahurupa) Daksni Bai, Bara Miyan, Chota Miyan, (Rahim Baksh), Nikki Bai, Brindavan Das, Firoz Khan (*rababi*) etc. are foremost among them. In our neighborhood, the resident of Chunchura [Chinsurah] Babu Ramacandra Shil, Babu Ramakanai Mukhopadhyay, Babu Ganganarayan Chattopadhyay, Hatkhola's Babu Radhikaprasad Datta, Bhawanipur's Babu Tolanath Chaudhuri, Srirampur's Babu Ramdas Goswami, Gharisha's Babu Candranath

> Gupta, etc. have studied instrumental music to the highest degree. Among those who are alive, Esadaulah, Amir Khan, Rasul Baksh, Hardar Baksh, Murad Ali Khan, Ramapati Bayu, Bishnu Bayu etc., are the ones who preserve the dignity of Bengal's knowledge of music today.
>
> (Nisacar 1865, pp. 29–31)

Hiding behind his penname, Nisacar's account shifts between mock oratory and precise documentary; most of his jibes are dependent on his readers being familiar with the personalities he namedropped. When he mentions the passage of master musicians from Hindustan, he is referring to those who came from Lucknow. Nisacar draws ironic parallels between a glorious past and an underwhelming present; the living *kalawant*s are mixed in with the giants of yore, beginning with the great Tansen. The first names on the list are canonical figures, who were enumerated as *nayak*s (maestros) in music treatises, from the Persian *Tohfat al-Hind* (c. 1675) through to the Bengali *Sangitataranga* (1818) (Williams 2016, p. 473). However, since Nisacar began by lamenting Bengalis' spurious grasp of musicology, including these names suggests that certain *babu*s had done *a little* reading and were clumsily displaying their erudition by casually associating legendary artists with today's musicians. The list not only flows from Tansen to Firoz Khan 'Adarang', a celebrated Delhi *kalawant*, but also goes outside the *kalawant* canon to include figures like Nikki Bai (fl. 1810s–1820s), one of Calcutta's celebrity *baiji*s (courtesan singers; Banerjee 1989, p. 12).[4] The reconfigured pantheon of great artists is then followed by a list of specific patrons in Calcutta and Bengal; Nisacar then reveals that they have now become musicians themselves, after studying with Hindustani *ustad*s, whom he then proceeds to list as well.

Nisacar's observations resonated with other texts, including later Bengali memoirs. Mukundadeb Mukhopadhyay (born mid-nineteenth century) recalled meeting one Nathu Khan, a singer from Delhi (Mukhopadhyay 1922, pp. 168–77). Mukundadeb first met him at the Sarkar *bari* (household) in Bahubazar (Bowbazar),[5] which was frequented by travelling musicians and appreciative listeners, including the Sanskrit scholars Nilmani (Mukhopadhyay) Nyayalankar (Professor at Presidency and then Sanskrit College) and Narasingha Candra Vidyalankar, who were entranced by the *ustad*'s perfect Sanskrit pronunciation. Nathu Khan claimed that he used to sing in the Delhi *darbar* in the three court languages – Persian, Sanskrit, and Urdu – but had now transferred to Calcutta and was increasingly singing in Bengali (Mukhopadhyay 1922, pp. 169–70). On that particular occasion, Ramlal Datta of Bhadrakali, a student of vocal music, was also in attendance, and exclaimed that Nathu was a true *nayak*, to which Nathu humbly replied that he merely sang *Bhajan*. This seems to be precisely the kind of 'erudite' praise that Nisacar wanted to satirise.

Based at the Sarkar household, Nathu Khan circulated between the mansions of his regular listeners, who took turns to convene new *mehfil*s. Like Nisacar, Mukundadeb listed the participants of these *mehfil*s at length. In Nilmani Nyayalankar's house he saw Jatindra Mohan Tagore, Srinath Das (who brought along his own singer, Kalinath Bandyopadhyay), Romescandra Mitra, and Kesabcandra

Mitra, all of whom Mukundadeb called *bisesajña* (specialist, discerning) in music (Mukhopadhyay 1922, p. 172). Kesabcandra Mitra and several other amateur musicians accompanied Nathu Khan in performance and took *talim* from him (Mukhopadhyay 1922, p. 175; c.f. Chatterjee 1996, pp. 211, 280). After some time, Nathu Khan would relocate to live with another host but would continue to perform across multiple households (Mukhopadhyay 1922, p. 176). Aside from the listeners and patrons, these gatherings were nodes in a network of Hindustani and Bengali musicians. Mukundadeb's prose ripples through circles of listeners and musicians who had public profiles but convened behind closed doors, indicating larger branches of hospitality, music making, and cultivation.

## The Lawyer and the Wizard

These literary recollections and directories of participants reflect the enthusiasm of elite Bengalis as they turned from patronising musicians to learning from them. Murad Ali Khan (born c.1839), who was mentioned briefly by Nisacar, provides an especially rich example of how musicians fashioned a working relationship with their patron disciples.

Murad Ali Khan was part of the cohort of artists from Lucknow who became a familiar face at these networked gatherings in Calcutta's households, over the 1860s–1890s. Bengalis remembered him principally as a *Dhrupad* artist (e.g., Mukhopadhyay 1980, p. 45; 1984, pp. 166–7), but it is possible that he is the same Murad Ali Khan identified in the Urdu *Ma'dan-ul Musiqi* (written towards the end of the 1850s, first published 1925). According to this text, Murad Ali was from a family of *Khayal* singers, the grandson of Shakkar Qawwal of Lucknow (Vidyarthi 1959–1960, p. 19), and sang *Khayal* and *Tappa* in the 'Lucknow style.' The text does not mention his singing *Dhrupad*, but this would not necessarily be an obstacle: it might even suggest, as with Nathu Khan (above), that Murad Ali adapted his repertoire later in life for his new clientele.

Murad Ali began to teach a *kulin* Brahmin attorney named Kishorilal Mukhopadhyay.[6] Due to health complications, Kishorilal spent intermittent periods away from his practice, when he would study singing with Murad Ali, whom he brought into his home in Tamluk, Midnapur (84 km from Calcutta). This house became a satellite node of Calcutta's networked sphere, especially the musicians associated with Bhavanipur. Two of Kishorilal's sons became well-known figures: Jadugopal Mukhopadhyay (1886–1976) was imprisoned for his revolutionary activities, while his younger brother, Dhan Gopal Mukerji (1890–1936), avoided a similar fate by emigrating first to Japan and then to the United States where he became a well-regarded litterateur.[7] Murad Ali evidently made a profound impression on the brothers as children, since both mentioned him in their memoirs (Mukhopadhyay 1956, pp. 155–6). Dhan Gopal's characterisation in particular provides a rare insight into the relationships forged between Hindustani Muslim musicians and their Bengali patrons-cum-disciples.

During his illness and recess from his legal practice, Kishorilal began performing professionally at the courts of local rajas, travelling by bullock cart between them. Murad Ali took this into account; he distinguished the professional training he gave to Kishorilal, from the 'training of a critic' he provided to Kishorilal's friends, which was designed 'so that when good musicians come you will know enough to support them and they will be able to remain good musicians' (Mukerji 2002, p. 57). Therefore, although this period saw many musicians from respectable Bengali families acquire practical training in music, the *ustad*s nonetheless maintained the older dichotomy between the knowledge of the practitioner and that of the connoisseur-patron. The *ustad* could offer both but reserved certain repertoires and techniques for his poorer disciples who had a financial incentive to their playing. When Kishorilal's health was restored and he returned to law, he continued to sing over his three-month vacation, but no longer charged for his performances (Mukerji 2002, p. 59).

In two works, *Caste and Outcast* (1923) and *My Brother's Face* (1924), Dhan Gopal Mukerji described Murad Ali as 'that white-haired, white-bearded, and white-clad old man telling his beads of amber' (Mukerji 1924, p. 130). Writing for an American readership that was largely unfamiliar with India, Mukerji wrote to not only inform but also enchant his audience. This had a significant impact on his writing style and his redaction of the historical kernels of his own life story. Murad Ali's musical skill was depicted in tandem with his charismatic presence in the Mukhopadhyay homestead, where he was at once the family's teacher, spiritual master, and storyteller.

These roles converged through Murad Ali's singing: he would sit with Jadugopal at his bedtime,

> a white wizard guiding a ship by the magic of his voice. Ah, what a voice! He was the only one left who could sing Dipak – the Fire and Thunder melody. His tones were deep and vibrant as a bull-frog's.
>
> (Mukerji 2002, p. 130)

Since the family was Hindu, Mukerji explained, Murad Ali taught the boys 'Vishnu hymns' (2002, p. 57) This might refer to *vishnupad* or perhaps indicate that, like Nathu Khan, Murad Ali had added Bengali *Bhajan* to his repertoire. Anecdotes about Murad Ali reflect how he was integrated into the family over their 12 years together: 'He had a terrific way of opening his mouth when he sang, and we used to tell him that he almost swallowed the universe' (Mukerji 2002, p. 57). Mukerji recalled how his mother would break the laws of their caste and cook meat for Murad Ali, since he 'had become my father's spiritual adviser, and therefore whatever he ate was spiritual' (Mukerji 2002, p. 57). Given that Muslim *ustad*s had been taking on Brahmin disciples in Bengal since at least the mid-eighteenth century (Scarimbolo 2014; Williams 2023), Mukerji's memoir offers a glimpse into the kinds of relationship that may have been forged through musical discipleship.

Mukerji gave a romantic account of how Murad Ali came to work for his father. He suggests that Murad Ali was 18 years old in 1857, which would place him in his early sixties when Mukerji knew him as a child. In his tale, Murad Ali was the former court musician of the Mughal Emperor (when, in reality, he was part of the retinue of the Nawab of Lucknow). During the Uprising of 1857, he saw the Emperor's son shot and in his terror abandoned his patron. The Emperor died shortly afterwards (according to Mukerji, in India rather than Rangoon) and in his last moments cried, 'Where is Moradali to sing to me now? I have paid him all his life.' The guilt-ridden musician composed a 'Remorse Song', which he would sing every evening from then on:

> O my king, for your sake I go as a mendicant of song from door to door, but desolation greets me as a great shadow on either hand! The glories are gone and wild animals prowl through the palaces. But the wild animals that prowl through my heart, who can take them away?
>
> (Mukerji 2002, p. 58)

Mukerji claimed that this 'terrible cry of anguish' could still be heard in India in his own time. Evidently his intention was to entrance his American readership with a tragic singer turned mendicant.

Mukerji's memories of Murad Ali gesture to how, at the turn of the twentieth century, the Hindustani *darbari* (court) musician became a meaningful trope and was reframed in Bengali writings. Mukerji was not alone in his representation of a weeping, nostalgic musician (e.g., Mukhopadhyay 1980, pp. 15–27). In Mukundadeb Mukhopadhyay's account of Nathu Khan, Aghorenath Cakravarty cried when he heard Nathu sing, and Nathu himself wept during his own recital, but also when he was discussing his earlier career in Delhi and uttered the name of Bahadur Shah (Mukhopadhyay 1922, p. 171). When he later performed at the house of Ganeshcandra Candra, his host asked him how best to honour (*khatir*) him. Nathu replied,

> I did not come for honour; music is my livelihood, I came for money. Ganesh Babu, what honour would you give me? I used to sit before the Emperor of Delhi, the *vazir* himself used to place the hookah pipe into my hand. Is there any other 'honour' after that?
>
> (Mukhopadhyay 1922, p. 175)

Whereas Murad Ali Khan was represented as an unworldly sage, in this passage, Nathu Khan explicitly stated that he saw music as his livelihood (*upjibika*). While music used to bring him both income and honours, as a court musician without a court, money was now the only crude reward he could expect. Representing *ustad*s as either wizards or disillusioned professionals were two sides of the same coin: Bengali elites listened to and studied with Hindustani musicians, often assimilating them into their families and began to reflect on the cultural transition these men had navigated over the nineteenth century. Evoking nostalgia, mourning, and disenchantment through music made it possible for the Bengali elite musician to imagine himself as the custodian of a splintered Mughal legacy, by appropriating the repertoires and tears of the Hindustani *ustad*.

## Conclusion

What did it mean to be a lineage artist in the age of amateur and non-hereditary musicians? This essay has qualified some of the assumptions about the modernisation of the musical economy under colonialism, and has cautioned against thinking in terms of a smooth transition from the model of the courtly patron to a public culture of celebrity artists, ticketed concerts, and institutional platforms for classical music, given the continued influence of small, networked gatherings of music enthusiasts.

From the 1860s onwards, writers in Urdu and Bengali reflected on the nature of the relationship between professional musicians and their patrons when they became students. These writers were conscious of how some of these new performers played as amateurs, while others became professional artists and teachers in their own right (see also Scarimbolo 2020). Urdu sources reflect anxieties around skills, repertoire, and uninitiated outsiders surreptitiously adopting lineage styles. The Bengali essays and memoirs discussed here were largely developed by the new patron class, who relished being part of a network of patrons, teachers, and disciples.

The case study of Kishorilal Mukhopadhyay and his *ustad*, Murad Ali Khan, highlights how teachers would offer different repertoires depending on whether their students were playing to be more appreciative listeners, or to perform as amateurs, or to earn a livelihood. Money was an ambiguous issue. Kishorilal alternated between working as an attorney and as a singer; he acquired a professional repertoire from Murad Ali, yet when he returned to the law, he began singing without seeking an income. As a non-hereditary musician, professionalism could be understood both in terms of money and expertise. For lineage musicians like Nathu Khan, however, livelihood was merely the base remnant of the profession, following the demise of Delhi and the Mughals.

Authors from the patron class reflected on how that culture relocated to the musical gatherings of Calcutta and rural Bengal. In the context of teaching and discipleship, the labour of musicians entailed more than a business transaction, and the incorporation of Murad Ali into Kishorilal's Brahmin household – and his sons' affectionate memories – indicates the emotional work and ritual negotiations involved. It is worth recalling that Murad Ali ultimately died in another student's household, so he perhaps went through the process of developing family-like intimacies multiple times. Hindustani musicians were long accustomed to searching for new patrons and moving between courts. Now in Calcutta, they made smaller migrations between networked households, which were neither wholly private or public but rather required a point of access or a personal introduction to unlock and operated through interconnected circles of musical professionals and enthusiasts, playing host to each other in their own residences. This culture did not seek to monopolise or institutionalise musical culture, or to reform its public presence, but rather served as an informal infrastructure for listening, learning, and sustaining the tradition.

## Notes

1 On discipleship, see Neuman (1990) and Qureshi (2009).
2 Portions of the material that follows have been selectively adapted from Williams 2023.

3 A rich example of this is Sanyal (1953). This literature continued into the 21st century, see Mukhopadhyay (2001).
4 On Mughal-era Delhi *kalawants*, see Schofield (2013).
5 Most likely home to the descendants of Radhamohan Sarkar, a music lover of the 1830s (Banerjee 1989, p. 103).
6 Kishorilal also attended events at the Bengal Music School in the late 1870s, but he was not actively involved in its administration or a member of the School's Committee (Tagore 1876, Supplement, p. 261).
7 See Chang's introduction in Mukerji (2002, pp. 1–40).

## References


Bakhle J 2005, *Two men and music: nationalism in the making of an Indian classical tradition*, Permanent Black, Ranikhet.

Banerjee, S 1989, *The parlour and the streets: elite and popular culture in nineteenth century Calcutta*, Seagull Books, Calcutta.

Brown, KB 2007, 'The social liminality of musicians: case studies from Mughal India and beyond,' *Twentieth-Century Music*, vol. 3, no. 1, pp. 13–49.

Capwell, C 1991, 'Marginality and musicology in nineteenth-century Calcutta: the case of Sourindro Mohun Tagore', in B Nettl & PV Bohlman (eds.), *Comparative musicology and anthropology of music: essays on the history of ethnomusicology*, University of Chicago Press, Chicago, IL, pp. 228–43.

Chatterjee, C 1996, *Śāstrīya saṅgīta and music culture of Bengal through the ages*, Sharada, New Delhi.

De Bruijn, T & Busch, A 2014, 'Introduction', in T de Bruijn & A Busch (eds.), *Culture and circulation: literature in motion in early modern India*, Brill, Leiden, pp. 1–20.

Erdman, JL 1985, *Patrons and performers in Rajasthan: the subtle tradition*, Delhi: Chanakya Publications.

Harder, H 2004, 'The modern babu and the metropolis: reassessing early Bengali narrative prose,' in S Blackburn & V Dalmia (eds.), *India's literary histories: essays on the nineteenth century*, Permanent Black, New Delhi, pp. 358–401.

Ikegame, A 2013, *Princely India re-imagined: a historical anthropology of Mysore from 1799 to the present*, Routledge, Abingdon.

Katz, M 2017, *Lineage of loss: counternarratives of North Indian music*, Wesleyan University Press, Middletown, CT.

Khan, A 2012, *My life*, trans. A Das Gupta & U Bhirdikar, Thema, Kolkata.

Khan, MMA 1863, *Ghunca-yi rag*, Naval Kishor, Lucknow.

McNeil, A 2007, 'Mirasis: some thoughts on hereditary musicians in Hindustani music,' *Context*, Vol. 32, pp. 45–58.

McNeil, A 2018, 'Hereditary musicians, Hindustani music and the "public sphere" in late nineteenth-century Calcutta,' *South Asia: Journal of South Asian Studies*, vol. 41, no. 2, pp. 297–314.

Metcalf, TR 1967, 'Landlords without land: the UP Zamindars today,' *Pacific Affairs*, vol. 40, no. 1/2, pp. 5–18.

Miner, A 2015, 'Enthusiasts and *ustāds:* early Urdu instructional books,' unpublished paper.

Morcom, A 2014, *Illicit worlds of Indian dance: cultures of exclusion*, Oxford University Press, New York.

Mukerji, DG 1924, *My brother's face*, EP. Dutton, New York.

Mukerji, DG 2002, *Caste and outcast*, Stanford University Press, Stanford, CA.

Mukhopadhyay, D 1980, *Bhārater saṅgīt guṇī*, pt. II, A. Mukherji, Kolkata.

Mukhopadhyay, D 1984, *Aẏodhẏar nabāb Oẏājid Alī Śāh,* Shankha Prakashan, Kolkata.
Mukhopadhyay, J 1956, *Biplabī jībaner smṛti*, Indian Associated Publ., Kolkata.
Mukhopadhyay, K 2001, *Maẏhphil*, Dey's Publishing, Kolkata.
Mukhopadhyay, M 1922, *Āmār dekhā lok*, Bhudeb Publishing House, Calcutta.
Neuman, DM 1990, *The life of music in North India: the organization of an artistic tradition*, University of Chicago Press, Chicago, IL.
Nisacar 1865, *Samaj-kucitra*, Notun Balmiki Press, Calcutta.
Qureshi, R 2002, 'Mode of production and musical production: is Hindustani music feudal?' in RB Qureshi (ed.), *Music and Marx: ideas, practice, politics*, Routledge, New York, pp. 81–105.
Qureshi, R 2009, '*Sīna ba sīna* or "from father to son": writing the culture of discipleship,' in RK Wolf (ed.), *Theorizing the local: music, practice, and experience in South Asia and beyond*, Oxford University Press, Oxford, pp. 165–83.
Roy, K 2013, 'From the mamluks to the mansabdars: A social history of military service in South Asia, c. 1500 to c. 1650,' in E Zürcher (ed.), *Fighting for a living: a comparative study of military labour 1500–2000*, Amsterdam University Press, Amsterdam, pp. 81–114.
Sachdeva, S 2008, 'In search of the *tawa'if* in history: courtesans, nautch girls and celebrity entertainers in India (1720s–1920s),' PhD thesis, School of Oriental and African Studies, University of London.
Sanyal, A 1953, *Smritir atale*, Mitralaya, Kolkata.
Scarimbolo, J 2014, 'Brahmans beyond nationalism, Muslims beyond dominance: a hidden history of North Indian classical music's Hinduization,' PhD thesis, University of California, Santa Barbara.
Scarimbolo, J 2020, 'On the secretive *ustād*: pride among musicians and patrons in North India,' *Indian Theatre Journal*, vol. 4, no. 1, pp. 59–76.
Schofield, KB 2013, 'Chief musicians to the Mughal emperors: the Delhi *kalawant biraderi*,' in ITC Sangeet Research Academy (Kolkata) (ed.), *Dhrupad, its future: proceedings of the ITC-SRA (West) Seminar*, ITC-Sangeet Research Academy, Mumbai.
Schofield, KB 2021, 'Emotions in Indian music history: anxiety in late Mughal Hindustan,' *South Asian History and Culture*, vol. 12, no. 2–3, pp. 182–205.
Subramanian, L 2000, 'The master, muse and the nation: the new cultural project and the reification of colonial modernity in India,' *South Asia*, vol. 23, no. 2, pp. 1–32.
Tagore, SM 1876, *Public opinion and official communications, about the Bengal Music School and its president*, Panchanun Mookerjee, Calcutta.
Vidyarthi, G 1959–1960, 'Melody through the centuries,' *Sangeet Natak Akademi Bulletin* vol. 11–12, pp. 6–14, 13–26, 33, 49–58.
Williams, RD 2016, 'Music, lyrics, and the Bengali book: Hindustani musicology in Calcutta, 1818–1905,' *Music and Letters*, vol. 97, no. 3, pp. 465–95.
Williams, RD 2017, 'Songs between cities: listening to courtesans in colonial North India,' *Journal of the Royal Asiatic Society*, vol. 27, no. 4, pp. 591–610.
Williams, RD 2023, *The scattered court: Hindustani music in colonial Bengal*, Chicago University Press, Chicago, IL.

# 11 The Hand in the Song

## Understanding Performative Labour, Gender, and Livelihood in the Arts of Chitrakar Women of West Bengal

*Priyanka Basu*

Walter Benjamin engages with the category of craft in his well-known essays, 'The Work of Art in the Age of Mechanical Reproduction' (1968 [1936]) and 'The Story-teller' (1963 [1936]). Both texts discuss the tactility of experience at length, the shift of art from its ritual to a political context, and, above all, the primacy of the hand in craft. In this paper, I analyse the 'hand in the song' or the conditions of labour in a performance within the Chitrakar community of West Bengal. This discussion involves two varieties of performance: tangible and intangible. The former consists of the performance practices of scroll-painters (*patua*s), and the latter, the *kobiyals*, those who perform *Kobigaan* (a song-theatre genre involving verse-duelling). The former is a traditional practice of Chitrakars while the latter is not. The analysis in this paper is based on a case study of both a female *patua* and a female *kobiyal* of the Chitrakar community to highlight the changing facets of such performance and art practices in relation to gender roles and the challenges of market conditions. The purpose behind choosing these two women from different performance practices is to highlight the variations between a mainstream (scroll-painting) and a non-mainstream (*Kobigaan*) profession practised by women in the Chitrakar community.

The Chitrakar community in West Bengal is commonly associated with the profession of scroll-painting. The scrolls are indigenously called *pata*s and the painters as *patua*s. The *patua*s are mainly Muslims that well-to-do Hindus earlier patronised. The community's name of 'Chitrakar' is a fairly new development, resulting from the emergence of folklore studies in Bengal in the early twentieth century. Gurusaday Dutt was one of the foremost proponents of folklore studies in Bengal. Around 1932, Dutt connected scroll-painters to the ancient Chitrakar (a pan-Indian painter caste), in order to save them from the 'state of decline' (Dutt 1932, p. 524) and promote their art. The community's acceptance of the generic surname helped them merge with the Hindu majority in the face of early twentieth-century communal riots as well as elevating their social status. The Chitrakars have thus remained a community of fluid Hindu–Muslim identities, that is, while they are Muslims, the generic Chitrakar surname has given them a Hindu identity.

The *Patachitra* or painted scrolls are traditionally long scrolls that the painter-performer unfold as they sing the narrative. Popularly referred to as a precursor to the bioscope by virtue of its audio-visual quality, these scrolls feature

DOI: 10.4324/9781351031028-12

subjects and themes centred on mythological stories and oral lore from epics like the *Ramayana* and the *Mahabharata*. The scrolls also depict medieval narratives, such as the story from the Bengali text, *Manasamangal*, of a widowed Behula carrying the corpse of her husband Lakkhindar to the abode of the snake-goddess, Manasa, to bring him back to life.

Over time, the medium of the scrolls has changed from paper to apparel, home décor, and other urban products, and the subjects of depiction have also undergone major shifts. The painters now portray diverse issues of contemporary social importance and relevance like HIV/AIDS awareness, the polio vaccination, women's empowerment, and literacy campaigns, or events such as the Tsunami and 9/11 attack. This transformation in the performative aspect of the scroll from being sung to being displayed as art objects is an interesting development that compels us to consider the nature of artistic agency, institutional and NGO patronage, and the effects of a global market economy. The change is also indicative of shifting gender roles within the ambit of scroll-painting in which women would previously be only engaged in domestic chores and in assisting the male painters. Anthropologist Frank Korom (2006) explains how women were not previously engaged in scroll-painting, being trained only from the 1970s by the master artisan, Dukhushyam, the senior-most painter in the village of Naya. Today, these women paint a lot more than their male counterparts and are also more actively engaged in selling their wares at festivals and fairs across West Bengal as well as within India and abroad.

*Kobigaan* ('song of poets') is a popular performance genre in the format of verse-duelling.[1] It involves two competing groups of poet-singers (*kobiyal*) with their respective chorus (*dohaar*) and accompanying instrumentalists and percussionists. The performance is marked by the virtuosity of the *kobiyal*s who are given a topic by the organising committee or patron to debate upon at the onset of the duel, and it is their ability to sustain the performance through logic, humour and verbal jugglery that decides the winner. In the first half of the nineteenth century, *Kobigaan*, along with several other allied performance genres, became exemplary of the popular dialogic traditions of Calcutta and the suburban spaces (see Banerjee 1998). These *kobiyal*s, comprising mostly male and fewer women *kobiyal*s, were an itinerant group of performers who regularly moved in and out of the city space and were well versed in religious narratives, theological debates, and popular mythologies. This enabled them to serve the dual purposes of *Kobigaan*: preaching and entertaining. The virtuosity of the *kobiyal* was determined by how seamlessly and convincingly they narrated episodes from Hindu mythology through which gods and goddesses became more like real to the listeners. Sumanta Banerjee (1998) writes how depictions of Hindu gods and goddesses in nineteenth-century visual and performing arts converged with real people from the contemporary Bengali society, and how satiric performance genres like *Kobigaan* emphasised gods and goddesses as ordinary men and women. For example, scenes of domestic conjugality and scuffle between the Bengali *babu*, his wife, and mistress were a common motif depicted in performing and visual cultures such as *patas* and *Kobigaan*.

Contemporary performances of *Kobigaan*, however, have shifted drastically from their early religious focus to incorporate contemporary socio-political issues.

The rural performances of *Kobigaan*, which usually last up to 10–12 hours of intense debate, have also been adapted to set formats of one to two hours. Much like the change of subjects and portrayals in the scroll-paintings, *Kobigaan* has now become a performance medium that is employed by the government to educate the rural public on issues such as polio vaccination or the need for literacy. Most of the *kobiyal*s are registered with the Folk and Tribal Cultural Centre in West Bengal who employ them for government-funded campaigns and shows. This shift in the nature of patronage of the folk performer from the rich feudal lord to the rural public and the government has also opened the performance space to historically marginalised female *kobiyal*s. However, their number is tiny in comparison to their male colleagues; for example, the number of documented women *kobiyal*s at the 15th State Kobiyal Fair (March 2013 in Murshidabad, West Bengal) was five, including a new entrant from the tribal Santhal community. It is also difficult to locate written records on female performers, especially in the nineteenth-century writings on *Kobigaan* practices.

The issues of physical and emotional labour are continuing to emerge as a central focus in performance studies. The recent explorations of the concepts of affective and gendered labour can be taken as an important framework in understanding the case study of *Patachitra* (see Foster 2013; Hardt 1999; Ridout 2013). It is also helpful to differentiate the terms labour, work, and action (Arendt 1998[1958]). In this chapter, therefore, I try to understand affective and gendered labour through the stories of two Chitrakar women. Since both these women come from the same performing community, frameworks of affective and gendered labour enable us to compare and contrast the nature of the work they do and the returns of the cultural labour in which they are engaged, that is the remuneration and pride attached to the work. The focus on labour in terms of performance is a crucial point of research enquiry since we can probe the immaterial aspects of labour in contemporary culture and society (Klein & Kunst 2012). In post-Fordist models of labour the social, imaginative and affective aspects are crucial to look at as they inform performance practices too (Klein & Kunst 2012, p. 2). By looking at two different female performers from the same Chitrakar community, and by reading their performance practices in terms of gendered and affective labour, I choose to understand how these performances can be analysed as work. Moreover, it also leads me to scrutinise the socio-economic aspects of this work in contrast to domestic labour, in both of which female performers take part. It is here that I emphasise the incomplete and marginal nature of the archival documentation of women performers, the loss of their historical identities, and the current cultural labour that they undertake to survive in the male spaces of performance; female performers have historically struggled to inhabit these male spaces of performances and their images as publicly performing women have aggravated their marginalisation. I argue that marginal rural female performers who combine their daily domestic labour with cultural labour in performance spaces constitute a significant subaltern group with respect to their cosmopolitan clientele. The stories of these female performers reveal global shifts in the capitalist market economy and changes in the objectification of art objects, from fairs and festivals to museum spaces and new media. It is thus crucial to read the agency and status of these female performers as they acquire greater mobility in the public sphere in relation to the larger issues of gender, development, and representation.

## Karuna Chitrakar

Fifty-one-year-old Karuna Chitrakar, or Kohinoor (her Muslim name), lives as a scroll-painter in the village of Naya in the West Midnapore district of West Bengal. Karuna learned scroll-painting and the songs that are sung as the scrolls unfurl in narrative from her father, Piyar Chitrakar, at the age of seven. As Kamala Devi Chattopadhyay has noted, 'Even though craftsmanship has always been considered hereditary, passed on from generation to generation, inheritance of actual skills was not assumed' (1984, p. 8). As Karuna related, it was only the scrolls with religious and mythological subjects that she inherited as part of her traditional learning.[2] Since very few in the Chitrakar community, including male scroll-painters, have any formal education, *patua*s depend upon oral tradition, picking up and remembering songs. Karuna's husband explained the process further by adding, 'Our songs reside in our stomach, and like a routine practice of saying night-time prayers we have to remember the songs before we sleep.'[3] Post-marriage, Karuna and her husband engaged themselves primarily as agricultural and day labourers for more than 20–25 years before reverting to their traditional scroll-painting 22 years ago. Karuna is one of the less promoted scroll-painters, if one considers the initiatives of collectors, and other present-day patrons NGOs.[4] Her rank as a second-grade artist among the *patua*s, and especially the female *patua*s, is underlined by a lack of access to the showcase venues of urban fairs and festivals based on the selection of NGO-patrons that is the key guiding factor behind such gradations.[5]

By comparison, Swarna Chitrakar, another female painter from the same village who travelled to the folk-art festival in Sweden in 2003, is hailed as a critically acclaimed artist both in India and abroad.[6] She has recently had her work displayed at the Centre for International Modern Art (CIMA) Mela in New Delhi.[7] Korom argues, 'What makes Swarna unique is that she is one of the few who can both sing and paint. But she has also moved beyond traditions. So, aesthetically, she is a cut above most of the rest.'[8] The gradation of scroll-painters, and an assessment of the hierarchy of their skills, points more towards discrimination caused by NGO-driven performative labour catering to an urban clientele, which relates to the principle of consumer sovereignty, whereby businesses must guarantee customers satisfaction to ensure repeat business. What is central to the potential threat caused by such focus is the consequent marginalisation of the worker if they cannot provide adequately for the 'experience economy' of the customer.[9] As Alan Bryman (2004) states, performative labour is 'the rendering of work by managements and employees alike as akin to a theatrical performance in which the workplace is construed as similar to a stage' (p. 104). The author also writes about 'the experience economy' in which the 'work of the person who stages the experience is crucial for the experience to remain in the customer's memory' (Bryman 2004, p. 104). The customer's memory is what is affected by NGO initiatives, because their market-driven initiatives aim at producing not only multiple copies of the tangible part of the craft but also the intangible part, that is the singing. For example, *patuas* often produce numerous short replicas of the motifs of longer narrative scrolls as per the guidance and instruction of the NGO patrons who do not necessarily require their painted product to be accompanied by singing, given the absence of the narrative on a single one-dimensional finished product, such as a greeting card. This is a potential threat not only for Karuna as an artist but also for the whole craft community as singing becomes more occasional than required.

However, Karuna has still managed to continue and to meet public taste by switching from 'traditional' scrolls to single-sheet horizontal, square, and vertical paintings (see Figure 11.1). She has also adapted the medium of the painting to textiles, such as t-shirts, scarves, stoles, and sarees. Occasionally, she is engaged to conduct workshops in West Bengal and other Indian states, imparting lessons in scroll-paintings to schoolchildren, and she is allowed to sell her work at the numerous fairs and festivals organised by the government of West Bengal. She informed me

> In those months of the year when we run out of employment and money, I and my husband pick up our old scrolls and sing them in the adjacent villages. Earlier they would shoo us away, but now, since they see us occasionally on television, we are welcomed to perform with our scrolls and are

*Figure 11.1* Greeting cards and horizontal single-sheet *pata* paintings that are more in demand in the urban markets (photo: Proshanto Mahato).

sometimes given gifts in cash and most of the times in kind (rice, vegetables, or fruits). This keeps us running![10]

Being visible in the media ensures cultural capital for the performing *patua* as it does for the performing *kobiyal*, many of whom have released video CDs (VCDs) to promote and preserve their oral tradition.

## Dulali Chitrakar

Dulali Chitrakar is the oldest of the female *kobiyal*s and perhaps the boldest in her statements against the male *kobiyal*s on stage. She comes from the Chitrakar community of the village of Gankar in the Murshidabad district of West Bengal. One of Dulali's poems, '*Amar Gram*' ('My Village'), in her biography, describes the colourful idols and dolls made in the Chitrakar neighbourhood; she also narrates her own memories of working as an idol-maker with her father when she was a child (Maitra 2012, pp. 13–4). It is worth mentioning that, unlike Karuna, Dulali has had formal education in the village school until the ninth standard, and that her own compositions and poems have been published in her biography. Her father, Shankar Chitrakar, who was also a performer in *jatra* (a form of indigenous theatre in Bengal), inspired her to take up *Kobigaan* as a profession alongside her long-term interests in *Jatra*. After a phase of discipleship under her guru, Sricharan Mandal, Dulali has been performing for the last 30 years. Dulali underlined, 'No platform can offer you what *Kobigaan* offers.'[11] She chose to forsake the community profession of scroll-painting and idol-making and asserts how she can comfortably speak instead of *samaj* (society), *sanskar* (reforms), *sachetanata* (awareness), and *sreni sangram* (class struggle) in her songs. It has not been an easy path for Dulali, as is evident from her biography (Maitra 2012), and my conversation with her. Threats and hindrances have surfaced both internally within the household in the form of domestic abuse by her husband and externally from the male *kobiyal*s who have tried to oust her from the profession.

An elected member of the village *panchayat* in 1983, Dulali has pursued the profession of her own choice and campaigned against the routine violation of human rights of women in her village. In her songs, she is not deterred by moral dilemmas or anxieties in speaking of sexual abuse, especially in the case of young girls, or of detailing the anatomy of the female body to her rural audience. This was highlighted in her *Kobigaan* contest with the male *kobiyal* Ranjit Das at the 15th *Rajyo Kobiyal Mela* ('State *Kobiyal* Fair') on 5 March 2013,[12] on the topic 'Past vs. Present' in which Dulali took up the role of the present. Humour and satire are intrinsic elements of any *Kobigaan* performance, and the performing *kobiyals* often resort to personal attacks to provide immediate entertainment and invoke laughter from the audience. The contesting *kobiyal*s often establish a relationship during the songs to make the act of insulting and belittling through arguments more convincing. In this performance, Dulali kept referring to the competing *kobiyal* as her 'grandfather,' which is synonymous with the old and the past, as well as a common trope for village performances of *Kobigaan*. Between her answers to the questions posed by the other side, she also drew the audience's attention to the practices of sexual abuse within the folds of the family committed by a girl's nearest male relatives. Dulali sang about how, as a child, a certain grandfather of hers attempted to kiss or touch even the private parts of her body and she was uneasy but unaware of the implications of the act. While the male *kobiyal* eulogised the past writ large for the sake of tradition and conservatism, Dulali portrayed through bodily images how societal relations have not only been gendered but also sexually exploited from time immemorial.

Dulali continues to travel across West Bengal throughout the year both at rural and urban fairs, festivals, and religious occasions, performing sometimes for a full month at a time. She is the sole breadwinner of her family.[13] She is deeply concerned about the younger generation of female *kobiyal*s who do not seem to be avid learners of the essential knowledge of mythologies, philosophies, and religious scriptures through rigorous practice. Dulali informed me, '*Kobigaan* is losing to "yankie culture"' and that it 'is not like before when the audience would be waiting eagerly for a *Kobigaan* performance. They are more drawn towards films and film songs, and that compels me to worry about the passion of my life.'[14] In a certain sense, she also seemed apprehensive about the question of mobilisation of more women into this performance as marriage is an obvious impediment to their career and, in a number of cases, female practitioners have quit the trade at an early age in order to get married. In contrast, for Dulali, who was a victim of domestic violence by her husband on a regular basis before she left for her *guru*'s house, performance has offered her an identity, mobility, and dignity.

## Gender, Labour, and Livelihood

The accounts of the two female performers bring us to the more specific aspects of livelihood, sustenance, endangerment, and gender roles within the greater debate between tradition and modernity. As women performers belonging to a marginal community, both as Muslims and scroll-painters, Karuna and Dulali face challenges that come from the performing community as well as the reception of their practices. For Karuna, the profession of a scroll-painter has travelled from being an oral-visual tradition, a community media to a folk art and then to an artefact. For Dulali, the practice of *Kobigaan* in the rural sphere still functions as community media, simultaneously informing and entertaining the rural populace. Kavita Singh (1996) has shown how government intervention in folk media in the 1970s was propelled by these communities of performers' access to an enormous network of remote rural-scapes hitherto inaccessible to the government. The craft market and those serving it have a greater stake now because of what Soumhya Venkatesan (2009) describes the 'vernacularism' of art and the 'politics of work' as 'the cultural produce of a community, the vernacular carries the mystique of symbolising the authentic voice of society … The politics of work provided craft with its moral core. Vernacularism gave craft its nostalgic and nationalistic character' (pp. 23–4).

The other major shift in the tradition was the transformation of the audience into customers. This is evident in what Michel Foucault (1986) terms the 'heterotopia of the festival' (p. 26), which highlights time in its flowing, transitory, and precarious aspect. Handicraft fairs, book fairs, and other such events that are governed by this distinct temporality are spaces in which performances of crafts, craftspeople, and performers are generated and exhibited. This change from traditional to festival spaces results in new demands from the urban customer that require the constant production of single-sheet paintings that can be readily framed for drawing-room décor, as well as greeting cards and various textiles. Nowadays, the nature of scroll paintings has shifted drastically whereby the scroll-painter and performer interweaves tradition and innovation to generate a 'cosmopolitan impression' that addresses and ensures an urban clientele (Ponte 2015). In urban exhibitions of these scrolls (e.g., the *Kalighat Patachitra* exhibition at the Nehru Centre, London, in 2015), the artisan is conspicuously 'absent,' although the visual object bears traces of the singing and storytelling performances that were once its main characteristic.

In comparison to the tangible art of *pata*, the intangible performing art of *Kobigaan* appeals to the changing taste of urban audiences through their cultural memory of films. The urban audience typically accesses the films made about these singing poets in the 1960s and 1970s and seeks a replication of this on stage in abridged, one-hour long performances of *Kobigaan.* Much in the format of the single-sheet paintings that the *patua* produces, the *Kobigaan* performer is required to present an essence of the art, something that aims towards what Benjamin (1968[1936]) terms the 'aura' of a work of art. In both the scroll painting and the performance, the aspect of narration or storytelling is reduced to the bare minimum to generate an ongoing demand for the craft itself and constant consumption, more for urban audiences of festivals than rural fairs.

Michael Hardt (1999) describes affective labour as directly constituted of 'communities and collective subjectivities' (p. 89). Hardt further asserts that 'immaterial labour' that has assumed a dominant position with respect to other forms of labour in the global capitalist economy (p. 90). In such economies, the production constitutes more and more the manufacturing of services and is hence informationalised. Here, one can see how performance forms and art forms get transformed into consumable products. Their process of production, thus, underlines the labour of the performer mainly as the informant. Hardt elucidates further on the nature of immaterial labour by saying:

> The passage toward an informational economy involves necessarily a change in the quality of labor and the nature of labouring processes. This is the most immediate sociological and anthropological implication of the passage of economic paradigms. Information, communication, knowledge, and affect come to play a foundational role in the production process.
>
> (1999, p. 93)

Through her cultural labour of practicing as a scroll-painter and singer, Karuna thus represents that aspect of affective labour that is part of her collective community-driven identity as a Chitrakar and as an individual female *patua*. While both the *patua* and the *kobiyal* belong to performing communities, the collective community-driven distinctiveness in the case of the Chitrakars is much more pronounced in terms of their caste-based identity. Coming from such a community of cultural labourers, Karuna, like her other fellow painters in the craft, contributes to the informational economy of the scrolls; it is here that she and many others incorporate information in the content of the scrolls in order to suit the taste of the urban clientele. New forms of documentation and preservation include those conducted by NGOs in the form of VCDs, fairs like the POT Maya organised by *patuas* themselves in their village in the month of November and collaborations with international participants (e.g. an ERC-funded project between London and the NGO Banglanatak Dot Com). They, thus, push the *patua* more towards re-thinking and re-inventing the affective possibilities of their art and craft. Karuna performs her role as a cultural labourer as a member of this community and as a collective subject.

Susan Foster (2013) writes about the performance of authenticity and gendered labour with respect to dance. In relation to the industrial body in dance as created by its presence on televised media, she writes how an important principle of the industrial body is the way it generates a 'gendered sexiness,' leading to hyperfemininity (Foster 2013, p. 131). The labour of the female *kobiyal* within the male platform of *Kobigaan* lies in negating 'gendered sexiness' and attaining a stature that makes the audience gaze shift from the body-feminine to the body-text, that is from the objectification of the female body to a woman asserting her identity as a performer. This body-text is crucial to the labour of the female *kobiyal* as a performer in performing like a man while not being a man. Dulali Chitrakar accomplishes this by the merit of her voice (loud and hoarse) and the minimal use of bodily gestures. Consequently, the passage from the body-feminine to the body-text of the female *kobiyal* like Dulali involves coming out of a collective subjectivity and a communitarian identity and instead asserting individual female identity as a performer within the patriarchal world of *Kobigaan*. It is herein that the cultural labour of Dulali ensures that she is exemplary of *Kobigaan* and situates her as a benchmark for other younger female *kobiyals* to aspire to. Unlike Karuna, therefore, who operates from within an existing caste community as a practitioner, Dulali's labour lies in building a possible community of female *kobiyals* to rewrite themselves back in their neglected histories.

## Conclusion

Labour and livelihood are two of the most important aspects of understanding marginal female performers and gendered everyday spaces of performance and the domestic sphere given the structural changes in performances owing to changing clientele. It is within these structural shifts and changes that female performers like Karuna and Dulali function as artists. Karuna faces challenges from other female scroll-painters of international repute from within her community, such as Swarna

Chitrakar, who has exhibited her scrolls all over India as well as abroad. This brings us back to the hierarchy of skills that informally grades the *patua*s. While both Swarna and Karuna paint about more recent themes like the 9/11 attack or violence against women, the hierarchy of skills highlighted by the acknowledgment of international repute decides the payment for their labour by patron organisations and audiences. In the case of Dulali, who has broken away from the traditional profession of scroll painting and has gained some education, the challenges come directly from male performers, for *Kobigaan* has always been a male-dominated world with a history oblivious to the existence of women singers. Both women operate between domestic and professional roles to varied degrees, in which the questions of the labouring performer can be extended to the home and the market. The greater question, however, remains as to whether tangible and intangible heritages like scroll painting and *Kobigaan* will witness similar later developments. While the *pata* can shift the medium of representation from paper to textile, will *Kobigaan* performances be further curtailed to be exhibited as museum pieces against a given seasonal wage or will they still circulate in rural locales and occasionally in carefully crafted urban fairs with rural essence? In both cases, the 'hierarchy of skills' as well as the proliferation of technological mediation under political intervention continue to guide the livelihoods of labouring performers, especially women.

## Notes

1 See Basu (2024) for a detailed study of the cultural politics of cross-border Kobigaan in India and Bangladesh.
2 Interview with Karuna Chitrakar, Naya, West Midnapore, May 2013.
3 Interview with Ajay Chitrakar, Naya, West Midnapore, May 2013.
4 I look at two NGOs – Asian Heritage Foundation in New Delhi and BanglanatakDotCom in Kolkata working with scroll-painters in Naya – to underline how the traditional *patachitra* and the work of the *patua*s have transformed so far. Much of Asian Heritage Foundation's work with the patuas have focussed on selecting a few from the community and upholding them as the face of the craft community for an international audience through festivals. BanglanatakDotCom, on the other hand, has worked consistently at the local level with the *patua*s, thus concentrating on the nature of the craft itself. It is, therefore, through both the organisations that we can see how the *patachitra* has evolved over time in its content, medium, and presentation. In this sense, patachitra has also opened up to a much broader clientele, that is urban, cosmopolitan, and international.
5 See <https://naya.research.wesleyan.edu/life-histories/>, accessed on 4 November 2015 for details on the women scroll-painters of the village of Naya.
6 See <https://bengalpatachitra.com/artist/swarna-chitrakar/> for a biographical account of Swarna's life and works.
7 See <https://www.cimaartindia.com/cima-art-mela/>, accessed 17 September 2023 for details on the artists featured at the CIMA Art Mela.
8 Quoted in Das (2010).
9 For details on the concept of 'performative labour,' see Bryman (2004, p. 104).
10 Interview with Karuna Chitrakar, 11 May 2013.
11 Interview with Dulali Chitrakar, Jindighi, Murshidabad, 5 March 2013.
12 I attended the *15th Rajya Kobiyal Mela* in Jindighi between 5 and 7 March, 2013, and documented this performance.

13 Dulali has also travelled internationally to Bangladesh and South Korea for *kobigaan* performances.
14 Interview with Dulali Chitrakar, Jindighi, Murshidabad, 5 March 2013.

## References

Arendt, H 1998[1958], *The human condition*, University of Chicago Press, Chicago, IL.
Banerjee, S 1998, *The parlour and the streets: elite and popular culture in nineteenth century Calcutta*, Seagull Books, Kolkata.
Basu, P 2024, *The Poet's Song: 'Folk' and its Cultural Politics in South Asia*, Routledge, London & New York.
Benjamin, W 1963[1936], 'The story-teller: reflections on the works of Nicolai Leskov,' trans. H. Zohn, *Chicago Review*, vol. 16, no. 1, pp. 80–101.
Benjamin, W 1999[1936], 'The work of art in the age of mechanical reproduction,' in H Arendt (ed.), trans. H. Zohn, *Illuminations*, Shocken Books, New York, pp. 217-251.
Bryman, A 2004, *The Disneyization of society*, SAGE Publications, London.
Chattopadhyay, KD 1984, 'Crafts and the future,' *India International Centre Quarterly*, vol. 11, no. 4, pp. 5–14.
Das, A 2010, 'She paints a scroll and strings a tune to tell a tale,' *The Telegraph India*, 16 April 16.
Dutt, G 1932, 'The art of Bengal,' *The Modern Review (Calcutta)*, (May), pp. 519–29.
Foster, S 2013, 'Performing authenticity and the gendered labor of dance,' in Y Hardt, M-L Angerer & A-C Weber (eds.), *Choreographie, medien, gender*, Diaphanes, Zurich, Switzerland, pp. 125–38.
Foucault, M 1986, 'Of other spaces,' *Diacritics*, trans. Jay Miskowiec, vol. 16, no. 1, pp. 22–7.
Hardt, M 1999, 'Affective labour,' *Boundary*, vol. 2, no. 26, pp. 89–100.
Klein, G & Kunst, B 2012, 'Introduction: labour and performance,' *Performance Research*, vol. 17, no. 6, pp. 1–3.
Korom, FJ 2006, *Village of painters: narrative scrolls from West Bengal*, Museum of New Mexico Press, Santa Fe.
Maitra, S 2012, *Kobiyal Dulali Chitrakar*, Bona, Kolkata.
Ponte, I 2015, 'Impressions cosmopolites sur une collection muséale de peintures *patachitra* contemporaines du Bengale, au Portugal (Cosmopolitan impressions from a contemporary Bengali patachitra painting museum collection in Portugal),' *Ateliers d'anthropologie*, vol. 41.
Ridout, N 2013, *Passionate amateurs: theatre, communism and love*, University of Michigan Press, Ann Arbor.
Singh, K 1996, 'Changing the tune. Bengali pata painting's encounter with the modern,' *India International Centre Quarterly*, vol. 23, no. 2, pp. 60–78.
Venkatesan, S 2009, *Craft matters: artisans, development and the Indian Nation*, Orient Blackswan, Hyderabad.

# 12 Kashmir's Crafts Women

## Tacit, Embodied Knowledge and its value in Post-conflict Reconstruction

*Neelam Raina*

Much has been written about Kashmiri crafts: their history and provenance, their value to the community that makes and sells them, and about those who buy into the notion of handcrafted. What is seldom examined, however, is the changing nature of these crafts and how they remain at the centre of Kashmiri culture, identity and economy even in times as turbulent as the present. Due to an intractable conflict, fed by ethnic and religious differences, along the Line of Control, which is the de factor border of Indian Kashmir with Pakistan, many generations of Kashmiris have grown up with a ringside view of violence. The conflict in Kashmir has resulted in limited investment and development, and the region risks falling into a spiral of poverty, unemployment and turmoil. Reconstruction is a long and arduous road. According to the World Bank, there are two main objectives: to facilitate transition from war to sustainable peace and to support the resumption of economic and social development, where post-conflict reconstruction entails rebuilding institutions and jump-starting the economy (Kreimer 1998). In this chapter, I argue that culturally embedded practices playing a key role in identity creation should also have a role in the reconstruction. Crafts in Kashmir are rich in social significance and cultural value, employ many people and generate significant revenue, which can potentially contribute to economic reconstruction.

In this chapter, I discuss the history of the famous Kashmiri shawl and examine the changes it has undergone over the last few decades, focusing on gendered conflict-driven shifts in the practices of making. I draw on empirical data from two decades of engagement in Indian Kashmir, district Srinagar; all names have been changed to protect identities of Kashmiri women (Raina 2009). Unless stated, all interviews and observations are from my own fieldwork since 2001. I attempt to tell the story of changing craft traditions and to capture the dynamic culture of making in the context of conflict in Kashmir.

There is a vast body of historical work about the Kashmiri shawl (Ames 1997; Lévi-Strauss 1986; Rehman & Jafri 2006) and a significant body of work on the politics of Kashmir (Bose 2021; Schofield 2021). However, these works rarely examine the cultural practices of the region or consider them as key to its future. This chapter will reveal deeper insights into how conflict, craft, and gender overlap, and what it means to make a Kashmiri shawl in 2023.

DOI: 10.4324/9781351031028-13

## A Brief History of the Shawls of Kashmir

The Kashmiri shawl can be traced as far back as the era of the great Hindu epics. In the *Ramayana*, King Janaka gifted shawls to Lord Rama (Mathur 2004). In the *Mahabharat*, the people of Kamboj are said to have presented King Yudhishtir with costly shawls embroidered with gold thread. Also, Lord Krishna is known to have been an emissary to the court of the Kauravas, and the gifts of the blind king, Dhritrashtra, included 10,000 shawls of Kashmir (Mathur 2004). In addition to the Hindu epics, shawls are a part of the long history of giving in South Asia. Kashmiri shawls were also among the several items given by the Sassanian King Bahram I (r. 273–276) to his contemporary ruler the Roman Emperor Aurelian (r. 270–275) after the fall of Palmyra. These references indicate that 'high quality Indian textiles were in vogue with the Sassanian elite and were valued highly' (Pathak 2003, p. 10).

The story of the Kashmiri shawl we know today starts with the fifteenth century ruler of Kashmir, Zain-ul-Abdin, who first introduced the weaving of twill tapestry shawls (the Kaanhi shawl) from Turkestan (Gillow & Barnard 1993). Zain-ul-Abdin, also known as *Badshah* ('great King'), is credited with developing shawl production in the Kashmir valley. He became ruler of Kashmir after spending seven years in Samarkand. Zain-ul-Abdin is said to have sent Kashmiri artisans to Iran and Central Asia to learn how to produce the artworks of Islamic culture (Sharrad 2004). The techniques, the designs and the processes of today remain very similar in Srinagar and surrounding districts to when these skills were brought to Kashmir in the fifteenth century.[1] Also, we know how shawls were made from lengthy details in all manner of court documents and accounts of travellers who visited Kashmir.

## Shawl Making in Contemporary Kashmir

Today's context of violence and fragility is markedly different from the Mughal times of relative peace, and the financial support that the rulers of Kashmir provided for the creative work of artisans has long since faded away, ceasing since Indian independence. Craft production now takes place in individual businesses. Shawls are sold through retail outlets, by word of mouth, and through the old shawl *walla* I remember from my childhood in Delhi who visits festivals and home celebrations (Hardy 2001; Koul 2003). Recent work in Kashmir (Dec 2022) also notes the start of the shawl being marketed and sold through social media platforms, with young and upcoming businesses requesting the need for training in this specific sector.[2] The shawl, however, retains its reputation, with the name 'Pashmina' evoking images of luxury and conspicuous consumption (Veblen 1899), like carpets from Iran or blown glass from Murano.

Crafts are made for domestic and export markets, where they face competition from machine made goods, as well as other hand-made craft goods. This situation is not unusual for crafts, especially textile-based products with a spectacular reputation and an equivalent price tag. An unembroidered pure pashmina shawl costs over £2000 in 2022, and a lot more if it features intricate hand embroidery. Shawl-making is labour intensive and often accomplished piecemeal, with each component of the process being done by a separate group of people who specialise in that component of the manufacturing process (Raina 2009). Whilst new methods have been adopted, the supply chain of each shawl consists of multiple specialists contributing to the final product. There are no examples of a complete vertically integrated unit of production in Kashmir.[3] Thus, the shawl is a product of a long line of interdependent relationships, which remain intact despite the politics of identity that drive the conflict.

The biggest investment is the yarn and the weaving. The Pashmina shawl begins its life as fibre from the goats. This fibre is collected and spun, sometimes in Ladakh (the North-Eastern region of Jammu and Kashmir).[4] Pure Pashmina fibre is so fine and delicate that it has not been possible to mechanise the spinning or weaving. The fibre length is short and fine, allowing for a very slight twist to be given to it during the spinning process, making it soft to handle. Hand spun yarn is made into large hanks by women, who make their first appearance in the informal sector of Kashmiri crafts at this stage. Continuing historical tradition, Kashmiri women are also currently involved in the spinning of yarn, which is an ancillary activity, often not noted or valued as highly as it should be. Spinning yarn is a role the women of Kashmir share with many other mountain communities of Central Asia and beyond.[5]

After spinning, the shawl-making process is taken over by men. Hand spun yarn is gently coated with rice paste and loaded onto a loom for weaving to keep the yarn stiff and slightly more robust. Often the weave is decided based on whether or not the shawl will be embroidered. This is not a design decision for the weavers, as most work on commission and are directed about what to make. There is little experimentation with weaving, with most weavers and designers preferring to conform to traditional designs like the *chashme bulbul* or lozenge design. When I questioned them about the lack of variety in the type of weaves found in Kashmir, most weavers attributed it to the lack of time and raw material for experimentation as well as the possibility of not being able to sell the 'new' product. I noted repeatedly during my work in Kashmir that experimentation here carries the invisible presence of privilege. There is also a causational relationship between the high value of the raw material, its ownership, and the space for weavers who never see themselves as the designer of the shawls to explore or experiment. Here, we see the juxtaposition of notions of identity, ownership, production, employment, and socio-economic status within creative labour.

Once woven, the fabric is taken for the first round of finishing. Here, the fabric is stretched taut across a wooden frame, and knots, stray yarns, and fine hairs that the loom did not catch are plucked off using a wide pair of tweezers. For shawls that are left a natural shade and are not dyed, this process is even more important, as dyeing can hide imperfections on the surface. The shawl is then dyed, a practice which has changed from its historic roots in many ways. Traditionally, dyeing used to be done using the fresh waters in the canals of Kashmir, with the water quality known to contribute to the dyeing process. Environmental damage caused by climate change and the mismanagement of water, as well as sewage links to the Dal Lake where shawls were washed and dyed, has made it imperative for Kashmiri dyers to seek other options. Historically used natural dyes are expensive and rarely used. Kashmiri shawl manufacturers also started sending shawls outside of the valley to be dyed as more careful methods of logging colours and shades in a batch and safer dyeing techniques were developed in Delhi as well as Amritsar. However, a vast amount of dyeing continues to be done in Kashmir by hand using hazardous chemicals. In Srinagar, men use their bare hands, boiling hot water and chemicals with little attention paid to the 'Danger' signs on the boxes of the chemicals. This is often laughed off and observers like me are told to not over think.

Once dyed, shawls are washed and pressed by passing them gently through mechanised heated rollers. This deviates from traditional methods in which shawls were left in the meadows after dyeing to be dried by the sun. Currently, with time and money short, and outdoors not always safe or warm, a domestic iron is used to iron out creases created by the dyeing process. After this, the shawl is ready to be sold as a plain shawl. If it needs embroidery, it travels to the *naqaash's* place straight after dyeing. *Naqaash*, or imprinting, is the process in which hand-carved wooden blocks are dipped in water-based blue ink or chalk and weak glue (depending on the base colour of shawl) and printed on the shawls. The blocks are made by a group of carpenters who have been trained to carve wooden blocks into fine designs, faint enough to be embroidered by a single line of thread. These ink marks provide guidance for the designs to be embroidered on the shawl. It is also important that the right amount of pressure is used for imprinting, as faded or blurred lines would confuse the embroiderer. Yet, this is not a design decision point, as each shawl usually comes with a design indication from the person who has commissioned or invested in the piece. Different types of embroidery require varying degrees of skill. The finer the embroidery, the more care needs to be taken in imprinting.

It is interesting to note that each process is led by individuals who are typically heavily critical of the process that precedes their engagement and see themselves as the upholders of high quality. When I first observed this in 2003, it was amusing to note each man who rolled his eyes at the amount of work needed to fix things. Over the years, it became clear to me that this innate Kashmiri self-deprecating humour, informed by sarcasm, masks the deep pride they feel in each object they finish, as well as the role they play in keeping their tradition and identity intact through their craft.

These traditional methods and processes of making shawls have been followed for many years now. However, due to the conflict, there are significant changes to this craft in terms of gendered labour. As the majority of actors producing a finished shawl are men, there is a gendered aspect of shawl production that is uncommon in other textile crafts across the world, which are mostly made by women in domestic settings or workshops. However, in recent years, there are increasing numbers of women working in this sector. In addition, data from Kashmir indicates that during the peak of the conflict, there was a rapid increase in the number of people working in the craft sector. The scale of this informal sector is astounding.

The production value of just woollen shawls in 2020–2021 was over £25 million, with 85 million people employed in the woollen shawls category alone. This data, contained in the statistics digest published by the Jammu and Kashmir government in 2020–2021, also reports the export value of woollen shawls in 2020–2021 to be over £17 million.

## The Current Political Context

The politics of Kashmir occupies many a bookshelf, song and film, yet creative cultures and the way they are impacted by politics, or the role they may play in peacebuilding, are largely ignored in the writing on international development. In the early 1990s, the situation in the Kashmir valley shifted from moments of relative peace to sharp escalations of frequent violence. Hence, whilst it does not classify as an 'active conflict', there exists an uneasy silence in the region which I experienced last in December 2022. The absence of war or active conflict due to a peace agreement or military victory is not necessarily peace (Licklider 1995); it can, for example, be called negative peace (Galtung 1969). According to Rothstein (1999), the ending of violence or a so-called post-conflict situation provides 'new set of opportunities that can be grasped or thrown away' (p. 224). This grey area is where Kashmir rests now in a post-conflict region where violence is sporadic, yet persistent. Military presence is reduced in comparison to the peak years of turmoil through the 1990s and into the middle of the first decade of the twenty-first century but is still there.

The violence and its socio-economic impact are plainly visible in Kashmir. While tourists return in larger numbers each summer, suggesting normality, the scars of long-term fragility that is uncertain, unpredictable, and unresolved remain. Quraishi (2004), for example, mentions the possibility of hiring men for killing as an alternative means of earning money. These scars also manifest themselves in poverty, with people living below the poverty line and social inequalities within the health and education sector, as well as little investment in industry and employment, all of which are well known as the impact of conflict.

However, there has been noticeable growth in the scale of handicrafts produced and sold, with steady increases in revenues and numbers of people employed. Income generation through dignified work in the sector of crafts promotes the development of Kashmir's economy and contributes to poverty alleviation, which, in turn, may lead to a decrease in violence. It also rekindles community relationships and, in many ways, harkens back to previous, more peaceful times when the joy of making overrode everyday challenges of poverty and violence. In the long term, crafts could thus be a source of economic reconstruction of this post-conflict area. In Kashmir in particular, we see this potential play out in gendered ways.

## Shifting Gender Relations in Kashmir

Kashmir has always been a Muslim majority state, with a specific cultural identity distinct to the region, accompanied and defined by cultural expressions that are visible through the arts. Being Kashmiri was always a primary identity and was actually a feature of many hilarious informal discussions about identity I have had over the years regarding how to define identity and in which order. Kashmiri, male, Muslim, Indian, district of parental origin, city- or rural-born, grandparental profession – multiple gendered, regional, religious, national, residential, historical, and professional layers all mixed together into a melting pot that created a uniqueness of being. A primary fissure resulting from the conflict is evident along religious lines, changing religious make-up of the population, as the Kashmiri Pandits (Hindus) left in 1992 to the neighbouring region of Jammu in what is often called an exodus. They remain a large internally displaced group, who never returned to Kashmir in large numbers.

As is common, the conflict also resulted in the skewing of the gender ratio, with the deaths and disappearances of many men. This has left behind many women-headed households, with Kashmiri Muslim women now the main bread winners for their families. This is a big shift from the traditional role women have played in caring within the home settings, which has brought about changes in the gender power balance and altered the perception of women in society. Women in a Kashmir-based NGO with whom I worked observed this shift away from a solely domestic role that promoted virtues of silence, obedience, chastity, domesticity, and motherhood. Men were traditionally considered protectors and income earners and those who left the home to provide financially for their families.

Kashmiri women in the early 2000s spoke about themselves as *bechaari* ('poor thing'), which denotes pity. Aziza, a woman from North of Srinagar wondered, 'In goliyon ne humari zindagai tabaah kar di hai. Hum bechaari kya karein?' ('These bullets have destroyed our lives, what should we women do?'). Bullets claimed many lives and have had a devastating impact on many homes in the region. In the city of Kashmir, there are numerous graveyards, increasing in size and numbers each year. This region also saw the use of pellet guns that did not kill, but blinded people, in most cases boys and young men (UNOCHR 2019). The UNOCHR report also discusses forced disappearances and arbitrary detentions, mainly of Kashmiri men.

Many Kashmiri women have been in direct or indirect contact with violence. I interviewed women who spoke about the physical insecurity they feel living in Kashmir. They hear news about sexual crimes in the valley and fear for their safety. The presence of security forces, who the women believed had limitless authority to interrogate and question them, made them nervous. Kashmiri women, like women across the world, are constantly watched and judged when present in public. They are expected to be religiously inclined and more pious than men and even to rectify religious shortcomings in husbands (Personal interviews, Kashmir University 2003). Kashmiri women are not only responsible for being good practicing Muslims but must also uphold the moral reputation of their families based on how they dress, as well as where they appear, at what time of the day, and with whom. This patriarchal structure is familiar in South Asia and, when combined with an intractable conflict, highlights the exacerbated burden women bear.

According to the teachings of Islam, in the Holy Quran, a woman has the 'noble task entrusted to her by Allah of childbearing and motherhood' (Surat Al Nisa':4, Ayah 34). She has duties towards her husband and children and these responsibilities should take precedence over other responsibilities. In Kashmir, women face a dilemma as the need to generate income conflicts with the expected traditional care-giving role. This often means children are left in the care of their grandparents and siblings (Kaul-Batra 2004). This has a knock-on effect as children are often not sent to school as they are required at home for caring and running the house (Kaul-Batra 2004). This clash of religious ethics with the reality of living in a post-conflict situation was observed as a cause of immense pressure, dilemma, and trauma for the women of Kashmir. The responsibility to earn is also hindered by low levels of literacy and skills necessary for gaining formal employment.

Due to the conflict and the loss of male relatives, domestic duties for women have also increased. Many women have relatives and older, sick, or disabled family members living with them. In poorer areas, there is also little access to childcare, which prevents women from leaving their homes. Farida told me in 2006 that she always felt ridden with guilt as she needed to work to keep her children and her in-laws fed and safe. She carries the grief of being the 'half widow' of a man who disappeared in 2002, now a status of numerous Kashmiri women (Zia 2013).

## The Role of Crafts the Politically Fragile Spaces of Kashmir

In this context, craft working from home, away from the harsh winters, and within sight and reach of those who need looking after, is appealing to most women. The duty of care, in all its dimensions, can be delivered through home-based practices of making. This work provides financial, social, and personal reassurance to the women who make crafts. The appeal of this work, engaging with arts and beautiful objects, is also therapeutic in many ways. There are bodies of research that speak about art as therapy, and in contemporary Kashmir, craft working functions as therapy. Here, the embodied knowledge of the maker, the landscape of work, the links between her cultural identity and the work she produces, the repetitive movement of hands, and the creation of objects that others will value and appreciate are all connected in positive ways. Sabah (2007) spoke about feeling disconnected from reality when she works on her embroidery. She expressed feeling distanced from her anxieties and her grief from the loss of her father and brothers. She found the textiles comforting and sustaining, and her anxieties of needing to be outside the house were laid to rest with this work. She was very young and faced loss at an early stage in her life, and craftworking felt safe and non-threatening.

I met Fahima, who had taken up this work, in Kashmir in December 2022. I remember her smiling at me, and saying, with the shawl draped over her legs and the needle in her hand as she embroidered delicate patterns onto the fabric, how it allowed her to zone out of the burdens of care and poverty that she carries each day. There is no need to travel, find childcare, or be in the company of strangers, she said. This is practical for women in remote locations with little access to public transport, or the money required for using it.

In a recent training workshop in Srinagar, Fareeda, one of the new craftswomen to join my group of makers, was surprised that craft-based income generation for women makers was being explored. She lives in downtown Srinagar and lost her son in 2010 to a 'brutal death' in police custody. Fareeda is part of a focus group for research on the Culture and Conflict project at the UKRI Gender, Justice and Security hub and had come for design and colour training. This research brings craft-made textiles from conflict-affected areas in South Asia to the British craft retail sector.[6] This traditional textile making is an avenue for the inclusion of women in the economy and their futures are linked to income generation, which changes many aspects of their lives in positive ways.

Tacit knowledge embodied within Kashmiri women has been key to their understanding of craft making and has also provided an incentive for them to select this area for earning an income. They have, in the past, received hand-made textiles as wedding presents, ancestral heirlooms passed from mother to daughter, and as matriarchs within their families they invested money in craft-made goods. These women have observed shawls being bought, used, gifted, made, saved, stored, washed, worn, and recycled. They have seen good quality fabrics; they have sold pieces of shawls when times were tough and cash was needed in the home; they have wrapped new-borns and older loved ones tightly for warmth through the arctic winters; and they have been closely attached to the unstitched cloth that is the Kashmiri shawl. They know, and now as they work in craft making, they recognise this tacit knowledge. Sharifa, one of the older women I have worked with for now over two decades, mentioned that working in this sector makes her realise how much she knows, and that this work helps her feel confident and she speaks about it, and the income she earns, with pride. She feels confident enough to want to help other women work on craft making too.

Craft making is also popular in Kashmir due to the ready availability of raw material, which makes it environmentally and financially sustainable. Local beauty inspires the design and making of crafts and severe winters confine people indoors, when income from agricultural labour reduces to nothing. The crafts sector evidences the presence of expertise and skills, systems of trading, supply chains for raw material, and the presence of local businesses that continue to trade. For women, this pre-existing structure enables them to enter the sector without prior financial or educational investment of any kind. The fluidity of employment in this sector is yet another reason why women choose to work in crafts. As freelance makers who can work on commission, they can earn without being formally employed by any business.

Individual memory of watching, buying, touching, and seeing crafts being made and used in their everyday spaces and places has embodied this tacit uncoded knowledge within Kashmiri women. Their craft speaks a language that is echoed and transmitted across generations as they live through fragilities. Numerous inequalities that women face on account of their intersectional identity are levelled to some degree by their work in this sector. Associated benefits also include achieving dignified livelihoods through engaging in locally valued and culturally relevant work. The conflict has destroyed much that shall need to be rebuilt. And yet, through crafts, what survives brutal geopolitics across generations is the identity of people, and their material cultures, embodied, tacit, resilient, and sustaining (Figures 12.1 and 12.2).

*Figure 12.1* Wooden *naqashkari* blocks, Srinagar, India. 2002. Photograph by author.

*Figure 12.2* Embroidery on Pashmina, Srinagar, India. March 2004. Photograph by author.

## Notes

1 This is an observation based on longitudinal research in the region by the author 2002–2023.
2 My research is built around training in the cultural and creative industries; hence, these were direct requests for bespoke training to be delivered in mid-2023.

3 Vertically integrated here means that one business would be able to complete a shawl without outsourcing any labour processes, in that they would be able to spin, weave, dye, embroider, and finish fabric, as well as retailing or wholesaling it.
4 This trade of fibre from Ladakh has a long history. This history and the politics of trade in Pashmina have a vast amount of literature written about them. See Ahmed (2004) and Maskiell (2002).
5 See works of Olcott (1991), Harris (1996), Ainley and Rainbird (2014), and larger bodies of work on women who spin, in Northern America, Mesoamerica, and Britain.
6 https://thegenderhub.com/projects/culture-and-conflict/.

## References

Ahmed, M 2004, 'The politics of Pashmina: the changpas of eastern Ladakh,' *Journal of Nomadic Peoples*, vol. 8, no. 2, pp. 89–107.

Ainley, P & Rainbird, H 2014, *Apprenticeship: towards a new paradigm of learning*, Routledge, London.

Ames, F 1997, *The Kashmir shawl and its Indo-French influence*, Antique Collectors Club, Woodbridge.

Ainley, P & Rainbird, H 2014, *Apprenticeship: towards a new paradigm of learning*, Routledge, London.

Bose, S 2021, *Kashmir at the crossroads: inside a 21st-century conflict*, Yale University Press, New Haven, CT.

Galtung, J 1969, 'Violence, peace and peace research,' *Journal of Peace Research*, vol. 6, no. 3, pp. 167–91.

Gillow, J & Barnard, N 1993, *Traditional Indian textiles*, Thames and Hudson, London.

Government of Jammu and Kashmir, 2006, Statistics Digest, Directorate of Economics and Statistics, Planning and Monitoring Department Jammu and Kashmir, Srinagar 2005–2006.

Government of Jammu and Kashmir 2007, *Economic survey 2007–08*, Directorate of Economics and Statistics, Srinagar.

Government of Jammu and Kashmir 2021, Statistics Digest, Directorate of Economics and Statistics, Planning and Monitoring Department Jammu and Kashmir, Jammu.

Hardy, J 2001, *Goat: a story of Kashmir and Notting Hill*, John Murray, London.

Harris, C 1996, 'Women of the sedentary population of Russian Turkestan through the eyes of western travellers,' *Central Asian Survey*, vol. 15, no. 1, pp. 75–95, https://doi.org/10.1080/02634939608400935

Kaul-Batra, A 2004, *Women in conflict*, film, Production Company, New Delhi.

Koul, S 2003, *The tiger ladies: a memoir of Kashmir*, Headline Publishing, London.

Kreimer, A, Eriksson, J, Muscat, R, Arnold, M, & Scott, C 1998, *The World Bank's experience with post-conflict reconstruction*, The World Bank. https://ieg.worldbankgroup.org/sites/default/files/Data/reports/postcon.pdf

Lévi-Strauss, M 1986, *The cashmere shawl*, Dryad Press, London.

Licklider, R 1995, 'The consequences of negotiated settlements in civil wars, 1945–1993,' *American Political Science Review*, vol. 89, no. 3 (September), pp. 685–7.

Maskiell, M 2002, 'Consuming Kashmir: shawls and empires, 1500–2000,' *Journal of World History*, vol. 13, no. 1, pp. 27–66.

Mathur, A 2004, *Indian shawls: mantles of splendour*, Rupa & Co, New Delhi.

Olcott, J. (2003). Miracle Workers: Gender and State Mediation among Textile and Garment Workers in Mexico's Transition to Industrial Development. *International Labor and Working-Class History*, vol. 63, pp. 45–62.

Pathak, A 2003, *Pashmina,* Roli and Janssen, New Delhi.

Quraishi, H 2004, *Kashmir: the untold story*, Penguin Books, New Delhi.

Raina, N 2009, 'Women, craft and the post conflict reconstruction of Kashmir,' PhD thesis, De Montfort University, Leicester. https://dora.dmu.ac.uk/handle/2086/8122

Rehman, S & Jafri, N 2006, *The Kashmiri Shawl, From Jamavar to Paisley,* Mapin Publishing, Ahmedabad.

Rothstein, RL 1999, (ed.) ' *After the peace: resistance and reconciliation*, Lynne Rienner, Boulder, p. 224.

Schofield, V 2021, *Kashmir in conflict: India, Pakistan and the unending war*, I.B. Tauris & Company Limited, London.

Sharrad, P 2004, 'Following the map: a postcolonial unpacking of a Kashmir shawl,' *Textile: The Journal of Cloth and Culture*, vol. 2, no. 1, pp. 64–78.

UNOCHR 2019, *Update of the situation of human rights in Indian-administered Kashmir and Pakistan-administered Kashmir from May 2018 to April 2019*, 22 January 2022. https://www.ohchr.org/sites/default/files/Documents/Countries/IN/KashmirUpdateReport_8July2019.pdf

Veblen, T 1899, *The theory of the leisure class*, Project Gutenberg.

Zia, A 2013, *The spectacle of a good-half widow: performing agency in the human rights movement in Kashmir*, UCLA: Centre for The Study of Women, 8 April 2019. https://escholarship.org/uc/item/3xx4n1zf

# 13 Kanchipuram as Brand Value

## Weaving, Marketing Tradition in South India

*Aarti Kawlra*

### Introduction: Culturally Valued Products and Globalisation

With the expansion of neo-liberalism, trade of artisanal products came under global regulations stipulated by the World Trade Organization (WTO) and the Trade-Related Intellectual Property agreements in the opening decade of the twenty-first century. New scholarship emerged on the commodification of craft labour, integration of artisans within international markets, and the advertising and consumption of craft products from the global South in the global North (Scrase 2005). What were the responses of artisans themselves to the sweeping changes brought on by a renewed nostalgia for a bygone era spurred by globalisation? The case of handwoven textiles opens the question of livelihood practices that sustain and validate the labour associated with a craft for both producers and consumers. In what follows, I take up the case of the iconic Kanchipuram silk handloom sari, whose design evolution, and cultural significance among Indians and the diaspora, paralleled the emergence of the Bharatanatyam dance-form in the 1930s and came to be recognised as the dress of the modern Indian woman of classic taste in the previous century (Kawlra 2018). This piece is an inquiry into how the branding and contemporary value of the Kanchipuram sari is predicated on notions of Kanchipuram as a place, well known for its weaving traditions in the past.

Historical and ethnographic studies of handloom weaving in twentieth-century South India have emphasised the rise of artisan capital, and the dynamic role played by weaver-merchants in organising production and labour in the colonial and post-colonial economy (Arivukkarasi & Nagaraj 2009; Basile 2013; Bharathan 1983; De Neve 2005; Haynes 2012; Kawlra 2018; Mahadevan & Vijayabaskar 2014; Niranjana 2004; Parthasarathi 2001; Roy 1993, 2002, 2007). At the other end of the spectrum is a growing body of literature focusing on artisanal products from the places of labour to international marketplaces, diversely addressing the question of voice, agency, and identity of artisans within changing regimes of value (Appadurai 1986; DeNicola 2004; Greenough 1996; Herzfeld 2004; Maskiell 1999; Mukherjee & Williams 2015; Nakatani 2020). This chapter focuses on the active role of artisan producers in adapting to global policy regulations and shifting markets for culturally valued products like the Kanchipuram sari. I inquire into how handloom sari producers and cooperative societies use place-based branding, associated with the

DOI: 10.4324/9781351031028-14

official and unofficial histories of Kanchipuram town, to validate their craft labour in the neo-liberal economy.

The commonly used phrase 'kanchipuram sari' or 'kanchi *pattu*' (literally 'kanchi silk') comes from an association with the historic temple town of Kanchipuram located in the Chengalpattu district of Tamil Nadu state in south-eastern India. Inscriptional evidence of Kanchipuram's association with silk and handweaving suggests the prevalence of mercantile corporations in the fourteenth century who made public donations, among whom were included the *Jayangonda Chilai Chettis*, or cloth merchants of Jayangondamandalam, which is the medieval name for the Kanchipuram region. An inscription from the town of Kanchipuram during the period of the Vijayanagar king Venkatapatideva Maharaya (r. 1585–1614) refers to custom duties levied on certain silk cloths brought in by the influential *nanadesi* (literally 'from many lands') merchants guild who were 'operating in southern India from the twelfth to the seventeenth century with strong trading networks as far as Malaya, Persia and Nepal' (Ramaswamy 2020, p. 69).

The twelfth and thirteenth centuries were an age of heterodox movements in South India, when medieval temple towns became the loci of intense sectarian activity in which weavers participated in large numbers (Ramaswamy 1985). Asserting their role in expanding markets, weavers achieved an elevated status in the caste hierarchy by claiming public honours through temple donations. It was during this period that the orthodox Sanskrit school of the Hindu sect of Vaishnavism 'shifted its centre from Tirupati to the Varadaraja Perumal temple at Kanchipuram' (Ramaswamy 1985, p. 113). Medieval urban religious centres like Kanchipuram also attracted skilled weavers who sought the patronage of temples that had come to own vast amounts of land and resources. Weavers set up residences in separate quarters, usually within the temple square, in contrast to the other temple artisans who lived in streets located outside the square. For instance, inscriptional evidence is available to show that 'During the period of Uttama Chola (tenth century), the Pattusales were settled in the four quarters of Kanchipuram (called Kachchipedu in the inscription) known as Karuvulanpatti, Karisahanappatti. Atimanappatti and Eruvalichcheri' (Ramaswamy 1985, p. 16).

Evidence from colonial documents suggests that by the nineteenth century, Kanchipuram (Conjeevaram) had become a specialised centre of fine cloth production, and weaving communities came to be associated with the specific varieties of cloths. The production of silk saris with contrast borders was particularly concentrated in certain towns and districts and became a full-time occupation for many weaving groups catering to wider domestic markets. In her article on 'The geography of weaving in early nineteenth-century south India,' Wielenga (2015, p.171) examines revenue data available on the distribution of looms, the tax paid, and the value of cloth produced from the district of Chingelput in the early nineteenth century, to reveal

> that about half the looms in the district were found in or around Kanchipuram and Arnee (Arani) and that these paid high loom taxes. Looms paying a tax of `4 to 4½ were found only in Kanchipuram. Those in Arani paid `3 ½ on

average. The remaining looms, scattered across the rest of the district, paid from 1 to 2 rupees. Though loom tax rates could vary widely within the same district, often for no discernible reason, a higher tax is usually indicative of fine-cloth production. From Forbes Watson's collection we learn that Arani was famous for fine muslins, dhotis and saris. Kanchipuram was also an important centre for the production of fine cloth. Thus Chengalpattu conforms to the pattern set out so far: while fine-cloth weaving was concentrated in towns or large villages, the production of ordinary or coarse varieties was dispersed.

## Politics of the Past: Emplacing Tradition

The imperial agenda of territorial integration and administrative unity was implemented through the geographical mapping of India's people, places, resources, and products. According to Wagoner (2003), Colonel Mackenzie, the first Surveyor General of India in early nineteenth century, is known to have meticulously collected oral histories of the places he visited, during the course of his travels in South India. Mackenzie's government-sponsored project of mapmaking and collecting, sedentarised India's populations and their pasts through the modality of caste-based census enumerations among other forms of governance (Irschick 1994; Ludden 1996). Communities came to be defined as culturally distinct endogamous groups bound by temporal, spatial, and qualitative characteristic features such as occupation and technical skills, dress, food habits, beliefs, and rituals, and whose membership was governed by rules of hereditary succession and hierarchy. This spatial structuring of colonial power through caste was legitimised through other forms of colonial knowledge like historical epigraphy and ethnology that fixed local communities to their pasts within a cartographic paradigm (Cohn 1996; Handler & Linnekin 1984; Wagoner 2003). Artisanal groups were now spatially identifiable in clusters based on their hereditary occupation and craft production was fixed to specific administrative districts and localities.

Knowledge production about crafts of India was part of a wider geophysical and techno-economic enumeration of the diverse commercial products of the colony (disambiguated into the raw material used, techniques employed, nature of ornamentation and provenance, or chronology of ownership and location) and meticulously documented in imperial gazetteers and monographs as part of a wider information network of techno-science governing a colonial locality. Among the early projects of documentation that recontextualised artisanal products for colonial interests include the series of 18 volumes produced by John Forbes Watson in 1866 and 1873, containing actual textile swatches with generalised labels such as fabrics 'plain' and 'ornamental,' 'coarse' and 'fine,' 'lower class wear' and 'upper class wear,' 'male' or 'female' wear (Driver & Ashmore 2010, p. 361). Watson included an appendix for ease of reference and accessibility which spatially marked each example according to 'the places of manufacture or markets from which they came carefully enumerated under name, district, Presidency, or country, right down to latitude and longitude' (Driver & Ashmore

2010, p. 366). Systemising local realities in the language of craft, featuring an 'informed selection of exemplary "types"' applicable throughout the length and breadth of the colonised territory, captured in a single sweep the geographical spread of the coverage (Driver & Ashmore 2010, p. 367). This colonial practice of place-based enumeration framed Indian artisanal products and producers within a craft tradition and spatially marked them according to their ascribed place of origin. The visual representation of the colony's products circulating in the colonial economy via museums, international expositions and fairs, department stores, catalogues, and journals reproduced the official ordering of artisanal production, stabilising an imperial vision founded upon cognitive, aesthetic and ethical notions of an imagined, Indian past (Appadurai 1986; Baringer & Flynn 1998; Cohn 1996; Dutta 2007; Mathur 2007; Metcalf 1989; McGowan 2009; Mitter 2002; Raina & Habib 1991; Sundar 1995; Tarar 2011).

The emplacing of artisanal products within a cartographic paradigm of craft production in British administrative texts not only linked specific producers and their products to specific places but also fixed standards of quality to discrete localities. Material samples of this project were actively collected, arranged, and displayed according to criteria that constituted criteria subsumed under the category of the traditional as defined and legitimated by colonial officials (Hoffenberg 2004; Maskiell 1999; McGowan 2005, 2009; Metcalf 1989; Sundar 1995). Artisanal products became synonymous with all that was deemed to be traditional in India in the eyes of British art administrators such as Sir George Birdwood, Lockwood Kipling, Cecil Burns, and Ernst B. Havell who were propagating 'the prevention of degradation' in the Indian arts in their search for authenticity (quoted in McGowan 2005, p. 273). Disparaging innovations and imitations as deviant, hybrid, or spurious, colonial officials, in their role as arbitrators of taste, attributed the decline in quality of craft products to the general tendency among native producers to digress from traditional principles and standards of practice set by their forefathers (McGowan 2005).

The identification of places as representing difference, both cultural and technical, continued post-independence and provided both state and non-state credence to the imaginary of a national crafts heritage flourishing in regionally located clusters of artisan settlements across the country. Among the many the nationalists who sought to bring a cultural reformation in India through an aesthetic understanding of tradition as found in its villages, Kamala Devi Chattopadhyay's work in the revival of India's regional crafts in the early fifties continues to shape the crafts agenda of the nation. As founder patron of the Craft Council of India, an elite nongovernmental organisation influencing craft policy and working to revive and promote the work of Indian artisans, she made remote and exotic handicrafts and handlooms available to urban consumers through regular exhibitions and fairs. India's first woman Prime Minister, Indira Gandhi (1916–1984), is known to have selected her saris to match the regional constituency in which she travelled. Indeed, maintaining a personal association with the country's diverse craft traditions were central to her political image as a cultural heritage conscious leader (Kawlra 2014).

The 1961 census of handloom weaving in Madras state reproduced this place-based identity of artisanal products and dedicated an entire volume only to the textile techniques, processes, and designs of handloom weaving in Kanchipuram (see Nambiar 1964a, 1964b). The nationalist revival and resurgence of regional Indian textile traditions culminated in the *Saris of India* series of documentations sponsored by the Development Commissioner for Handlooms and initiated during the 1980s. This colonial practice of emplacing tradition crystallised, post-independence, into regionally distinguishable handloom textiles with locally contingent designs and technologies which, in turn, has had a bearing on the present-day definition of the 'Kanchipuram sari' as the queen of all silk handloom saris from South India.

A more recent appropriation of tradition by state-authorised legal and administrative functionaries anticipates the neo-liberal commoditization of artisanal production in the twenty-first century. The Geographical Indications of Goods (GI) mark of quality is a legal branding instrument instituted by global economic and regulatory regimes and implemented by individual nations seeking proprietary rights for artisanal products produced within their territories. In India, the GI (Registration and Protection) Act of India 1999 was enacted in 2003 following a global agreement of trade and intellectual property between nations, under the auspices of the WTO. The GI for the Kanchipuram sari provides a useful entry point for conversations on the politics of place-based tradition. In an earlier paper, I demonstrated how the GI in fact delegitimises production outside of the administrative boundaries of the town of Kanchipuram; and that an authorised version of the Kanchipuram sari has spawned the proliferation of a new genre of what are called 'duplicates' (Kawlra 2014). In this paper I discuss how weavers, producers and designers appropriate the colonial place-based typology of craft to brand the Kanchipuram sari as an authentic product of an inalienable tradition for a heritage-conscious market.

## Branding Inalienable Culture

According to Hann (2002), the selective valorisation of local traditions and identities can be traced to the political project of burgeoning cultural nationalism in Europe, at the turn of the twentieth century. In India, the place-based typology of traditional craft, discussed earlier on in this paper, was part of this wider trend in the making of national selfhood through a presumed congruence of state and culture at the international. However, with the renewed interest in local, lived realities of craft products, the idea of a singular national culture has weakened. Scholars have pointed to the need to bring back to the table historical contingencies and predilections to unveil a politics of culture from the lived experiences of the local which, according to Hann (2002), must emerge as *C*ongealed, *R*econstituted … Intersubjectively *M*eaningful … *E*volving … *S*ociality" (pp. 275–6). From the perspective of artisans and their patrons then, craft products are culturally encoded memories of past (and present) realities imbued with meaning for a variety of stakeholders to use for diverse ends. Esther Leslie (1998) notes how, for Walter Benjamin, the shift from artisanal to industrial production, and the concomitant redundancy of the labouring hand, has a bearing on the different facets of memory and experience available for imagining future possibilities. For Benjamin, craft objects are invested with both intimacy and imagination and, like storytelling, imprint 'themselves into listeners' fantasy, awaiting retransmissions, after-lives' (Leslie 1998, p. 5).

Producers of silk saris in Kanchipuram use a range of tags or labels to mark the quality of their saris for the benefit of their customers. The certifications of standard include the Handloom mark, the Silk mark, the mark of the production organisation or Cooperative Society mark, and the gold thread or *zari* mark. Yet, it is the Kanchipuram sari, which references the town of Kanchipuram, that triggers memories of a bygone place-based past. Kanchipuram has crystallised as brand-value for different marketing constituencies who, with their 'often incommensurable perspectives,' are able to deploy the culture concept within a single semiotic framework (Manning 2010, p. 35). In what follows, I explore how the discourse of the Kanchipuram sari results in multiple mediations of an inalienable past in the present, even as it anticipates new narratives of tradition among weavers, producers, and designers of the famed silk sari.

In a market of specialised cloth production in medieval South Indian urban centres of production, the claims of many weaving castes to professional legitimacy were contested, and many had to find ways to demonstrate their inks with Kanchipuram town. In 1879, British administrator CS Crole recounted a dispute between two groups of weaving castes – the Kaikolars and the Saliyans – who 'trace their allocation in Conjeevaram to the time of Karikala Chola, whom they date in the 12th century' (Crole 1879, p. 33). Kanchipuram continues to be the geocultural site for the assertion of silk weaving as a hereditary practice among many groups and the accrual of symbolic capital (mythic and ritual) in the socioeconomic and religious region of caste. At the Kamakshiamman temple's 10-day festival, the right (*urimai*) to sponsor the cloth for the temple flag at the flag hoisting ceremony every February is held by the Padma Saliyars, a Telugu-speaking community of silk weavers who, in exchange, receive *kovil mariyaathai* ('temple honour') in the presence of the *shaiva* deity (Kawlra 2018, p. 84). In his book, *Work is* Worship, Nalli Kuppuswami (1983), the proprietor of the oldest and largest family-owned silk sari concern in Tamil Nadu reminisces about his humble beginnings from the town of Kanchipuram.

The common adage among weavers, 'Kanchipuram *ponal kalatti pozhaikalam*' ('One can go to Kanchipuram and survive by pressing one's feet (on the loom)'), refers to an image of Kanchipuram as a place of self-reliance and sustenance in the face of myriad uncertainties characteristic of their profession. Kanchipuram is not only renowned as a place that attracts weavers with skill but also the place where they can be found in large numbers. In the 1930s, when Rukminidevi Arundale set up a weaving unit at Kalakshetra in present day south Chennai, members of silk weaving castes, renowned for their hereditary skill, were summoned and relocated from Kanchipuram, to cater to a new demand for the costume of the classical Bharatanatyam dancer (Kawlra 2018). Many weavers are proud of their hereditary skill and association with silk and are not afraid to challenge new entrants into the

*Figure 13.1* The Kanchipuram sari's most recent avatar as a high-end 'designer' or 'studio' sari for the heritage-conscious yet fashionable Indian Woman.

*Source:* Kanakvalli.com (used with permission).

field. In 2006, Kanchipuram-based Padma Saliyar weaver-designer V Sundarajan filed a formal objection to the Intellectual Property Rights office in Chennai against the RMKV group (a relatively new silk sari firm from a non-weaving caste background) to contest their patent on a reversible Kanchipuram sari (Kawlra 2018, p. 148).

Kanchipuram's caste-based organisational forms and networks of production have supported economic reform in the weaving sector, by creating cooperatives and led to being recognised for its oldest and largest silk production and sales cooperative societies. According to Arterburn's study done in the 1970s, Kanchipuram's cooperatives became vote-banks for political parties, and many weavers joined the labour movement and union organisation via the Communist Party of India (Arterburn 1982). The street on which The Kamakshiamman Silk Weavers Cooperative Society is located and named after KS Parthasarathy, an elected leader of the Marxist Community Party of India and member of the Padma Saliyar community of silk weavers. That this Kanchipuram town continues to be synonymous with the labour and skill of silk handloom weaving in popular imagination is evident from the 2008 film *Kanchivaram*, which depicts the struggle for survival of silk weavers in Kanchipuram, their awareness of their subalternity, and the eventual emergence of the weavers' cooperative movement in the first half of the twentieth century. According to writer and director Priyardarshan, the title of the film draws from its reference to a *varam* (blessing) of the skill of weaving from goddess Kanchi bestowed upon the weavers of Kanchipuram.

For producers of silk saris in Kanchipuram – both private manufacturers and cooperative societies – the coming of the national-level GI protection regime in 2009 was a matter of choice, that of producing the official version or original Kanchipuram sari or some version of the same. In 2013, of the 50 authorised user certificates that were issued for Kanchipuram saris, 23 were cooperative societies in the town, 27 were private producers, and the rest were in various stages of inspection and awaiting certification (Kawlra 2014). Many producers belonging to hereditary weaving castes saw in the GI an opportunity to recast tradition as a marketing strategy and to valorise Kanchipuram town's geo-physical and cultural past, in the language of authenticity. For many producers, the GI was a prospect of quality assurance that they could provide to discerning customers. One of them remarked that it was a way of marking the difference between a 'horse and a donkey,' or the original and the fake, whilst differentiating themselves amidst competition. Many producers even went to the extent of emphasising the inalienable worth or 'divine look' of the sari on account of it having been 'produced in the holy abode of the gods, the town of Kanchi,' comparing it to an 'investment' equivalent to its value in gold, and equating it to wearing precious jewellery, as part of their branding of tradition (Kawlra 2014, p. 19).

In an interview with the author, a Handlooms department official in Kanchipuram noted that only six cooperative societies, the ones that are prominent in Kanchipuram, had opted to conform to the weaving specifications of the GI and to market their products with a GI label. The official added that none of the private producers who had previously applied for the GI tag have renewed their user certification in 2019. Moreover, many of the small producers who were functioning outside of the approved parameters of the GI continue to cater to a segmented market for silk saris. The allure of the original Kanchipuram sari has spawned a whole new genre of saris, popularly referred to as the duplicate Kanchipuram sari, often in demand for its more affordable price and unmistakable visual likeness to the original. The duplicate sari's appeal is not credited to any externally authorised mark of quality but to its invocation of the word 'Kanchipuram.'

Kanchipuram conjures culture and tradition for connoisseurs and purveyors of the authentic contrast-bordered, silk and gold handloom sari. The Kanchipuram sari is integral to weddings, life-cycle ceremonies and festivals, and classical music and dance performances in South India. It is known for its legendary nexus, not only with its place of origin but also with its hereditary weavers who are deemed specialists in augmenting well-being and mitigating misfortune for their clients. For the tradition-conscious, purchasing wedding saris from certain hereditary weaving family concerns is believed to be auspicious for newlyweds on account of their ethical business practices. The cultural value ascribed to these saris refers not only to the price of the precious metals and silk yarn used but also to the non-monetary worth or *raasi* (the Tamil term for 'auspiciousness') that is woven so to speak into the sari by the producers (Kawlra 2018, pp. 150–3).

The recent trend in studio or designer silk saris is yet another branding strategy that uses the silk sari's identity with Kanchipuram town for the benefit of consumers with a cosmopolitan sensibility but with a taste for the handmade. Fashion designers with a taste for culture and tradition curate saris that are somehow imbued with the spirit of the past, whilst emphasising the wearer's personal style and need for an aesthetic grounded in tradition in the world of global fashion. The website of a Chennai boutique selling silk saris under label Kanjivaram echoes the curator's desire for building 'a sanctum santorum for the Kanjivaram' in order 'to celebrate the queen of silks and house it befittingly in a spot' and 'underline the highest standards in craft, provenance and process, all of which go into the creation of the (Figure 13.1).'[1] The Kanchipuram sari now personifies tradition – both national, regional, and personal – and

> is considered an heirloom piece not only for its heritage value, but also for its place in our families and in our hearts ... becoming a repository of memories and stories that we hope will live on in its weavers, as it is handed down from one generation of women to the next.[2]

## Concluding Reflections

The legitimation of Kanchipuram as a brand through the lens of tradition elevates the contrast bordered silk and gold sari of Kanchipuram to the level of an archetypal product. Its importance amidst discursive narratives of identity, and standards of quality and taste, is obtained through a demonstrable semiotic nexus with a place of origin, each time produced anew, in response to changing regimes of value. Ironically, in the neoliberal global economy, place of origin and the handmade have now become a global good. It anticipates the universalisation of globally sanctioned programmes valorising locality and heralds the commodification of the 'local,' eminently eligible for high status within what Herzfeld (2004) has called 'the global hierarchy of value.'

Yet, as we have seen in the case of the Kanchipuram sari, the contenders for such valuations are a range of protagonists – weavers, producers, cooperative societies, and designers – and not merely state functionaries, like those implementing the GI, who brand tradition within national and global standards. The singular congruence between state and culture is easily lost in the myriad claims to culture and sites of meaning, be it for collective labour and livelihood or for more individualistic, creative, or aesthetic consumption ends.

## Notes

1 Kanakavalli.com n.d., 'The Kanakavalli Story.' https://kanakavalli.com/pages/the-kanakavalli-story.
2 Kanakavalli.com 2017, 'My first love....' https://kanakavalli.com/blogs/kanakavalli-journal/my-first-love.

## References

Appadurai, A 1986, 'Introduction: commodities and the politics of value,' in A Appadurai (ed.), *The social life of things. commodities in cultural perspective*, Cambridge University Press, Cambridge, pp. 3–63.

Arivukkarasi, N & Nagaraj, K 2009, 'Some aspects of socioeconomic change in rural Arani with special reference to silk weaving industry,' paper presented at the International Workshop on 'Market Town, Market Society, Informal Economy,' Contemporary South Asian Studies Programme, Oxford, 8–9 June.

Arterburn, YJ 1982, *The loom of interdependence: silk weaving cooperatives in Kanchipuram*, Hindustan Publishing Corporation, New Delhi.

Baringer, T & Flynn, T (eds.) 1998, *Colonialism and the object: empire, material culture and the museum*, Routledge, London and New York.

Basile, E 2013, *Capitalist development in India's informal economy*, Routledge, London and New York.

Bharathan, K 1983, *The cotton handloom industry in Tamil Nadu: some characteristics and aspects of change from the post-independence census data*, Madras Institute of Development Studies, Chennai.

Cohn, BS 1996, *Colonialism and its forms of knowledge*, Princeton University Press, Princeton, NJ.

Crole, CS 1879, *The Chingleput, late Madras, district: a manual compiled under the orders of the Madras government*, Lawrence Asylum Press, Chingleput. https://books.google.co.in/books/about/The_Chingleput_Late_Madras_District.html?id=J6oPAAAAYAAJ&redir_esc=y

De Neve, G 2005, 'Weaving for IKEA in South India: subcontracting, labour markets and gender relations in a global value chain,' in CJ Fuller & J Assayag (eds.), *Globalising India: perspectives from below*, Anthem Press, London, pp. 89–118.

DeNicola, AO 2004, 'Creating borders, maintaining boundaries: traditional work and global markets in Bagru's handblock textile industry,' PhD thesis, Syracuse University. https://surface.syr.edu/ant_etd/34

Driver, F & Ashmore, S 2010, 'The mobile museum: collecting and circulating Indian textiles in Victorian Britain,' *Victorian Studies*, vol. 52, no. 3, pp. 353–85.

Dutta, A 2007, *The bureaucracy of beauty: design in the age of its global reproducibility*. Routledge, New York and London.

Greenough, P 1996, 'Nation, economy, and tradition displayed: the Indian Crafts Museum, New Delhi,' in C Breckenridge (ed.), *Consuming modernity*, Oxford University Press, New Delhi, pp. 216–48.

Handler, R & Linnekin, J 1984, 'Tradition, genuine or spurious,' *The Journal of American Folklore*, vol. 97, no. 385, pp. 273–90.

Hann, CM 2002, 'All *Kulturvölker* now? social anthropological reflections on the German-American tradition,' in RG Fox & BJ King (eds.), *Anthropology beyond culture*, Berg Publishers, New York, pp. 259–76.

Haynes, DE 2012, *Small town capitalism in Western India: artisans, merchants and the making of the informal economy, 1870–1960* (No. 20), Cambridge University Press, Cambridge.

Herzfeld, M 2004, *The Body impolitic: artisans and artifice in the global hierarchy of value*, University of Chicago Press, Chicago, IL.

Hoffenberg, PH 2004, 'Promoting traditional Indian art at home and abroad: "The Journal of Indian Art and Industry," 1884–1917,' *Victorian Periodicals Review*, vol. 37, no. 2, pp. 192–213.

Irschick, E 1994, *Dialogue and history: constructing South India, 1795–1895*, University of California Press, Berkeley.

Kawlra, A 2014, 'Duplicating the local: GI and the politics of place in Kanchipuram, Tamil Nadu,' *Nehru Memorial Museum and Library Occasional Paper*, Perspectives in Indian Development N.S. 29, NMML, New Delhi.

Kawlra, A 2018, *We who wove with lotus thread: summoning community in South India*, Orient Blackswan, New Delhi.

Kuppuswami, N 1983, *Work is worship*, Arunothaya, Madras.

Leslie, E 1998, 'Walter Benjamin: traces of craft,' *Journal of Design History*, vol. 11, no. 1, pp. 5–13.

Ludden, D 1996, 'Caste society and units of production in early modern South India,' in B Stein & S Subrahmanyam (eds.), *Institutions and economic change in South Asia*, SOAS Studies in South Asia. Understandings and Perspectives Series, Oxford University Press, New Delhi, pp. 105–33.

Mahadevan, R & Vijyabaskar, M 2014, 'The making of non-corporate capital: some historical & contemporary entrepreneurial narratives from Tiruppur, Tamil Nadu,' *Nehru Memorial Museum and Library, Occasional Paper*, Perspectives in Indian Development N.S. 33, Teenmurti Bhavan, New Delhi.

Manning, P 2010, 'The semiotics of brand,' *Annual Review of Anthropology*, vol. 39, pp. 33–49.

Maskiell, M 1999, 'Embroidering the past: Phulkari textiles and gendered work as "tradition" and "heritage" in colonial and contemporary Punjab,' *The Journal of Asian Studies*, vol. 58, no. 2, pp. 361–88.

Mathur, S 2007, *India by design: colonial history and cultural display*, University of California Press, Berkeley.

McGowan, AS 2005, '"All that is rare, characteristic or beautiful": design and the defense of tradition in colonial India, 1851–1903,' *Journal of Material Culture*, vol. 10, no. 3, pp. 263–87.

McGowan, AS 2009, *Crafting the nation in colonial India*, Palgrave Macmillan, New York.

Metcalf, TR 1989, *An imperial vision. Indian architecture and Britain's Raj*, Faber and Faber, London.

Mitter, P 2002, 'Mechanical reproduction and the world of the colonial artist,' *Contributions to Indian Sociology*, vol. 36, no. 1–2, pp. 1–32.

Mukherjee, I & Williams MG 2015, 'Branding authenticity, global–localization and technology: thematic analysis of two West Bengal urban–rural handicrafts NPO websites,' *Connnexions*, vol. 4, no. 1, pp. 91–130.

Nakatani, A (ed.) 2020, *Fashionable traditions: Asian handmade textiles in motion*, Lexington Books, London.

Nambiar, PK 1964a, Census of India 1961a. *Handlooms in Madras State,* IX, Part XI-A. Government Publication, New Delhi.

Nambiar, PK 1964b, Census of India 1961b. *Silk weaving of Kanchipuram*, IX, Part VII-A, Handicraft Survey Monograph, No. 1, Government Publication, New Delhi.

Niranjana, S 2004, 'Thinking with handlooms: perspectives from Andhra Pradesh,' *Economic and Political Weekly*, vol. 39, no. 6, pp. 553–63.

Parthasarathi, P 2001, *The transition to a colonial economy: weavers, merchants and kings in South India, 1720–1800*, Cambridge University Press, Cambridge.

Raina, D & Habib, SI 1991, 'Technical institutes in colonial India Kala Bhavan, Baroda (1890–1990),' *Economic and Political Weekly*, vol. 26, no. 46, pp. 2619–24.

Ramaswamy, V 1985, *Textile and weavers in medieval South India*, Oxford University Press, New Delhi.

Ramaswamy, V 2020, 'The culture and economics of silk weaving during the Vijayanagar era (1336–1646) in south India,' in D Schäfer, G Riello, & L Molà (eds.), *Seritechnics: historical silk technologies*, Max Planck Research Library for the History and Development of Knowledge.pp. 61–72. Available from https://cadmus.eui.eu/handle/1814/69268

Roy, T 1993, *Artisans and industrialisation: Indian weaving in the twentieth century*, Oxford University Press, New Delhi.

Roy, T 2002, 'Acceptance of innovations in early twentieth–century Indian Weaving,' *The Economic History Review*, vol. 55, no. 3, pp. 507–32.

Roy, T 2007, 'Out of tradition: master artisans and economic change in colonial India,' *The Journal of Asian Studies*, vol. 66, no. 4, pp. 963–91.

Scrase, TJ 2005, 'Crafts, consumers and consumption: Asian artisanal crafts and the marketing of exotica,' in R Julian, R Rottier, & R White (eds.), Community, Place, Change: TASA 2005 Conference Proceedings Australia: The Sociological Association of Australia (TASA). Conference Proceedings, University of Tasmania, 6–8 December 2005.

Sundar, P 1995, *Patrons and philistines: arts and the state in British India, 1773–1947*, Oxford University Press, Oxford.

Tarar, NO 2011, 'From 'primitive' artisans to 'modern' craftsmen: colonialism, culture, and art education in the late nineteenth-century Punjab,' *South Asian Studies*, vol. 27, no. 2, pp. 199–219.

Wagoner, PB 2003, 'Pre-colonial intellectuals and the production of colonial knowledge,' *Comparative Studies in Society and History*, vol. 45, no. 4, pp. 783–814.

Wielenga, KD 2015, 'The geography of weaving in early nineteenth-century South India,' *The Indian Economic & Social History Review*, vol. 52, no. 2, pp. 147–84.

# 14 Drumming, Value, and Patronage in a Himalayan Village Economy

*Stefan Fiol*

Drumming evinces a paradox of value across South Asian ritual contexts. How can we reconcile the heightened value of drumming with the stigma of being a hereditary drummer? Given the importance of drumming to the proper functioning of society and the cosmos, how and why has the social status of the drummer eroded to the point that young people from hereditary drumming families regularly refuse to perform? Why is the Dalit drummer often (dis)regarded as a remnant of an earlier way of life?[1]

This chapter contributes to the limited scholarship documenting the experiences of traditional, Dalit performers in India in the face of capitalist expansion. It is critical to dispel the notion that the hereditary drummer is an anachronism rooted in a pre-modern, pre-capitalist way of life. It is more accurate to say that he (for in this part of the world, drummers are almost exclusively male) is caught between two concurrent economic systems: one rooted in local ritual practice, and another rooted in the capitalist marketplace. Each of these economies operates through its own logic of order, authority, and value.

The ritual economy is ordered through sets of customary obligations between people, and between people and their gods. In theory, all devotees are equal in relation to the divine. In practice, some have more authority than others, leading to a ritual economic and political system that is inherently hierarchical, unequal, and transactional. Artisans provide ritual labour and essential services, patrons provide benefaction in the form of money or in-kind offerings, and local divinities receive praise and redistribute sacralised offerings (*prasād*). For drummers and other artisans at the bottom of the social and ritual order, there is little possibility of imagining a different social organisation. The ritual economy supports unequal and exclusionary practices that devotees often interpret as part of the natural and divine order, and not as discriminatory or exploitative.

These hierarchical relations, naturalised through ritual action and dogma, are more or less consistent across the region; crucially, however, the drummer's labour is only intelligible within a local field of knowledge. Drawing upon Qureshi (2002), we can understand ritual drumming as a part of an exchange of elements between human and divine agents, and as a kind of labour that has no exchange value, but instead only a use value. Drumming is valued for its ability to transcend the mundane human realm and to awaken the gods to divine play (*līlā*), whether

DOI: 10.4324/9781351031028-15

through corporeal possession or some other manifestation. Drumming also marks auspicious time, communicates messages across distances, and brings people together in song and dance, forging a sense of community grounded in the locality and the land. The central goal for drummers is to perform their duties efficaciously. A drummer has fulfilled his duty if and when the gods and patrons are pleased.

The hereditary drummer also operates within a quintessentially capitalist economic context. In spite of the ambiguity surrounding Marx's assessment of whether music is productive labour, drumming is a means of generating social capital for oneself or for others (Mason 2013). Moreover, and in contradistinction to the use value of drumming, capitalist relations demand that drumming have an exchange value that can be determined by such factors as the amount of time that it takes to perform, the skill and reputation of the performer, the availability of other drummers in a field of competition, and the laws of supply and demand. When a patron hires a drummer, he is essentially buying a value of abstract labour that is converted into money. Following Marxian economic theory, this conversion is exploitative because the cost of abstract labour is always going to be less than the value of what the labourer can produce. Like the ritual economy, capitalism also naturalises a hierarchical order, with those controlling the means of production (i.e., landowners or patrons) exploiting an economic advantage over those who do not (i.e., labourers or artisans).

The distinctions I am drawing between ritual and capitalist economic systems (see Table 14.1) are overly crude, and I do not seek to impose a sharp dichotomy of practice or history. While it tends to be the case that ritual economic relations are more firmly rooted in villages, and capitalist economic relations are more firmly rooted in cities and towns, this is by no means a rule. Across much of rural South Asia, ritual and capitalist economic logics have become so intertwined that it would be unproductive to try to separate them. Moreover, the intensification of capitalist forms of exchange can result in an intensification of non-capitalist forms of exchange, such that these are overlapping and embedded rather than opposing systems (Morcom 2015, pp. 304–5).[2] In Uttarakhand, there are places where the gods have registered bank accounts, and many of the most successful capitalist entrepreneurs in South Asia show a penchant for lavish displays of ritual. While there is no hard and fast line that can be drawn between ritual and capitalist economies, then, a different logic about musical value and labour can be identified in each (Table 14.1).

*Table 14.1* Characteristics of the Ritual Economy and the Capitalist Economy

| *Ritual Economy* | *Capitalist Economy* |
|---|---|
| Primacy of use value | Primacy of exchange value |
| Rural | Urban |
| Labour framed as obligatory service or offering | Labour framed as autonomous work |
| Divinely sanctioned hierarchy | Socially sanctioned hierarchy |
| Capital in the form of localised knowledge | Capital in the form of money and status |

When, where, and how do capitalist and ritual notions of value and labour become conflicted or conflated? How do drummers and their patrons switch between these economic logics? What is at stake in lifting the drums to perform for different kinds of patrons at different kinds of events? This chapter interrogates such questions by focusing on the everyday experiences of one hereditary drummer. Garib Das was my drumming teacher for the five months of 2016 that I lived in Salood-Dungra, a village in the Chamoli District of Uttarakhand, North India, close to the Nepalese and Tibetan borders. During my time with Garib, I became interested in the conditions that would determine where, when, how, and ultimately whether, he would play the *ḍhol* and *damāūṅ*.[3] These conditions included Garib Das's personal devotion to local divinities, his identity as a widower with five children, and his inherited, subservient position within the local caste hierarchy.

## The Das and His Patrons

I was taken aback when my drumming teacher first introduced himself, for his name, Garib Das, translates as 'poor slave/servant.'[4] Garib was born into a caste of drummers formally labelled *Bājgī* or *Aujī*, but colloquially referred to as Das (lit. 'servant,' or 'one who is in servitude'). Until the last few decades, nearly all hereditary drummers used the surname Das, and many still do. When I asked Garib what the term Das meant to him, he stressed its religious significance. 'Das shows a special relationship to the gods,' he said. 'We are the gods' chosen servants (*Bhagwān ke Dās*).' Within the discourse of the ritual economy, this interpretation of Das as one who offers service to the divine is positively valued. Arguably, there was no greater value than being the god or gods' servant; even if the rewards were not always evident in this lifetime, they would be in the next. Yet this interpretation of Das can be juxtaposed with a more pejorative interpretation that circulates in the capitalist economy, in which a servant is one who had the least amount of capital and thus the least social value. With the capitalisation of the cultural economy and the impact of anti-untouchability and social reform movements, this interpretation of Das has become more prevalent, and it carries such stigma that most drummers now reject this name. Garib continues to use the surname Das even as his children and many of his relatives use more caste-ambiguous surnames such as Lal or Bharti.

This paradox of value stems from a philosophical distinction between the ontology of sound and the embodied behaviours that produce it. Within a central Himalayan cosmology, drumming is a primordial vibration that comes from sacred sources and is offered back to divinities through elaborate ceremonies. At the same time, drummers inherit an element of original sin whereby Viswakarma, or another divine progenitor, knowingly or unknowingly committed an act of pollution (e.g., killing a deer for its skin, or putting skin to the mouth in the act of making a drum), thereby forever marking his descendants with a lower status. Retelling this narrative could be understood as a way of naturalising the social order, of rationalising a subjugated position in a rigid caste hierarchy. And yet, depending on when, where, and how they were told, such narratives could also ridicule the social order and elevate the position of the drummer.

Garib Das' family and the other Dalit families lived in a small hamlet at the bottom of the village. This site had a water source separate from the rest of the village, a fact that was vitally important to the higher caste residents of the village, who feared pollution from the intermixture of substances. Approximately 200 families resided in the village, and their homes were distributed among two dozen hamlets spread across the western-facing side of the mountain. Each hamlet was made up of one to three clans sharing the same caste surname, each with their own narratives of dispersion and resettlement. Many of the families in the village settled at their present location more than a century ago, when a cholera outbreak at lower elevations sent people fleeing to unoccupied tracts of higher land. Garib Das's family was one of eight drumming families in the village, and he claimed that his ancestors and those of one patron family were first to settle in the locality.

Each of the drumming families in the village had inherited a group of patron families for whom they performed all of the necessary family-level rituals, including weddings, naming ceremonies (*nāmkaraṇ*), haircutting ceremonies (*muṇḍan*), and family healing rituals (*jāgar*). Garib Das and his brother inherited from their father the drumming duties for the approximately 15 families living in 3 adjacent hamlets, each located about a 30-minute walk up the mountain. Garib compared the work that he does as a drummer to that of the Brahmin priest: both labour in the ritual economy, serving as intermediaries between patrons and divinities, conveying the genealogies of their patrons, and relying upon customary offerings for their services. The only difference, Garib claimed, was that the Brahmin performed his service inside the home, whereas the Das performed outside.

Hereditary drummers uniquely possess the knowledge and skills needed to invite, move, and propitiate the gods; because of this, they feel a special connection to the divine. Garib's relationship to the presiding god (*devtā*) of the village, Kshetrapal-Bhumiyal, was that of a personal servant (Dās) to a king. He felt intense devotion and gratitude to the god. During possession rituals, Garib's drumming summoned Bhumiyal *devtā* to possess the body of his human medium(s), typically a high-caste man. In a stereotypical movement, the possessed man held the straps of the *ḍhol* and embraced Garib around the neck while dancing animatedly. Such intimate physical contact between a high-caste man and a drummer was unknown in other contexts; but under the influence of the god, this intimacy was allowed and even encouraged. Still, there were limits to the ways that Garib can know Bhumiyal. According to the customary laws of the village, drummers and other lower castes could not enter Bhumiyal's temple or directly touch any of his sacred implements for fear of pollution.

As devotees of Bhumiyal *devtā*, Garib and the other village drummers performed for a variety of large-scale religious festivals that occur every one to three years (Ramman, Pandava Nritya, Nanda Ashtami). These festivals, which last from 3 to 14 days, required enormous sacrifices of time, money, and other resources on the part of the entire village. Garib and his fellow drummers performed in processions and in front of the temple for hours each day, rain or shine. The eight families

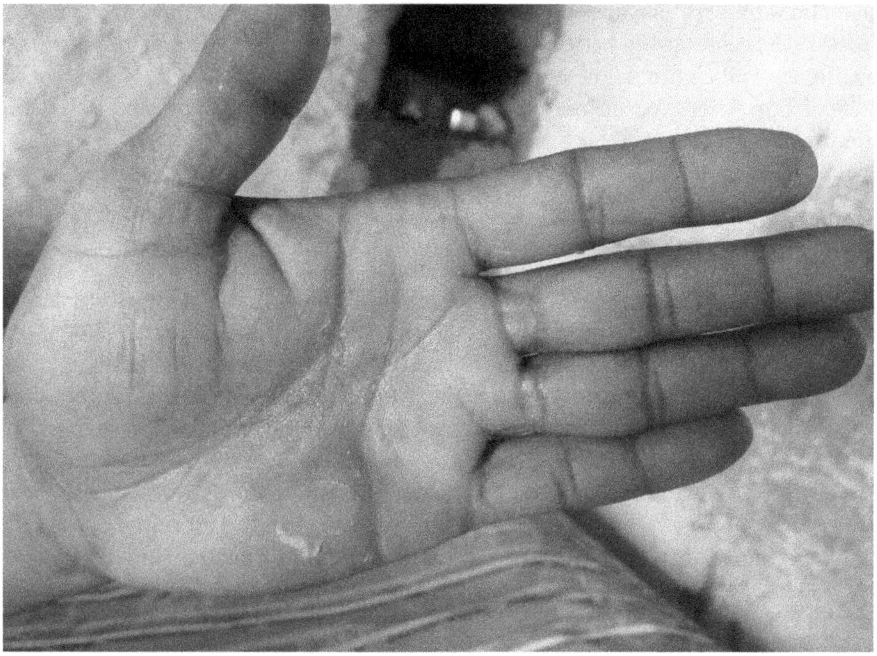

*Figure 14.1* Garib Das's calloused hand. Photograph by author.

of drummers had an established rotation system according to which they performed during these festivals; when any drummer found it difficult to perform because of age, illness, or fatigue, his kin stepped in to support him (Figure 14.1).

At the end of festivals, Garib and each of the other drummers were offered sanctified rice (*prasād*) by each home in the village, alongside a portion of the sacrificial goat meat, and a monetary offering ranging from INR 51 to 251 (USD $1–5). This amount was determined by what is remaining in the gods' fund at the end of the festival. This fund, in turn, consisted of the monetary offering (usually INR 101) of each family in the village, which was used to purchase the ritual implements and ingredients for communal feasts. When I asked drummers about compensation for their labour, they acknowledged that such a small amount of rice and money was woefully inadequate. Nevertheless, in their conversations with each other, they tended not to think about drumming through the discourse of work (*kām*), but rather as an offering or service (*sevā*) to the gods, one that was in many ways a repayment of blessings bestowed. In this way, drummers framed their compensation not in the crude capitalist terms of exchange for services rendered, but rather as a ritual act of duty and love that was part of a reciprocal and essential relationship with the divine.

Regula Qureshi (2002) has written insightfully about the financial obligations between the patrons and labourers in the ritual economy, which she labelled the feudal economy, saying, 'Remuneration was a gift to the person, not a reward for an amount of labor performed … it was given in return for labor offered as needed' (p. 93). The relationship between Garib and his patrons rested on a platform of inequality as well as mutual responsibility. Garib was required to follow convention and perform whenever his patrons requested; in turn, his livelihood, and indeed his life, was contingent on their beneficence.

## Monetisation and Survival

If such festivals were evidence of the continuing importance of the ritual economy, there was also little doubt that capitalist economic values and relations were deeply entrenched in the central Himalayas, and that they had intensified over time. As Sahai (2006) has documented in the context of eighteenth-century Rajasthan, monetisation and capitalism led to a deepening of (already) unequal relations between artisan and patron classes, in many cases undermining the economic viability of artisanal production altogether (p. 165). In Uttarakhand, caste-based occupational groups like woodworkers, smiths, tanners, and basket-makers have gradually been replaced by migrant labourers or rendered irrelevant by cheaper imports from the southern plains and China. Scanning the entire bazaar of a central Himalayan town like Uttarkashi, Srinagar, and Joshimath, one is hard-pressed to find any locally manufactured, non-agricultural products. Even local alcohol stills have dissipated wherever English *sharāb* (*pakki*) is locally distributed in the mountains.

In some respects, however, the challenges that market capitalism had inflicted on other artisan communities were less severe for hereditary drummers. In contrast to artisans who crafted materials, drummers produced a non-material form of labour that was contingent on their knowledge of local power dynamics and local cosmologies.[5] While it is possible to substitute one agricultural worker, blacksmith, or tanner with another, it is usually not possible to substitute a *ḍhol-damāūṅ* drummer from one region with one from another, for the simple reason that drumming repertories have developed in response to local conditions of ritual and sociality. For instance, only a small portion of Garib's drumming repertory was interchangeable with that of drummers from the other side of the mountain valley. Even drummers in the adjacent village articulated many of their rhythmic patterns differently. Drumming compositions are orally transmitted as an inheritance from male relatives, and crucially, they are of divine provenance. Most drummers extolled Lord Shiva as the progenitor of the *ḍhol* and *damāūṅ*, but their repertory was crafted specifically to propitiate the specific divinities that inhabited their village.

The key question here is to what extent these two predominant forms of value in the ritual and capitalist economy—money and localised knowledge—are exchangeable. Capitalism may not have rendered the hereditary drummer obsolete, but monetisation has led to drastic and uneven effects on musical production in the region. Seemingly everyone I met commented on the abundance of cash in today's economy. Drummers once exclusively dependent on payments in kind (called *kar* or *ḍaḍwār*, generally a customary amount of agricultural products given to the drumming families by each home in the village) were now more likely to negotiate cash payments with specific patrons in exchange for services. This arrangement was becoming more common within a village, but it was the norm when drummers and patrons lived in different villages. The decreasing numbers of hereditary drummers in many parts of Uttarakhand has paradoxically given the remaining drummers more negotiating power with their patrons. Perhaps as a result, some patrons shared with me their perspective that drummers have become too greedy. Some felt that *ḍholī-s* (those who play *ḍhol-damāūṅ*) had turned away from their traditional obligations and were now seeking only the most profitable opportunities. A common attitude among patrons was that drummers regularly exploited the patron's ritual need for drumming, commanding large fees in the process. On several occasions I heard people say that drummers were becoming quite wealthy, despite evidence to the contrary. When I asked about the reason for the abject living conditions of almost all hereditary drummers, the response was often that drummers had no ability to save their money, or that they only knew how to waste it on alcohol. Few of the upper-caste patrons with whom I interacted were able to reflect on the condition of dependence and caste stigma that continued to drive poverty and alcoholism within this community. Their comments were rooted in attitudes of privilege that remained mostly unexamined. According to Sainath (2002), '[untouchability] is, and has been for a very long time, an extremely sophisticated economic and political strategy for ensuring a perpetual pool of demoralised, cheap labour that has no sense of its bargaining power' (para. 13).

Drummers had a very different understanding of the causes and effects of monetisation. They often felt squeezed between ritual obligations to patrons and the financial burden of supporting their household, and several drummers expressed the opinion that superior knowledge of drumming—or even a stellar musical reputation—did not necessarily translate into higher monetary income. Garib felt that patrons exploited relationships of obligation, demanding that he perform for little or no pay whenever it suited them, and discounting the need for cash in today's economy. Garib regularly complained about the rising costs for such things as rations, school fees, and utility payments. I have only met a handful of drummers for whom drumming alone provided a living wage. Historically, Das households laboured as tailors as well as drummers, but in contemporary households, family members were more likely to move between any number of income-generating activities, including farming, driving, hotel service, and manual labour.

Garib Das's story was not atypical in this regard. His wife died of tuberculosis when she was only 28, leaving him with 5 children to care for singlehandedly. Although he could have remarried, he chose not to. Sustaining a livelihood has been incredibly challenging for their young family. Two of his daughters were married, but the third is 75% visually impaired, and he feared that he may never find a suitable marriage prospect for her. His two sons, aged 11 and 15, attended school only rarely, and openly talked of moving to live with extended kin in other places.

Garib Das engaged in many different forms of labour in order to sustain his family. Drumming was only an economically sustainable activity during wedding seasons and major festival occasions. At other times of the year, he hired himself out as a manual labourer on road crews, made and sold *ḍhol-damāūṅ* drums, performed small-scale agricultural work, and, during the months of March and

April, ascended to the high Himalayan ranges to gather caterpillar fungus and other prized herbs that could be sold to middlemen for a profit.[6] Although he inherited a small plot of land from his father, he gradually sold most of it after his wife passed away. Even though agricultural labour might arguably bring the most benefit to the family, Garib chose not to pursue it. Like many others in the region, he regarded field labour as primarily women's work, and his daughter's visual impairment prevented her from doing this form of labour.

Garib's story is part of a discernible trend in which Das families have abandoned or sold off most of their cultivable land holdings in recent decades. This has happened for various reasons, including changes in climate resulting in less water and less yield from the land, systematic land encroachment by upper-castes, the experience of hostility or violence resulting from high-caste prejudices about the tilling of the land by lower-castes (some feel this would make the land barren), and a sense among earlier generations that land would be unnecessary because of traditional forms of patronage based on in-kind exchange for drumming services (*ḍaḍwār*). One Das householder in the village worked as a sharecropper on land belonging to a migrant family who lived in the plains; his labour was a way of paying off a loan that he inherited from his father.

Drumming for weddings was by far the most profitable activity for Garib. In a few days, he and a partner could take home between INR 5,000 and 8,000 (approximately US$100–150). Earning the equivalent by breaking rocks on a road-building crew took more than a week's worth of labour at the daily payment rate (*dīūrī*) of INR 300 (approximately US$7). Yet drumming for weddings carried significant risk. In July 2016, I joined the wedding procession (*barāt*) for a high-caste Rajput friend who was marrying a girl from a village on the other side of the valley. Garib and his brother led the procession to the bride's village and back, carrying and playing their drums for hours at a stretch while traversing treacherous mountain pathways, often in the dark. After a two-hour drive followed by a six-hour hike, we reached the bride's village after dusk. Because of the stigma of caste pollution, Garib and his brother were given separate sleeping quarters from the rest of the wedding party, and were offered food and drink only after every other guest had had their share.

One of the ways that male wedding attendees assessed hospitality was by the amount of alcohol offered by the host. Garib was continually subject to harassment from drunk men, who had to be dealt with carefully; some drunks could be violent, while others were very good tippers. Garib was not normally a heavy drinker, but during the festivities he imbibed frequent pegs of local moonshine (*kacchī*). Garib later told me that it was considered rude to refuse alcohol if offered by a patron. In some regions, I have observed drummers being compensated for their playing with bags of liquor. But it became clear to me that drinking was also a means of coping, inuring Garib from the elements and from verbal abuse and physical harassment. Watching Garib perform for inebriated patrons late into the night, it was as if his hands and face told two different stories. His hands moved with a grace and determined strength that belied his long, gaunt frame. There was no hesitation in his playing. But his face betrayed more vulnerability, as if he wanted to alternately shrink into himself, cry, or pass out from exhaustion.

*Figure 14.2* Garib Das playing *ḍhol* with his son Shankar accompanying on *damāūṅ*. Photograph by author.

It was often the case that Garib and his drumming partner had to share the entertainment duties with a more prestigious wedding band or dee-jay. Hosts hired other musical entertainment because the younger generation demanded it or because the higher cost and status of these groups conveyed a higher status of the patron. Garib felt that it was disrespectful to have to compete with other musicians, who were usually much louder, and on one occasion I saw him get angry about this. Yet privately, he also confessed that the presence of other musical entertainment helped him find opportunities to rest (Figure 14.2).

Ironically, Garib's eldest son, 15-year-old Shankar, supplemented the family income by playing music in a wedding band (consisting of a Western-style bass drum, electric keyboard, and cymbals) as well as by gathering and selling wood and wild seasonal greens in the bazaar. Shankar was already a competent *ḍhol* player, and Garib wanted to teach him more, but Shankar was ambivalent. He spoke of wanting to leave home and learn to drive a taxi in the nearby town Gopeshwar, where he had relatives. In Shankar's presence, Garib admitted disappointment that young people did not want to learn drumming because of caste discrimination. He joked that kids listen to their fathers playing '18 talas' (a phrase that expresses deep knowledge) all night long, but in the morning, they would ask who Sita's father is (conveying that they do not understand basic ritual narratives). Summarising the feeling that drumming has become a necessary evil, he remarked that *ḍhol* playing 'brings both problems and earnings' (*pareshanī bhī hai kamāī bhī hai*).

## Conclusion

This chapter has endeavoured to show 'how value systems produce musicians' (Mason 2013, p. 448), or how the distinctive logics and values of ritual and capitalist economies condition the labour and livelihood of Dalit drummers. Every transaction with a patron required a balance of monetary, social, and divine responsibilities. In the face of an eroding patronage system in which drummers would have been compensated in kind, they necessarily negotiated cash payments with their patrons. Doing so inevitably reframed drumming as a form of utilitarian labour or work (*kām*) that could be evaluated based on quantities of time, effort, and skill. Yet drummers and their patrons simultaneously upheld the values of the ritual economy. They did this out of a sense of obligation to their ancestors and divinities but also because it gave them a sense of collective identity, a feeling of purpose and local belonging that could not be found in capitalist forms of exchange. As Lord Shiva's chosen servants, Das drummers implicitly valued performing for the gods. Even in the face of caste oppression, Garib Das articulated feelings of pride and self-worth in his service to the gods and patrons. Moving back and forth between ritual and capitalist obligations and notions of value thus entailed a kind of code-switching on the part of drummers and patrons. Drummers emphasised their ritual duty in one context only to stress the 'market rate' in front of a potential patron.

Here I return to the paradox of value. The social and ritual value of drumming contrasted starkly with the stigma of being a hereditary drummer. Caste identity was overdetermined within this socio-economic context. The ritual value for drumming did not adequately translate into monetary or social capital for the people playing the drums. Rather, it drove them into a state of subservience and servitude. Within the capitalist marketplace, choice was a value imagined to create parity and equity in the labour market. Yet in the village ritual economy in which Garib Das operated, he did not have much of a 'choice' to drum. As a devotee to local divinities, as a healer who channelled divinities through bodies, as the inheritor of sacred knowledge passed on to him from his ancestors, as a landless and illiterate Dalit musician, there was intense social pressure to drum, and few alternatives to earn a sustainable livelihood.

## Notes

1 The short film *Auji* (2017) depicts many of the challenges that drummers face as they experience poverty and social discrimination, are deemed old-fashioned, and are overwhelmed by electronic music. The film is available on YouTube with English subtitles at: Auji 'औजी' - Award winning Garhwali short film || ddniff award 2017 || Abhishek Maindola.
2 Tim Taylor (2015) similarly describes capitalism as 'a system of economic value production that competes with existing systems, usually becoming hegemonic, but co-existing and feeding off of other forms of value in complex and never-ending processes' (p. 104).
3 *Dhol-damaun* are the most ubiquitous set of instruments in the soundscape of the central Himalayas. The *dhol* is a large, two-headed, barrel-shaped drum slung over the shoulder with a cloth strap, and played on one drumhead with an open hand, and on the other drumhead with a stick. The accompanying *damaun* is a shallow kettledrum slung around the neck of a second performer and played with two thin sticks.
4 Coincidentally, Gibb Schreffler (2014) shares that his *dhol* teacher is also named Garib Das and he writes about similar issues of value and hereditary labour in the Punjab.
5 It is tempting to assert here that the forms of labour used in ritual contexts cannot be outsourced as easily as those in other contexts. However, the Sanskrit recitations of Brahmin priests are largely interchangeable across the region. This suggests that drumming has a unique relationship to locality in the ritual economy that is not present in other kinds of labour.
6 Income diversification is a broader trend for Dalits in rural areas of India (Gang et al. 2017).

## References


Gang, IN, Kunal, S, & Yun, MS 2017, 'Is caste destiny? occupational diversification among Dalits in rural India,' *The European Journal of Development Research*, vol. 29, no. 2, pp. 476–92.

Mason, K 2013, 'Musicians and the politics of dignity in South India,' in P Bohlman (ed.), *The Cambridge history of world music*, Cambridge University Press, Cambridge, pp. 441–72.

Morcom, A 2015, 'Terrains of Bollywood dance: (neoliberal) capitalism and the transformation of cultural economies,' *Ethnomusicology*, vol. 59, no. 2, pp. 288–314.

Qureshi, R 2002, 'Mode of the production and musical production: is Hindustani music feudal?' in R Qureshi (ed.), *Music, Marx and money*, Routledge, New York, pp. 81–105.

Sahai, NP 2006, *Politics of patronage and protest: the state, society and artisans in early modern Rajasthan*, Oxford University Press, New Delhi.

Sainath, P 2002, 'Dalits in India 2000: the scheduled castes more than a half century after independence,' *Asia Source* [online]. https://asiasociety.org/dalits-india-2000.

Schreffler, G 2014, '"It's our culture": dynamics of the revival and reemergence of Punjabi jhummar,' *Asian Music*, vol. 45, no. 1, pp. 34–76.

Taylor, T 2015, 'World music, value and memory,' in D Helms & T Phleps (eds.), *Speaking in tongues*, transcript-Verlag, Bielefeld, pp. 103–17.

# 15 Globalities and Temporalities of Artisanship

## Lessons from an Indian Wood Art Industry

*Thomas Chambers*

Somewhere in your house you may have a small wooden box with a carved lid. Perhaps the box is adorned with some brass elephants or a carved floral pattern. It may have an ivory effect inlay made from fine plastic and be lined with velvet or felt. Chances are that the box comes from India, and if so, the narrow *gallīs* (lanes/narrow roads) of the woodworking *mohallas* (neighbourhoods) of the North Indian city of Saharanpur are quite possibly the origin. Drawing on Marxist and related understandings of craft, artisanship and labour, this chapter combines engagement with literature on craftwork, precarity, affect, and temporality to think through change and continuity in Saharanpur's Muslim dominated woodworking cluster. The chapter explores the increasing incorporation of the city's artisanal traditions into global production networks; considers the ways in which production in the city intersects with globalised representations of craft; and, through an engagement with temporal contestations emanating from artisanal desires to exert a degree of control over work time, examines moments of contestation and resistance. In so doing, I argue that representations of craft as entrepreneurial, artisanal, and independent can conceal particularised modalities of exploitation. I also show that contemporary forms of structuring within craft sectors continue to contain moments of potentiality that emerge in relational, spatial, and temporal contexts.

### Artisans, Craftwork and the Global Economy

Within Karl Marx's (2011[1887]) illustration of transformations in the labour process under industrial capitalism, the artisan takes a central position. Artisans, for Marx, represent a pre-capitalist, pre-proletarian mode of production within which the craft product is intimately connected to the skill and labour of the producer. As Marx argues:

> [W]hat distinguishes the worst architect from the best of bees is this, that the architect raises his structure in imagination before he erects it in reality. At the end of every labour-process, we get a result that already existed in the imagination of the labourer at its commencement. He not only effects a change of form in the material on which he works, but he also realises a

DOI: 10.4324/9781351031028-16

> purpose of his own that gives the law to his modus operandi, and to which he must subordinate his will.
>
> (Marx 2011[1887], p. 198)

With the emergence of industrial capitalism, labour becomes, for Marx, increasingly alienated from commodities as craft skills fragment into various stages of low-skilled factory production (cf. Braverman, 1998[1974]). Drawing on Marx, Tim Ingold (2000) argues that, although historically recent and globally variegated, the transformation of craftwork under industrial production also results in increasing separation between artist and artisan as well as between art and technology. These processes have been commonplace across craft sectors in the global south and global north but persistence and re-emergence of craftwork are also present (Wilkinson-Weber 1999; Mollona 2005; Antrosio and Colloredo-Mansfeld 2016; Holmes 2015; Mohsini 2016).

Within some research, however, the analytical location of craft has moved beyond the study of sectors with clear artisanal groundings. Richard Sennett (2008), in particular, has attempted to collapse craft-based, pre-industrial contexts and industrial or post-industrial modes by situating various skilled and semi-skilled sectors as constituted through craft. For Sennett, the distinction between master and apprentice amongst construction workers, chefs, lab technicians, nurses and musicians – along with sectors more often associated with craft such as carpentry – is grounded in notions of experience and dedication. Pivotal, Sennett argues, in identifying the craftsman is that one's labour is not merely defined in terms of efficiency or productivity, but also through a 'dedication to work for its own sake [which…] represents the special human condition of being *engaged*' (p. 10, original emphasis). This substantially broadens craft to incorporate various forms of labour that retain a sense of making for its own sake. However, Sennett also makes clear that craftwork is not defined by unrestrained creativity but is an inherently controlled process within which apprentices must learn the rules and become accepting of a high degree of discipline to reach the position of master.

Linking this to the writings of Plato and Aristotle, Sennett (2008) notes the long-lasting ambiguity of the crafts*man* within which gendered hierarchies are reproduced to reify masculinised skillsets while maligning craft skills in occupations seen as feminised (cf. Chambers and Ansari 2018; Wilkinson-Weber 1999). Whilst acknowledging these ambiguities, Sennett draws on the Homeric hymn to the Greek God Hephaestus throughout his opening to show how ancient Greece situated the craftsman as central to the civilisation of humanity and as a natal middle-class producing, not only for its own sake, but also for the public good. The twist deployed by Sennett is to take archaic articulations of craftwork and apply them to relatively new spaces of production. Specifically, he identifies programmers who contribute to the free, open access operating system Linux as constituting a modern craft community and traces this into various other tech sectors. Others, too, have discussed the ways in which programmers, or digital artisans, articulate their labour in craft terms due the need to attend to aesthetics, not just utility, in their work (DeNicola 2016).

There is, however, a tendency in some of this work to reify craft and dissolve forms of differentiation in everyday experiences of labour. Sennett (2008) is pertinent when indicating that the lived reality of those labouring in sectors which may, on the surface, espouse 'craft' values are often constituted through long hours of work, precarity and dissociated labour. However, his vision of the modern craft worker is somewhat nostalgic and tends at times to valorise 'craft' forms of organisation as productive of positive problem-solving potential, whilst leaving aside the relations between capital and labour within which they remain enmeshed. The broadening of 'craft' as a category of labour engagement has led others to articulate various sectors in craft terms. Drawing on Sennett, Helen Holmes (2015), for example, identifies many facets of craft tradition – apprenticeship, experience-based hierarchy and specific skillsets – in hairdressing salons of Northwest England. Although skill and use of tools are very much a part of working in the trade, hairdressing and related sectors, such as nail salons and beauty parlours, are also sites of intense labour precarity, insecurity, and exploitation. In addition, they are not detached from the broader demands decreed by other sites of labour and production. Thus, Laurie Ouellette (2017) emphasis the role of aesthetic labour by relating it not only to the stylist or nail technician but also to female clients who often work in feminised service industries that link female employability with specific notions of grooming and beauty. Importantly, Ouellette additionally ties the growth and feminisation of beauty industries to the reification of aesthetic labour in the media, citing U.S. shows such as *Nail Files*, *Nail'd It*, *Blow Out,* and *Shear Genius,* which actively cultivate an ideal of self-enterprise, entrepreneurialism and 'craft' whilst concealing the drudgery and exploitation that constitute many realities of salon and beauty work.

Against this background, then, a craft aesthetic becomes as much aligned with affective forms of labour control and discipline as it does with notions of craft, skill and experience. One of the key traits of neoliberal capitalism has been the expansion of precarity to sectors often associated with skilled, well paid, middle-class jobs, not least in the types of fields identified by Sennett (2008) as comprising degrees of craftsmanship. In European cultural industries such as film making and web designing, new creative classes increasingly work in engagements based on ostensibly entrepreneurial yet precarious work (Gill and Pratt 2008). These emerging forms of economic structuring, Rosalind Gill and Andy Pratt (2008) argue, have created new degrees of exploitation but also, within a Marxist autonomist framework, potential spaces of labour resistance. Gill and Pratt do not explicitly discuss craft work or artisanship in detailing creative industries, but their identifications of a sector that is defined by irregular hours, piecework, creativity and a breakdown in the spatial demarcation of home and work, echo many features of artisanal production.

Within the post-Fordist moment, Gill and Pratt (2008) trace the emergence of a new socialised worker who labours in factories without walls. This socialised worker is controlled not through the discipline of the factory floor but through embedded and affective appeals to, for example, religiosity and family, aspirations, dreams and desires or the aesthetic of craftwork and artisanship (Moreton 2006; Rudnyckyj 2009; Cross 2014; Schmidt 2018). These critiques are echoed in a variety of ethnographic contributions that have nuanced representations of the entrepreneurial craft worker through the detailing of forms of exploitation, alienation and subordination (Elyachar 2005; Prentice 2015; Mezzadri 2016; Schmidt 2018). In the following section, I employ this background to situate everyday experiences of labour in Saharanpur's woodworking *mohallas* within a supply chain which, whilst grounded in an artisanal sector with roots in the 1700s, is also created by a variety of global circulations, accumulations, and localised forms of exploitation.

## Wood Crafting and the Supply Chain

While some Indian craft industries have seen a decline in quality, the desire for authentic Indian craft goods in the UK drove a campaign in the early 1900s to protect artisans from the ravages of industrialisation (Venkatesan 2009) but also, along with other factors, laid the foundation for incorporation of various Indian craft sectors into global production networks driven by consumer demand for exotic and authentic products. As with many other artisan clusters, slippages between artisanal and industrial modes in Saharanpur's wood working industry is not historically new (e.g., Beinin 2001). A dip into the District Gazetteers for the United Provinces (1909) reveals increases in production being associated with declines in quality as the wood industry gradually mechanised. Yet, within degrees of fragmentation, mechanisation and alienation, small-scale artisanal production remains the primary mode (Figure 15.1).

Tirthankar Roy (1999) discusses a shift away from the master-craftsman approach in India during the late colonial era towards that of employee/employer. He identifies a decline in the *ustād-shāgird* (master-apprentice) system, as production became de-skilled. Whilst there was a period of decline in production levels, changes in quality and moves towards mass manufacturing, colonialism did not lead to the collapse of the industry in Saharanpur. Instead, it pre-empted a change in structural arrangements of production and involved the emergence of factory-style manufacturing alongside the older cottage industry in the late colonial period. Indeed, it was from the craft community that a new capitalist class emerged in Saharanpur. Abdul, the owner of a large factory on the edge of town, highlighted these factors to me when we met in 2011 as he narrated his family history. Having started as small scale artisans, it had been his great grandfather who began to expand from the position of craft producer, as the result of orders arriving in his workshop from British businessmen. Today his factory employs around 3,000 workers with many more working on a subcontracted or outsourced basis and other family members running similar large-scale operations.

Although there had been a period in which some artisans emerged as a local capitalist class, for the majority, undertaking such a transformation in their class status today is only the remotest of possibilities. Kathakheri, formerly a rubbish dump, was a relatively new market having been established in the 1980s. The original, located at Purāni Mandi, had been there since the colonial era. In Kathakheri, I started to work as a brass overlayer. I began as a *shāgird* (apprentice) and gradually learnt the trade over a year and a half. Each day, as I sat in the small, rented

*Figure 15.1* A woodcarver at work in Saharanpur. Photograph by author.

space with Islam, my *ustād* (master), I watched the comings and goings in the narrow *gallī*. At the heart of the organisation of production were the carving shops. These units completed their own stage of production and organised others. Amongst the *kārīgars* (artisans), carvers would often be the first port of call for direct customers, outsourcing factories and showroom owners. From here carvers sent items to neighbouring shops for completion. A combination of higher skill and status along with their position as orchestrators placed the carving shops at the top of the production hierarchy and produced slippages, not only between positions of artisan and labour but also artisan and *ṭhekedār* (contractor/middleman/broker).

Next came other specialised trades such as brass inlay work and after these, the *mistrī* (tradesperson/craftsman) trades such as carpentry, cutting and polishing. In some cases, carvers would recruit a carpenter or cutter to operate in their shop and at other times the work would be sent out.[1] Whilst carvers orchestrated a lot of putting out (subcontracting), others were also involved. In Islam's shop, we received items for brass overlay. Usually this consisted of panels or sections with carving completed that would later be assembled. Although low in the chain, Islam would then negotiate with the buffer to have the brass section shined up. Indeed, across all sections of the *gallī* chain 81% of workshops received outsourced work and a further 52% engaged in further outsourcing themselves. At the bottom of the status hierarchy in the *gallī* were those jobs perceived as dirty work (see also Mohsini 2010), such as buffing, with its associated levels of dust. This was not the only issue that led to it being seen as lowly. Ishan, to whom Islam and I took our buffing work, was already feeling the physical effects of his labour. His thin frame regularly heaved with the hacking cough so common amongst those for whom work consisted of long hours breathing in wood dust.

Regardless of occupation, craft production in the *gallīs* was universally characterised by precarity. Work came and went. Whilst, at times, *kārīgars* and others would often labour late into the night, periods of *mandī* (recession) were common. During my time in the brass shop, and over various visits since, I watched as several workshops folded. This was often a result of a temporary fall in orders, which meant that workers could not be retained, debts for wood taken on credit could not be repaid, and demand for rents from landlords, who owned most of the *gallī* shops, led to eviction. Sometime after my initial fieldwork, Islam, too, closed his small shop and found himself working as a *mazdūr* (labourer) in a nearby factory. Artisans often spoke of themselves as independent business owners engaged in *apna kām* (own work). However, as with the aesthetic of craft discussed in the previous section of this chapter, the complex networks of subcontracting within which daily labour played out meant that for many the reality of work was often closer to that of *mazdūr* (labour) than *kārīgar* (artisan) (cf. Breman 1996; Mohsini 2016).

For artisans in the *gallīs*, the challenges were stark, but elsewhere in the supply chain they could be even more extreme. Small items, such as the box mentioned in the opening of this chapter, would be taken into the narrower lanes behind the workshop *gallīs* by rickshaw *wallahs* (rickshaw pullers) who would knock on steel doors or shout through simple curtain partitions to the women inside, notifying them that work had arrived to be sanded, touched up and varnished. Women homeworkers were engaged in the latter stages of the supply chain primarily undertaking finishing work on smaller wood items and experienced the lowest status and incomes of all the actors in the supply chain. For women, working in Saharanpur's wood industry, domestic and industrial spaces of production were deeply intertwined (see Chambers and Ansari 2018) with many moving between paid work in their own home and the factory space. Whilst the factory offered a marginally better income, home-based paid work was less problematic for one's reputation and character (Chambers & Ansari 2018; Grover et al. 2018). In either case, though, earnings were meagre, generally ranging from ₹50 to ₹100 per day for homework to ₹100–₹150 for factory work,[2] with long hours and the need for high rates of productivity, which created a variety of health issues from chronic back pain to poor eyesight and, in a couple of cases, prolapsed wombs. Whilst woodcraft provided livelihoods for large numbers in the city, the aesthetic embodied in the small wooden box with its caved lid and brass elephants concealed much. The authenticity is one produced not merely through the inalienable labour of the artisan but through ambiguities and slippages between artisanship, craft, brokerage and labour which act to shroud various layers of exploitation and extraction. As Andrew Ross (2004) argues:

> Just because artisans are not factory wageworkers does not make them free, or any more capable of controlling their time and labor value ... an artisan can be a skilled, apprenticed craftsman (especially if he is male) who is functionally flexible in the application of those skills. But (and especially if she is a woman) she is more likely to be an off-the-books homeworker who accepts job enlargement (as opposed to job enrichment) as a matter of familial sacrifice or self-exploitation.
>
> (Ross 2004, p. 216)

When exploring contemporary craftwork in Saharanpur's woodworking cluster it is, therefore, critical to situate artisans and workers within a broader framing that considers transformations regarding the imagined, as well as the material, position of craft workers under late capitalism. Those labouring in Saharanpur's wood *gallīs*, from the large manufacturer to the artisan employing two or three *shāgirds* (apprentices) and the labourer employed on a piece rate basis, are increasingly, and often adversely incorporated within global production networks. This can be a transformative process, stretching the supply chain, driving down prices (and earnings), and leading to the emergence of new niches of wealth extraction (Carswell & De Neve 2013; Phillips 2011).

However, unlike the barista forging newly found craft credentials or the programmer making claims to digital artisanship, there is much in Saharanpur's wood industry that is constituted not through change but continuity. Indeed, even for the barista, hairdresser or worker in an artisanal bakery, much of the everyday experience of work is little different from that experienced by previous generations, only its status and representation (although often not pay) has changed. Artisanship and crafting, then, not only represents the (re)crafting of self (as a form of self-making) but is also a classificatory project that rearticulates and redefines what may already be present. More explicitly, the reconstitution of the artisan or craft worker as an egalitarian figure that cuts across class position and relative wealth acts to conceal long-established inequalities and hierarchies. Whilst craft industries and the subjectivities of craft workers are by no means static, the glorification of craftwork, micro-enterprise, and 'self-employment' by international institutions, national governments, NGOs, and others have left many in Saharanpur fulfilling a new ideal type of which they themselves are not aware and that provides little in the way of positive change.

## Crafting Temporalities

Temporal patterns embedded in craft production in Saharanpur are also present in analytical engagements with precarity in the global north where 'the temporality of life becomes governed by work … long working hours … [and] 'bulimic' patterns of working, in which periods with no work can give way to periods that require round the clock working" (Gill & Pratt 2008, p. 17). EP Thompson's (1967) classic text, 'Time, Work-Discipline, and Industrial Capitalism,' describes the reconfiguration of temporal rhythms brought about by the arrival of clock time within industrial manufacturing. For Thompson, the transformations brought about by processes of clocking on and clocking off not only led to the end of temporal rhythms governed by day and night or by the seasons, but also a loss of control by labour over patterns of working. Often missed, however, in Thompson's text is a concluding note in which he reflects on the re-emergence of a-post clock temporality within industrial capitalism. Here, Thompson argues:

> [I]f the purposive notation of time-use becomes less compulsive, then men might have to re-learn some of the arts of living lost in the industrial revolution: how to fill the interstices of their days with enriched, more leisurely, personal and social relations; how to break down once more the barriers between work and life.
>
> (Thompson 1967, p. 97)

Conflict between labour and capital in Saharanpur's wood *mohallas* has rarely been large-scale and never unionised. A spatial context that bounds and even ghettoises the city's Muslim population creates a sense of bordering and enclavement at the spatial and subjective level (see Chambers 2018, 2019, 2020a; Carswell et al. 2019). This enclavement produces pressures which bind residents of the *mohallas* together, resulting in the situating of wealthier households alongside poor, working-class homesteads (cf. Jaffrelot & Gayer 2012; Jasani 2008). The intersectionality produced creates a common bond that, on the one hand, can be communally activating and community forming but, on the other, leads to the suppression of class politics through appeals to an imagined common Islamic identity. Because of this, and a variety of other factors (i.e., limited regulation, no unionisation and little state intervention), political activity tends to be orchestrated by local elites as opposed to being constituted through the kinds of bottom-up resistances envisaged by autonomist Marxists (Gill & Pratt 2008; Hardt & Negri 2005; for some ambivalences see Chambers 2020b; Ansari & Chambers 2022).

One of the few sites of contestation between labour and capital in the *mohallas* was time. The temporality of craftwork often required long hours of labour. However, many craft workers resisted clock-time working and preferred the relative independence offered by *apna kām* (own work), citing the need to give time for society as well as for work. For many, this meant time for family, attending events such as weddings, and the cultivation of neighbourhood and friendship-based networks, often a critical source of help in times of need. For others, dedicating time to society was also tied up with a desire to engage in religious pursuits, charitable activities or missionary work. Money, pay, and conditions were all concerns, but many craft workers rejected the marginally better and more stable earnings offered by factories to retain a degree of control over their time. The extent to which much of this labour could truly be seen as *apna kām* was questionable. However, so prominent were resistances around control of time that many factories sought to capture the rhythms of the bazaar and the motivating aesthetic of *apna kām* through the incorporation of artisanal modes of production within the factory walls, a practice that connects with the utilisation of craft aesthetics as a form of governmentality discussed earlier in this chapter. Yet, the value given to time for society, friendship and other concerns illustrates that, within this craft industry at least, the colonisation of all areas of life by the temporalities of work was not complete and remained contested even in an artisanal cluster that has long experienced conditions that have elsewhere been conceived as recent or exceptional.

## Conclusion

Under late capitalism, and contrary to substantivist narratives of ongoing dis-embedding (Polyani 2001[1944]), we have seen both a persistent re-embedding of economy in the social (e.g., Mollona 2005), and the activation of a variety of affective forms of discipline of which the call to artisanship and craft is but one. Sennett's (2008) identification of dedication and engagement as markers of the craftsman are also activated in calls to increase labour efficiency and discipline amongst those engaged in various forms of alienating and mundane work. The temporal and aspirational experiences this evokes may be relatively new to some but represent continuity for many. In contributing to this edited volume, I have made a call that echoes a familiar tension within anthropology, that which lies between the universal and the particular. This chapter has drawn out universalising discourses which reify artisanship and crafting as constitutive of idealised forms of modern self-making and economic organisation. Through attending to the particularities of Saharanpur's wood working cluster, I have also illustrated some of the areas these discourses act to conceal and have sought moments of potentiality that emerge in relational, spatial and temporal contexts. Finally, there is a further underlying contribution in this text. In her chapter on digital artisans in a recent edited volume, Lane DiNicola (2016) opens by describing a conversation with a publisher who expressed a strong preference for ethnographic work dealing with new frontiers of anthropology, such as computer hacking or digital cultures, as opposed to more 'traditional' sites of anthropological interest. This chapter, however, illustrates that niches of the global economy which could be conceived as traditional or old remain important constituents in the global circulations involved in processes of place making, affect and capital accumulation.

## Notes

1 *Mistrī* is applied more generally then *kārīgar* and includes mechanics, electricians, and plumbers.
2 Around USD 0.75 to USD 1.50 and USD 1.50 to USD 2.30, respectively.

**References**


Ansari, A & Chambers, T 2022, 'Gendering the everyday state: Muslim women, claim-making & brokerage in India,' *Contemporary South Asia*, vol. 30, no. 1, pp. 72–86.

Antrosio, J & Colloredo-Mansfeld, R 2016, *Fast, easy, and in cash: artisan hardship and hope in the global economy*, University of Chicago Press, Chicago, IL.

Beinin, J 2001, *Workers and peasants in the modern Middle East*, vol. 2, Cambridge University Press, Cambridge.

Braverman, H 1998[1974], *Labor and monopoly capital: the degradation of work in the twentieth century*, NYU Press, New York.

Breman, J 1996, *Footloose labour: working in India's informal economy*, Cambridge University Press, Cambridge.

Carswell, G, Chambers, T, & De Neve, G 2019, 'Waiting for the state: gender, citizenship and everyday encounters with bureaucracy in India,' *Environment and Planning C: Politics and Space*, vol. 37, no. 4, pp. 597–616.

Carswell, G & De Neve, G 2013, 'Labouring for global markets: conceptualising labour agency in global production networks,' *Geoforum*, vol. 44, pp. 62–70.

Chambers, T 2018, 'Continuity in mind: imagination and migration in India and the Gulf,' *Modern Asian Studies*, vol. 52, no. 4, pp. 1420–56.

Chambers, T 2019, '"Performed conviviality": space, bordering, and silence in the city,' *Modern Asian Studies*, vol. 53, no. 3, pp. 776–99.

Chambers, T 2020a, *Networks, labour and migration among Indian Muslim artisan*, UCL Press, London.

Chambers, T 2020b, '"Lean on me": Sifarish, mediation & the digitisation of state bureaucracies in India,' *Ethnography*, https://doi.org/10.1177/1466138120940755

Chambers, T & Ansari, A 2018, 'Ghar mein kām hai (there is work in the house): when female factory workers become "coopted domestic labour",' *Journal of South Asian Development*, vol. 13, no. 2, pp. 141–63.

Cross, J 2014, *Dream zones: anticipating capitalism and development in India*, Pluto Press, London.

DiNicola, L 2016, 'Forging source: considering the craft of computer programming,' in CM Wilkinson-Weber & AO DeNicola (eds.), *Critical craft: technology, globalization, and capitalism*, Bloomsbury, London, pp. 35–56.

Elyachar, J 2005, *Markets of dispossession: NGOs, economic development, and the state in Cairo*, Duke University Press, New York.

Gill, R & Pratt, A 2008, 'In the social factory? Immaterial labour, precariousness and cultural work,' *Theory, Culture & Society*, vol. 25, no. 7–8, pp. 1–30.

Grover, S, Chambers, T & Jeffery, P 2018, 'Portraits of women's paid domestic-care labour: ethnographic studies from globalizing India,' *Journal of South Asian Development*, vol. 13, no. 2, pp. 123–40.

Hardt, M & Negri, A 2005, *Multitude: war and democracy in the age of empire*, Penguin, London.

Holmes, H 2015, 'Transient craft: reclaiming the contemporary craft worker,' *Work, Employment and Society*, vol. 29, no. 3, pp. 479–95.

Ingold, T 2000, *The perception of the environment: essays on livelihood, dwelling and skill*, Routledge, London.

Jaffrelot, C & Gayer, L, 2012, *Muslims in Indian cities: trajectories of marginalisation*, Hurst & Co., London.

Jasani, R 2008, 'Violence, reconstruction and Islamic reform: stories from the Muslim "Ghetto",' *Modern Asian Studies*, vol. 42, no. 2–3, pp. 431–56.

Marx, K 2011[1887], *Capital: a critical analysis of capitalist production volume I*, Dover Publishing, New York.

Mezzadri, A 2016, 'Class, gender and the sweatshop: on the nexus between labour commodification and exploitation,' *Third World Quarterly*, vol. 37, no. 10, pp. 1877–900.

Mohsini, M 2010, 'Becoming an "asli karigar": the production of authenticity among old Delhi's Muslim artisans,' PhD thesis, University of London, School of Oriental and African Studies.

Mohsini, M 2016, 'Crafting Muslim artisans agency and exclusion in India's urban crafts communities,' in CM Wilkinson-Weber & AO DeNicola (eds.), *Critical craft: technology, globalization, and capitalism*, Bloomsbury Publishing, London, pp. 239–58.

Mollona, M 2005, 'Factory, family and neighbourhood: the political economy of informal labour in Sheffield,' *Journal of the Royal Anthropological Institute*, vol. 11, no. 3, pp. 527–48.

Moreton, B 2006, *To serve God and Wal-Mart: the making of Christian free enterprise*, Harvard University Press, Cambridge.

Nevill, HR (ed.) 1909, *Saharanpur: A Gazetteer, Being Volume II of the District Gazetteers of the United Provinces of Agra and Oudh*, Allahabad, Printed by F. Lukar, Supdt., Govt. Press, United Provinces. British Colonial Administration for the British Crown.

Ouellette, L 2017, 'Dream jobs? the glamourisation of beauty service work in media culture,' in AS Elias, R Gill, & C Scharff (eds.), *Aesthetic labour: rethinking beauty politics in neoliberalism*, Springer, London, pp. 183–98.

Phillips, N 2011, 'Informality, global production networks and the dynamics of "adverse incorporation",' *Global Networks*, vol. 11, no. 3, pp. 380–97.

Polyani 2001[1944], *The great transformation: the political and economic origins of our time*, Beacon Press, Boston, MA.

Prentice, R 2015, *Thiefing a chance: factory work, illicit labor, and neoliberal subjectivities in Trinidad*, University Press of Colorado, Boulder.

Ross, A 2004, Made in Italy: the trouble with craft capitalism, *Antipode*, vol. 36, no. 2, pp. 209–16.

Roy, T 1999, *Traditional industry in the economy of colonial India*, Cambridge University Press, Cambridge.

Rudnyckyj, D 2009, 'Spiritual economies: Islam and neoliberalism in contemporary Indonesia,' *Cultural Anthropology*, vol. 24, no. 1, pp. 104–41.

Schmidt, SC 2018, 'Precarious craft: a feminist commodity chain analysis,' *Migration and Development*, vol. 9, no. 3, pp. 1–18.

Sennett, R 2008, *The craftsman*, Yale University Press, New Haven, CT.

Thompson, EP 1967, 'Time, work-discipline, and industrial capitalism,' *Past & Present*, vol. 38, no. 1, pp. 56–97.

Venkatesan, S 2009, 'Rethinking agency: persons and things in the heterotopia of traditional craft,' *Journal of the Royal Anthropological Institute*, vol. 15, no. 1, pp. 78–95.

Wilkinson-Weber, C 1999, *Embroidering lives: women's work and skill in the Lucknow embroidery industry*, State University of New York Press, New York.

# 16 The Gramophone, the Concert Stage, and the Hindustani Musician as Commodity Fetish

*Dard Neuman*

Within the literature of a political economy, it is well established that the transition from pre-capitalist to capitalist modes of production involved a fundamental shift in the status of labour: the producer entered the marketplace no longer to sell the products of labour but also his/her labour itself (Marx 1978[1972], pp. 319–29).[1] This shift produced forms of alienation that were triply marked: the alienation of producer from consumer, producer from the products of their labour, and humans from their full subjectivity. And yet, the distinction between producer and product is blurred in oral music traditions; there is no tangible object that stands apart from the performance, as there are other forms of artistic expression, such as a musical score, a painting, and a written text. The gramophone provided a fundamental shift, enabling the musical performance to exist apart from its live expression, and to be sold and circulated as a commodified object. This chapter examines the impact of that transformation on the new buying public in South Asia through readings of encounters with professional musicians at the turn of the twentieth century and around the time of Independence. Through these encounters, I consider the gendered logic of the commodity fetish as it structured a relationship between the modern consumer and producer, a relationship mediated not by alienation per se, but through a new kind of intimacy, a type of commodity fetishism specific to conditions of South Asian modernity.

## Gramophone: The Artist as Commodity Celebrity

Any examination of the musician's place in the twentieth-century public sphere must include the place of the gramophone. Its reach in turn-of-the-century India was significant; it required no electricity, and its price point was low enough that it could be purchased second-hand in villages. Also noteworthy was the content; a large number of the recorded musicians were from the professional community of female singers known as the *tawaif*s. The gramophone entered South Asia in 1902 when FW Gaisberg, a representative of the English Gramophone Company, began a world-circuit tour in 1902 in search of music for the nascent record industry. Travelling to India in 1902, he made the very first recordings of Hindustani music (Gaisberg 1942). Working from the offices of the superintendent of the Calcutta police, he recruited musicians from the red-light district, most of whom were

DOI: 10.4324/9781351031028-17

women and, therefore, of the courtesan class. The male professional musicians (*ustads*) had, according to him, 'only high-pitched effeminate voices' and so were left largely unrecorded (Gaisberg 1942, p. 56).

The gramophone company made over 500 records in the first year alone (Manuel 1989, p. 73). Female professional musicians became the first mass phenomenon in the Hindustani music community, and some found a lucrative place in the twentieth-century recording industry. Most notable of these singers were Gauhar Jan, Janki Bai, Malka Jan, Mandala Sundari Dasi, Bai Sundara Bai, and Zohra Bai. The new listening public encountered these singers not in person on stage but as bodiless entities, 'heard without being seen' (Weidman 2006, p. 112). Because of their disreputable standing in middle-class India, *tawaifs* would not otherwise have been allowed a place in the household. Hindustani music, a princely cultivated but Victorian-condemned tradition, found a backdoor into the new public sphere. With this backdrop in mind, we move to the discursive construction of one such musician, Gauhar Jan, one of the first and most highly compensated, musicians to be recorded.

## My Name Is Gauhar Jan

A salient and peculiar feature of gramophone recordings from their beginnings in India in 1902 until the 1940s was the artist's announcement of his or her name at the end of the three-minute recording. It turns out that this practice, which was born of clerical necessity – to serve as an aural catalogue – provoked a certain public delight. We note this in an article by an unnamed author titled 'My name is Gauhar Jan' and published by *The Indian Music Journal* in 1912.[2]

> Miss Gouhar [sic] is known through the Gramophone records even to the villager. Her records are enjoyable but there is a disparity between the copy and the original leading to disappointment. She has made a name and fortune far above the reach of even masters in the arts, of whom there are plenty in India, and if the key to such success is to be sought for, it will be found to lie in the invisible and effective self-advertisement through the Gramophone 'My Name is Gouhar Jan.'
>
> [W]e failed to notice in her rendering any of those intelligent flourishes of Hindustani music that we are accustomed to find in first-rate Gavois [sic]. The pieces she sang, though suited to the middle class of hearers, were not adorned with any skilful improvisations which an expert cannot possibly avoid even in ordinary singing. The mode of combining notes, or of expanding them, was not above average.

To anyone growing up during the second half of the twentieth century, these statements come across as rather jarring; most musicians and connoisseurs I know hold Gauhar Jan in high regard. The author of this editorial, however, posits Gauhar Jan as little more than what the gramophone has fashioned. Gauhar Jan achieves her fame through her proper name; she is known by her advertisements and is better enjoyed as a copy. It is not that she fails to come across as advertised. Rather, the advertisement itself creates her arrival. Moreover, what makes her advertisement so effective ('the key to such success') is that it cannot be seen ('will be found to lie in the invisible ... self-advertisement'). Thus, when Gauhar Jan comes on stage in concert with a visible presence, she does so as a disappointment. From this perspective, the concertising musician emerges, post-gramophone, as an original, as something that exists in relation to her copy. However, it is the copy that is preferred and privileged, while the original appears other than itself.

The critical tone of the editorial is clearly patriarchal and elitist. Yet those male 'masters in the arts, of whom there are plenty,' are unnamed and unmarked, except in their abundance. How are we to account for these positionings? Turning to the historical context of colonial modernity in South Asia, we note that from the 1830s to the turn of the twentieth century, the gendered groupings of professional musicians underwent significant transformations, with the most dramatic being the semiotic reduction of multiple categories and classes of female musicians to that of courtesan and prostitute (Schofield 2012). This burden of association was most often carried by the *tawaif* and, by association, her accompanist and teacher, the bowed-fiddler, the *sarangiya* (Bor 1986–1987). In public, they became linked as a notorious pair. This larger history is multifaceted but can be signposted by the following shifts.

To begin with, the place of elite courtesans underwent significant changes in the early 1830s due to new policies of succession established by the British for Mughal rule. As Margrit Pernau (2013) argues, prior to the 1830s, it was not uncommon to find courtesans rising through the social ranks of respectability and even the political ranks to sovereignty. After the 1840s, however, such mobility was cut off when the British redefined succession 'on the basis of biology' as opposed to inheritance rights defined 'socially' (Pernau 2013, pp. 135–6). After the great rebellion of 1857, issues of succession shifted to panic over contagion. As Veena Oldenburg (1990) asserts, the British were surprised to realise that they suffered more deaths due to illness than to battle, with a quarter of the soldiers having contracted venereal diseases (Oldenburg 1990, p. 260). Professional women from a wide range of classes and occupational categories became seen as potential carriers of disease and therefore a threat to the biological health of Europeans. Configured now as prostitutes, they were to be 'regulated, inspected, and controlled' through multiple Contagious Diseases Acts, the first of which was passed in 1864 (Oldenburg 1990, p. 260). By the end of the nineteenth century, colonial policies converged with national discourses and reformist efforts into what would be called the anti-nautch campaign. Courtesan culture in the North was thereafter implicated as a moral threat to the social fabric.

This history was not, however, hegemonic. Print capitalism and post-1857 migrations from the imperial centre brought the expressive culture of the Mughal elite from Delhi and Lucknow to other urban centres, opening a space for professional women to inhabit the new public sphere as figures of literati sophistication. Shweta Sachdeva (2015), Sumata Banerjee (1998), Anna Morcom (2013), and Richard Williams (2017) all demonstrate how *tawaif*s engaged colonial modernity not just as passive victims to the anti-nautch movement but also as creative entrepreneurs.

Print capitalism put poetry and biographical portraits into mass circulation, positioning professional women as celebrities of elite sophistication.

The figure of the courtesan celebrity, then, had a dual placement in the late nineteenth and early twentieth century, mediated first through the printing press as a published poet and then through the gramophone as a voiced singer. In both cases, the *tawaif* could achieve a celebrity status, paradoxically, through the alienation effect of the commodity form, which detached the in-person presence from a traditionally intimate encounter. The musician's greeting on the gramophone, however, complicated the situation.

## Intrusion of the Real

I would like to suggest that both the public delight and the editorial ambivalence that attended to Gauhar Jan were structured around an oscillation between song and speech. In this dynamic, the spoken greeting served as an 'intrusion of the real' that disturbed social boundaries that were in a state of historical transformation: the elite and popular; the public and private; the professional and respectable (Zizek 1995, p. 17). Slavoj Zizek (1995) positions the Lacanian concept of the 'intrusion of the real' as an uncanny encounter, as that which both disrupts and reveals a constructed boundary (pp. 15–8). Mladen Dolar (1991) goes one step further and brings the concept of the uncanny away from its phallocentric register and into history: he argues for 'a specific dimension of the uncanny' that emerged in conditions of modernity (p. 7).

It is in this spirit that I would like to explore the emergence of the Hindustani musician as a commodity celebrity in colonial modernity. In the 1912 article on Gauhar Jan, we note a series of crossings that the musician's spoken announcement provoked. To begin with, the announcement comes at the end of the performance, something that occurred after a musically coded finish line. And yet, the announcement emanates from the record, within the commodity form itself. The announcement, therefore, does not disrupt the musical performance so much as it disrupts the commodity performance: insofar as the signifier Gauhar Jan points to a commodified presence, the effect of Gauhar Jan's being emerges with her greeting, as if the speaking voice were introducing the person from behind the cult of the singer. The real voice provided the fetishistic idea of an intimate encounter at a time when actual encounters were becoming historically inappropriate. Indeed, the 1912 article was written two years after Gauhar Jan entered the public eye as a figure of controversy. As Vikram Sampath (2010) writes, the Government of the United Provinces planned an exhibition featuring Gauhar Jan in 1910. As news of her upcoming performances spread, so too did public protest. Letters to the editors of local newspapers decried the inclusion of a *tawaif* in a public function (Sampath 2010, pp. 142–3). While many segments of South Asian society delightfully consumed Gauhar Jan's disembodied voice on the gramophone, some segments vehemently opposed her embodied presence in public venues.

Gauhar Jan's name was clearly implicated in the moral politics of the anti-nautch campaign. It is even possible that her celebrity status helped propel the campaign from the legal confines of colonial legislation to the public exposure of national outcry, mass-marketing the semiotic ambiguity of the professional musician. In a paradoxical way, then, the gramophone both dislodged the professional musician from the political economy of feudal culture while also attaching her more (in)visibly to a scandalised figure of colonial provocation. The speaking voice provided, for a time, a different kind of intimate encounter, one mediated by commodity fetishism whereby the gramophone object produced a subjectivity of sorts through the spectral presence of a disembodied voice, a voice that introduced the effect of a person from behind a song.

## The Concert Stage and The Birth of the National Celebrity

As we move from the early to the mid-twentieth century, another important shift takes place: professional musicians, once castigated in the new public sphere as carriers of moral unease and venereal disease, then celebrated as printed poets and recorded singers, now emerge on the concert stage as biographical figures of the nation and national celebrities. How did this occur? As I have argued elsewhere, it would take nearly 50 years for in-person performance to become a regular feature of urban public life (Neuman 2009). One of the implications of this deferred encounter was that the social panic of the anti-nautch campaign would give way to anti-colonial politics. Consequently, the public place of the professional musician faded from notoriety to irrelevance, heard on the gramophone and radio but otherwise ignored. This marginalisation of the musician had certain productive effects, for when musicians, both female and male, re-emerged in the public eye, quite literally on the concert stage, they did so through a new dialectical burden of possibility; they were not only castigated but also celebrated as traditional bearers of elite art culture. The figure of the musical master exploded on the social scene after the masters of the old regime died: the colonial master, who was sent home at Independence in 1947, and the feudal master, who was consigned to history with the Zamindari Abolition Act of 1950.

The new figure of the master musician as a national protagonist owes itself, in part, to the changing form of the commodity fetish, attached as it was to the figure of the recorded musician who now stepped onto the national concert stage. Zizek (1989) provides a Lacanian reading of Marx's analysis of the commodity fetish, arguing that there were two 'parallel' but 'incompatible' forms of fetishism in the passage from pre-capitalist to capitalist societies (pp. 25–6). In the old world, exchange was not alienated, but relations between people were hierarchically ordered: fetishism was marked, for example, by the auratic power that subjects attribute to Masters. In the 'new world,' relations between people became alienated but also de-fetishised, 'free of all the lumber of veneration of the Master' (Zizek 1989, p. 25). In this arrangement of legally free and equal people, the fetish gets displaced from the dead Master onto commodities (Zizek 1989, p. 26). In the case of Hindustani music, a slightly different itinerary of displacement takes place. As the feudal master dies, the feudal servant, in the form of the former court musician, takes the stage as a new master, with music and reputation fully imbued with a modern aura.

**His Master's Voice**

One of the earliest post-Independence concert reviews that I have come across appears in *The Bharat Jyoti* on 14 November 1948, by the music critic Mohan Nadkarni. He writes a review of Sawai Gandharva (1886–1952), a disciple of the famed hereditary musician, Abdul Karim Khan (1872–1937). According to Janaki Bakhle (2005), Abdul Karim Khan trained his non-hereditary student to serve as a *khandani* (of a hereditary lineage) response to a national charge: namely, that Muslim hereditary musicians were an impediment to the modernisation, classicisation, and democratisation of Indian classical music. Abdul Karim Khan answered this charge by producing a musician in the nationalist image but of exceptional training: Sawai Gandharva was an outsider to hereditary lineages but, as a Brahmin, an insider to the national ideal of the modern subject.

Turning to this concert review, one notes a difference in how the listener awaits the singer. As we saw in the previous section, in the editorial on Gauhar Jan, this anticipation had been directed towards a disembodied greeting 'my name is ...' 50 years later, 'a feeling of great expectancy' is now attached to another type of appearance, that of a voice attaching itself to the body of the musician. But this reunification was interestingly fragmented. As Nadkarni writes,

> A musical concert was being held in Hubli on the occasion of the death anniversary of the late Khan Saheb Abdul Karim Khan some years ago ... There was pin-drop silence as Sawai Gandharva appeared on the dais with joined hands. The eyes of the audience were riveted on him. A feeling of great expectancy was abroad. Soon the Tamboras were tuned to the Nishada note, and in the quiet hours of the star-lit autumn night, the solemn strains of puriya steadily flowed from his divine voice ... We were being transported as it were from this mundane ... life to a new world of fancies—of musical fantasies. The worthy disciple was rendering Ragas after Ragas in *His Master's Voice* [the insignia of the Gramophone Company]. Hours were fleeing away like minutes. Our souls were lost in his melody. Many of us shed silent, idle tears when he plaintively sang.
>
> It was in his early teens that Sawai Gandharva was once captivated by the heavenly music of Abdul Karim Khan ... How ... did this pupil sing *in His Master's Voice* in later years? ... Sawai Gandharva had had thorough training under the sympathetic guidance of his Ustad... And therein lies the secret of his success as an eminent vocalist. His more recent recorded songs ... deserve special attention in this respect. One marvels at the rich, pliable, flexible and sonorous voice of the renowned singer. ... He charmed his audience by singing the Khansaheb's well known Thumris and Bhajans with that typically emotional fervor.
>
> (Nadkarni 1948)

Note the sense of expectation, of visual excitement. The 'eyes of the audience' are 'riveted' on the musician, and with this ocular orientation comes a 'feeling of great expectancy.' The writer and his audience, so accustomed to the gramophone and radio, finally get a chance to see and hear the musician on stage. And when the master's voice issues forth from a singing body, Nadkarni evinces no sense of disappointment, no disjuncture between the original and the copy, as did the editorial reviewer of Gauhar Jan. Instead, the voice explodes as the central topic of discussion; it becomes an aesthetic vehicle to a sublime experience.

This encounter bears some resemblance to what Michael Chion (1999) terms the *acousmetre*. For Chion, the acousmetre marks a filmic voice that lacks a bearer but is nevertheless present in the diegetic world of the narrative being presented. The acousmetre draws its uncanny power through its spectral presence, being neither the third-person voice of the narrator nor the first-person voice of a subject in narrative. The process of de-acousmatisation serves the opposite purpose: it evacuates the acousmatic voice of its auratic power. The deferred emergence of the musician on the mid-century concert stage presents an interesting twist to this structure. The disembodied voice was never an acousmatic presence until it retroactively emerged as such when voice and singer met on stage. This process of de-acousmatisation, then, did not neutralise but rather provided the singing voice with its captivating power. As voice and body reunited in the form of the singing body, however, the voice became refracted through its multiple references: to the voice of the concert musician, Sawai Gandharva; to the voice of his master, Abdul Karim Khan; to His Master's Voice (HMV) on gramophone recording; and to the gramophone logo of HMV. It was as if the voice detached from a singular subject in its very attachment to a single body, as if the singer became a kind of spectral presence in his physical being.

## His Master

It might be tempting to argue that Indian nationalism opened a space for the male Brahmin musician and, in so doing, centralised a subject who could replace and eventually overwrite what some viewed as historical imposters, the Muslim *ustad* and the *tawaif*. This reading, however, would miss the fact that hereditary musicians, both male and female, had a central place on the post-Independence public stage for several decades. I suggest that as hereditary musicians became heard in the public concert, their music referenced not just a gramophone standard – a song – but also the idea of a national repertoire that threatened to disappear. The professional musician became valued both as an archival repository and a performer of a national aesthetic, a live concert imbued with a modern aura, as that which could not be captured and reproduced. We note this in one of the first biographical mentions of a male Muslim hereditary musician in twentieth-century writing. This column comes in the form of a memorial to Sawai Gandharva's teacher, Abdul Karim Khan:

> By the sad and sudden demise of Sangita Ratna Abdul Karim Khan, the world of Indian Music has lost a remarkable and forceful personality and a brilliant exponent of classical Hindustani music. The void left by him is not likely to

> be filled, as even in the north, there is a dearth of first-rate musicians … The writer's most precious memory of Abdul Karim is his Lalit, that he sang once but could never duplicate. Not all the gold of the Indies could buy that Lalit.[3]

Note how this remembrance identifies a performance in its particular instance, as something that occurred once and never again. This performance stood out because its singularity was tied, negatively but inextricably, to purchase and duplication. The concert, then, was structured by means of the commoditized logic of mechanical reproduction even though it was neither heard through the gramophone nor recorded by one. Until the late 1950s, the full-length concert performance was neither recorded nor recordable, neither purchased nor purchasable. The concert, removed as it was from the domain of commodified posterity, thus took on the quality of evanescence.

Note a similar encounter with another hereditary Muslim master, Bade Ghulam Ali Khan (1902–1968).

> In 1944, [a concert] was held in the Bombay University Convocation Hall. An artist from Punjab presented Raga Marwa and a thumri, as they had never been presented before, and will never be presented again. This was how Ustad Bade Ghulam Ali Khan introduced himself to lovers of classical music in Bombay.
>
> (Joshi 1984, p. 52)

Music is typically understood as ephemeral; unlike other art forms, it exists only when it is articulated. In the Hindustani context, however, music was described as ephemeral only after it became mechanically reproducible and was then encountered as a live performance. After nearly half a century of listening in a manner determined by mechanical repetition – one could always place the needle back to the beginning – the new listening public was suddenly confronted by the ephemeral, the performance that could not be replayed. The commodity fetishism structured this expectation, but in negation: where the gramophone consumer obtained an intimate encounter with the singing and speaking musician, the concert attendee could experience the sublime, that which could not be represented and reproduced. But this sublime aura was not that which 'withered in the age of mechanical production' as Walter Benjamin famously argued, but was produced by it (Benjamin 1969, p. 220).

## Conclusion

This chapter has explored how technologies of mechanical reproduction created a complicated space of celebration for the Hindustani musician. This space emerged against a greater historical trend that would have seen the professional practitioner die out with the feudal and colonial master, and give way to the new, middle-class artist. In particular, I argued that the professional musician emerged as a national protagonist due to the commodity fetish effects of the gramophone that intersected with the public concert stage. At the turn of the twentieth century, some professional musicians obtained a celebrity status through print and gramophone media, a status that prepared the way for the post-independence placement of the master musician as a national protagonist. Put differently, the post-colonial figure of the master musician qua national subject owed itself, in part, to the phenomenon of the commodity fetish, attached as it was to the recorded musician who, after 1947, increasingly found him and herself on the national concert stage after half a century of being heard primarily on the gramophone and radio. There were co-constitutive links, in other words, between the ennoblement of the musician, the technologies of reproduction, and the experience of music as ephemeral: the professional musician sat on stage as the singer of a live concert, and the attendee bore witness to an ephemeral, sublime and auratic experience, that of a national legacy that disappeared as it was encountered.

## Acknowledgements

The author would like to thank Kathy Chetkovich for her deeply engaged readings, feedback, suggestions and overall encouragement. The author would also like to thank Daniel Neuman, Anna Morcom, and Anjali Arondekar for their comments on this chapter.

## Notes

1 My reading of Marx is indebted to Michael Taussig (1980) and Slavoj Zizek (1989). It is also influenced by Walter Benjamin (1969) and his linking of the commodity fetish to his notion of aura. My readings of Benjamin are influenced by Susan Buck-Morss (1983) and Michael Taussig (1993).
2 'My name is Gauhar Jan,' *The Indian Music Journal* vol. 2, no. 1 (March and April 1912), p. 16.
3 *The Journal of The Music Academy of Madras* vol. 5, no. 1–4 (1934), emphasis added.

## References

Bakhle, J 2005, *Two men and music: nationalism in the making of an Indian classical tradition*, Oxford University Press, New York.

Banerjee, S 1998, *Dangerous outcast: the prostitute in nineteenth century Bengal*, Seagull Books, Calcutta.

Benjamin, W 1969, 'The work of art in the age of mechanical reproduction,' in H Arendt (ed.), *Illuminations*, trans. H Zohn, Schocken Books, New York, pp. 217–51.

Bor J 1986–1987, 'The voice of the sarangi,' *National Centre for the Performing Arts: Quarterly Journal*, vol. XV & XVI, nos. 3, 4, & 1, pp. 1-183.

Buck-Morss, S 1983, 'Benjamin's passagen-werk: redeeming mass culture for the revolution,' *New German Critique*, vol. 29, no. 29 (Spring-Summer), pp. 211–40.

Chion, M 1999, *The voice in cinema*, Columbia University Press, New York.

Dolar, M 1991, '"I shall be with you on your wedding-night": Lacan and the uncanny,' *October* vol. 58 (Autumn), pp. 5–23.

Gaisberg, FW 1942, *The music goes round*, The Macmillan Co., New York.

Joshi, GN.1984, '*Down Melody Lane*. Orient Longman Limited'.

Manuel, P 1989, *Thumri in historical and stylistic perspectives*, Motilal Banarasidass, New Delhi.

Marx, K 1978[1972], 'The fetishism of commodities and the secret thereof,' in RC Tucker (ed.), *The Marx-Engels reader*, W.W. Norton & Company, New York, pp. 319–29.

Morcom, A 2013, *Illicit worlds of Indian Dance: cultures of exclusion*, C. Hurst & Co., London.

Nadkarni, Mohan.1948, 'A Great Exponent of Khayal--Sawai Gandharva.,' *The Bharat Jyoti*, 14 Nov. 1948, pp. unknown.

Neuman, D 2009, 'The production of aura in the gramophone age of the "live" performance,' *Journal of the Society for Asian Music*, vol. 40, no. 2, pp. 100–23.

Oldenburg, V 1990, 'Lifestyle as resistance: the case of the courtesans of Lucknow, India,' *Feminist Studies*, vol. 16, no. 2, pp. 259–87.

Pernau, M 2013, *Ashraf into middle class: Muslims in nineteenth-century Delhi*, Oxford University Press, Oxford.

Sachdeva, S 2015, 'Tawa'if as poet and patron: rethinking women's self-representation,' in A Malhotra & S Lambert-Hurley (eds.), *Speaking of the self: gender, performance, and autobiography in South Asia*, Duke University Press, Durham, NC, pp. 141–64.

Sampath, V 2010, *My name is Gauhar Jan*, Rupa & Co, New Delhi.

Schofield, KB 2012, 'The courtesan tale: female musicians and dancers in Mughal historical chronicles, c. 1556–1748,' *Gender & History*, vol. 24, no. 1, pp. 150–71.

Taussig, M 1980, *The devil and commodity fetishism in South America*, The University of North Carolina Press, Chapel Hill.

Taussig, M 1993, *Mimesis and alterity: a particular history of the senses*, Routledge, New York.

Weidman, A 2006, *Singing the classical, voicing the modern: the postcolonial politics of music in South India*, Duke University Press, Durham, NC.

Williams, R 2017, 'Songs between cities: listening to courtesans in colonial North India,' *Journal Royal Asiatic Society*, vol. 27, no. 4, pp. 591–610.

Zizek, S 1989, *The sublime object of ideology*, Verso, New York.

Zizek, S 1995, *Looking awry: an introduction of Jacques Lacan through popular culture*, The MIT Press, Cambridge.

# 17 The Business of Kollywood Dance in Chennai, India

*Kristen Rudisill*

The attitude towards popular dance in Chennai has undergone a dramatic shift over the past 20 years. Middle-class dance practice has expanded beyond classical forms, and established Indian dance hierarchies are starting to dissolve as styles are remixed and recombined into cohesive freestyle performances that are associated with modernity, global culture, and consumption. As Bollywood dance (and following close behind it, Kollywood, or Tamil-language film dance) has become gentrified, careers in the field of dance have become more viable and respectable for middle-class women and (especially) men (see Shresthova 2011; Morcom 2014). In the Tamil industry, dancing in films as a back-up dancer is still not viewed as respectable, so upper-middle-class dancers and choreographers have created new avenues for dance careers both within and outside of the film industry. They control these segments of the dance industry by normalising language, dress, and financial requirements to access dance classes and studios, television reality shows, and school/college competitions. In this chapter, I explore these alternative dance careers, focusing particularly on two reality television dance competitions, arguing that class status plays a central role in determining the appeal and viability of various dance careers.

## Class, Respectability, and Dancing in the Film Industry

Pallabi Chakravorty (2018) argues that

> Despite the fact that Bollywood dance has broken through its prior "low culture" status due to factors such as its association with glamorous figures like Shiamak Davar and its popularity among the diaspora and demand in weddings … its artistic value remains questionable among cultural pundits. (p. 179)

This is especially true in the city of Chennai, famous for its annual classical dance festival, where *Bharatanatyam* dancers flock from all over the world, vying for the opportunity to showcase their technique and virtuosity (see O'Shea 2007). Still, both boys and girls perform in school cultural programs, competitions, and weddings, where it is no longer a requirement to perform classical or folk dances as semblances of

DOI: 10.4324/9781351031028-18

them are blended into freestyle dances that incorporate both along with Western-style dance movements. The semblances are often lumped together under the moniker 'semi-classical,' which indicates the preservation of signature movement vocabularies from *Bharatanatyam* without requiring the rigorous training, complexity, or reach of the classical dance, favouring fluidity and affect over precision and form.

Though dance is central to both tracks of a film career – dancer/choreographer and actor – the two paths are very different in terms of status and earning potential. Being a dancer/choreographer in the Chennai film industry offers a stable career. However, the Film Dancers and Dance Directors Union has been successful at keeping non-union members away from the back-up dancing and choreography jobs, at least for dance sequences shot within the state of Tamil Nadu. Access to the union in Chennai is also severely limited. In order to join, one must train with a union dance director for a minimum of five years. There are two paths to get there, and there is currently a shift from one to the other that parallels the rise in prestige of the college competitions and the increasing number of middle-class dance students and upscale studios. An example of the first type is Upathi, who teaches at Jayanthi Akka's studio in T Nagar. As a child, he took two hours of dance classes per day with Jayanthi, later becoming one of her teaching assistants. Jayanthi's sister, the Kollywood choreographer Kala Master, recommended him for an audition, and he paid for the union card with the money he had saved from teaching and performing, eventually building a stable career teaching and dancing back-up in films. The second trajectory is the narrative of Prabhu Master, owner of Spring Boots Dance Academy in Besant Nagar. He did not begin to dance seriously until college when he choreographed a team for a competition. The team did extremely well, so after he graduated, the college continued to hire him. He started taking a few students and was soon making enough money teaching that he could quit his day job as a mechanical engineer. He made friends in the film industry and worked with a dance director, getting an audition for the union after seven years. He said that there was not a need for dancers, so auditions were not held every year, and the year he was selected they took only 12 dancers out of several hundred hopefuls. Once he had his union card, he was eligible to dance in films, and did a few, but mostly bided his required two years until he was eligible to act as assistant dance director, then two more until he could be a dance director. In 2008, he was starting to get contracts as a dance director.

Financially, joining the Dancers Union is more stable than becoming an actor, because there is always work, but it also requires more investment up-front. When this research was done in 2012, joining the union was a flat fee of INR four lakhs (INR 400,000) and the compensation was approximately INR 3,500 for a three-day shoot. The average back-up dancer does about five songs a month, earning INR 15,000–20,000, so it takes approximately two years to recoup the investment one makes in the card, unlike the situation in Bollywood, where the card costs only INR one lakh (INR 100,000) and dancers recoup the money in three months. Operating as a non-union dancer in the Bollywood industry is also easier (Morcom 2014, p. 133).

In Kollywood, one executive film producer told me that a choreography assistant is paid INR 20,000 per song and dance directors vary widely from about INR 70,000 up to INR 500,000 per song. He also mentioned that back-up dancers still tend to be lower caste and from struggling families and that 'film dance is kind of defined by socio-economic factors.' Middle-class dancers are the new trend, but it is a slow transition as there are limited places available in the union, so existing members must retire to make room for new members. Most of these middle-class dancers do not want the grunt work of back-up dancing, however, preferring to make better money teaching classes and doing private choreography, making their names through those circles and on television until they can get the more lucrative and prestigious work of dance directing for film. There are many well-known choreographers in Chennai who simply do not bother with the dancers' union and therefore cannot do dance direction for films. There are possible workarounds, but producers prefer to follow the rules of the union, and the choreographers want credit for the work they do.

The actor's union, in contrast, does not require any up-front fee. Dues are based on a percentage of income (approximately 10%), and the union card comes with one's first role. This makes it easy to do a single project, as there is no large up-front investment. Additionally, actors get paid varying rates that are far more negotiable, making it more attractive for middle-class dancers. An actor's role can be choreographing and dancing lead in a song, and as long as they have a line or two in the film to justify their categorisation as 'actor' rather than 'dancer,' they can join the actors' union. Middle-class dancers and choreographers are willing to take small roles in films for minimal pay because the recognition and prestige from those roles can benefit their studio careers, attracting business and allowing them to charge higher rates in non-film ventures.

## Non-film Dance Careers

In thinking about Bollywood dance careers in Mumbai, Anna Morcom (2014) identifies the same avenues I found in Chennai, 'With the dance schools, the film industry, the wedding sangeets, and all the shows at which dance is performed, dance is much more than just viable in terms of a career' (p. 132). What is fascinating is that while the film industry is central and provides the music and much of the inspiration for movement in all these fields, it is now possible to construct a dance career outside of films. One of the differences I find in Chennai compared to Mumbai is that avoiding the film industry can actually heighten a dancer's respectability and decency, even though that move sacrifices 'association with fame, fortune, desirability, and a chic globalized image' (Morcom 2014, p. 132). However, I would note that Chennai has not yet reached the level of at least parts of Mumbai, where 'middle class girls now perform what are often sexy numbers in public in sometimes skimpy costumes, without being seen as disreputable or equivalent to prostitutes, but rather, as normal and trendy' (Morcom 2014, p. 117).

Owning a dance studio can be lucrative in Chennai, as this career path promises a variety of ways to make money and can be started with minimal capital. A middle-class teacher, with middle-class students, involves less risk to reputation than working in the film industry, where the population is more mixed and less controlled. The two main requirements for setting oneself up as a teacher are a space and some business acumen. The 50 or so biggest studios in Chennai have their own dedicated, air-conditioned spaces with mirrored walls and wood flooring, but countless others are housed in smaller, less ideal or rented spaces. The primary income source for most studios is teaching. In 2012, students paid an average of INR 1,000 per month for two one-hour classes per week. Middle-class families are happy to pay for their children to learn dancing, if not pursue careers in it, and the summer camps are especially popular, costing around INR 2,000 in 2012 for daily classes over two weeks plus final performance (see Figure 17.1).

Many of the top studios have professional dance teams that perform at corporate events, which pay extremely well and are often the goal of a studio as they allow a focus on complex and original choreography, quality costumes, and the ability to hire the very best dancers. For middle-class dancers, corporate events can be a classy way of performing, and keeping visuals away from family or gossiping busybodies, which is impossible with film or television. Annual recitals and summer dance camps provide opportunities to advertise professional teams as students may have family connections to the corporate world.

Studios can also use television to promote their classes, choreography, and professional teams. John Britto Dance Studio and Raack Academy of Dance once had contracts with Vijay TV to provide choreography and back-up dancers for their reality dance competitions, and their logo and name were mentioned in every episode. Once they had a big enough name, these studios chose to focus more on teaching and their professional teams. They no longer work in television regularly, though their names are reinforced to viewers when their students compete. When they bowed out, newer studios like Flyerz and Sherif's Dance Company stepped up.

*Figure 17.1* Author at Flyerz Dance Studio in Nungambakkam, Chennai. Author's own photograph.

The next most lucrative enterprise after corporate events for a studio is choreography. As competitions for school and college teams become more common and competitive, they become more likely to hire professional choreographers. In 2012, these teams and corporations were paying upwards of INR 30,000 for this service. Providing four minutes of choreography for four people costs an average of INR 5,000, and additional people and additional minutes add up fast. The growing trend of sangeet nights is also adding well-paying customers for choreographers. This started as a night of traditional music before a wedding in Punjabi culture, but thanks to Bollywood, it has expanded in both geographic range and concept, spanning the country by 2005 (Morcom 2014, p. 136). These performances celebrate the new couple and also the bond between the two families, members of whom dance together on this night, very often in film-style dances choreographed by professionals.

## Reality Television Dance Competitions

Dance reality shows in India have grown in popularity since the 1996 debut of the Hindi *Boogie Woogie*, which was quickly followed by a number of similar shows in both Hindi and regional languages. There have now been at least a dozen Tamil-language reality television dance competition programs (many with multiple seasons), and while there is overlap of concept, audience, judges, hosts, contestants, choreographers, and back-up dancers, each offers viewers and performers something distinct.[1] These shows target specific types of contestants and encourage them in dance careers that can take a variety of creative economic trajectories.

My research on two reality dance shows that were shot in 2012 in Chennai – the seventh season of Kalaigner TV's *Manada Mayilada* (*MM*) (*The Deer Dances and the Peacock Dances*) and the second season of Vijay TV's *Ungalil Yaar Adutha Prabhudeva* (*UYP*) (*Who is the Next Prabhudeva?*) – reveals class distinctions between contestants and variations in the opportunities provided by each show. *MM* is a mixed-gender couples competition directed by one of Kollywood's top choreographers, Kala Master. *UYP* is a search for someone of comparable talent to dancer and choreographer Prabhudeva, who is often referred to as the 'Indian Michael Jackson' or 'the original "item boy"' (Chakravorty 2018, p. 93). Reality television dance competitions, which offer exposure to prospective clients, as well as professional connections within the film industry and owners of top dance studios, have become a steppingstone for those looking to turn a hobby into a career as well as an accelerant for those looking to advance fledgling careers in television or film. I examine some of these opportunities and creative career paths with particular attention to the intertextuality of television and film as they play out in the lives of contestants and choreographers from these two programs in the city of Chennai. Both shows have Kollywood film personalities behind them, and the reputations and roles in the film industry of these individuals help determine the style of dance as well as the direction of the program and the future careers of the dancers associated with it.

*MM* is arguably the most professional Tamil reality dance competition and is a space for dancers from other shows to extend their celebrity. All the women, and some of the men, are spotted in other capacities and invited to participate, and they are paid like the professionals they are for doing so. In addition to being paid for each performance, the top three *MM* pairs each receive substantial cash prizes, as does the winning pair's choreographer (INR 10 lakhs, 5 lakhs, and 3 lakhs, respectively). The *MM* contestants with whom I spoke can support themselves on their income from the show, and most would not have considered participating without payment, as they would have preferred to accept opportunities for paying work elsewhere. However, contestants did recognise that participation could be a major benefit to their careers in terms of association with the branding of the show and the exposure, face value, and professional connections it provides.

The *UYP* contestants I met are amateur dancers who are not paid for performing on the show, though housing was provided for the duration of the shooting for those from outside Chennai. Most are secondary school or college students whose middle-class families support their dancing. Some work part-time in the dance field, teaching or dancing for a professional troupe, and some older contestants have other jobs. Only the winner of this program is awarded a prize, though it is a game-changing one: an apartment valued at 40 lakhs, provided by Om Shakti Homes, the sponsor of the season. The difference in payment affects who can afford to compete, as *UYP* contestants require support from savings or families in order to commit to participating and forgoing income for this length of time.

Most of the dancers I met at *UYP* aspired to have their own studios or to teach and choreograph for their current studio, perhaps in addition to jobs in the fields they were studying for or planned to study for at university. Those at *MM*, however, mostly aspired to be part of the film industry. This is partly a difference between amateurs and professionals, but also a product of the shows themselves. Some *MM* contestants were already working in films, and others were trying to transition from television acting to film. In response to the question 'Who would you say has benefitted most from the show [*MM*]?' Kala Master replied, 'The choreographers, undoubtedly. Some of these people are incredibly talented but had no way of expressing themselves' (Srinivasan 2010). *MM* choreographers who were already part of the dancer's union could use their work on the show to convince film directors to hire them as dance masters.

Although the premises and approaches of the two shows are different, there are some notable overlaps between them. Like the Mumbai-based shows, both have high production values and present dance as 'hard work, and an activity to be taken seriously and respected' (Morcom 2014, p. 119). The style of dance rewarded by the two shows provides hints about the aspirations of contestants, as does the post-show self-branding work that former contestants do via social media. Their internet savvy and access belie the middle-class roots of contestants from both programs, though they reveal little about caste. While caste was not something I could politely ask interviewees about, class markers, particularly level of English language education, were more easily ascertained. Most participants in both shows spoke English. About one-third of the contestants in each show, however, were not confident with their English skills, suggesting lower middle-class status or roots outside an urban centre.

## Dance Careers Post-Reality Television Competition

*MM* debuted in 2005 and has completed ten seasons, making it the longest-running (and one of the earliest) reality dance competition in Tamil. This show is viewed as a route into the film industry by insiders and outsiders alike, though perhaps more so for choreographers than contestants, and a means to boost an existing career in entertainment. Bobby and Swarna, who won season seven, for example, both went on to perform in films.[2] Runner-up Puviarasu has also become a popular serial and film actor, and his *MM7* partner Anusha was originally selected because of her work as an assistant dance master in the Telugu film industry. Other contestants went back to their careers in serials or elsewhere in the entertainment industry. *UYP* only ran for two seasons (2009 and 2012), and while it was connected to the film industry through its judges, most dancers went on to either open their own dance studios or teach and choreograph for their teachers' studios while pursuing a career in a different field. A few finalists also choreograph, dance, or act for films. After winning season one in 2009, Sherif moved from Coimbatore to open Sherif's Dance Company in Chennai and has now choreographed for over 100 film songs. Sai Pallavi, from season one, has danced with a number of heroes since 2015, especially shining in 'Rowdy Baby' from the 2018 film *Maari 2.* While others may aspire to be in films, there are the social, financial, and time-related roadblocks discussed earlier.

*UYP*'s winner, Kartik, opened Provoke Dance Company in his hometown of Erode. The popularity of organised dance schools teaching hip-hop and freestyle dance in Tamil Nadu has increased astronomically over the last 15 years, in concert with the popularity of televised dance competitions and the growing respectability of dance. Rajesh, a contestant from the first season of *UYP*, opened his studio Dance World specifically to cater to reality show hopefuls: 'Apart from dance-aerobics, filmy stunts and freeze styles are a hit among those who aspire to enter dance reality shows … sophisticated dance styles such as Salsa and Jazz are pursued by people aiming for reality shows' (Shrikumar 2015). The situation in Chennai in the 2010s is different from what Shresthova and Morcom witnessed in Mumbai in the 2000s, where '[Shiamak] Davar's institute meets a popular demand for Bollywood-inspired dance classes as it simultaneously helps shape current trends within the film dance industry itself' (Shresthova 2011, p. 10). Chennai boasts many Hip-hop, Zumba, and freestyle classes, but the only cinematic dance class I found was the one run by Jayanthi Akka. Most classes were not designed to propel students into the film industry, but rather to excel at school or college competitions, family functions, or the studio's annual show in addition to reasons of fitness and fun. Classes that cater to competitions are likely an expanding trend across the country as the number of competitions continues to rise at all levels.

## Social Media and Maintaining Momentum

Whether they go into film or another dance career, former reality show contestants must keep up the momentum after the show finishes with Facebook pages, YouTube channels, and Instagram feeds. The shows themselves help to keep relevant those who appeared in previous seasons by inviting them to guest choreograph, dance, or otherwise be involved with later seasons of the show, especially for the finales, which celebrate the brand of the show as much as the finalists for that particular season. The brand can later be activated by individual participants, who can forever be described as having been on that show and thus connected to the networks of celebrities associated with it. This branding can extend to their hometowns, teachers, studios, and fellow students, as their success on the show transfers to those associated with them. Maintaining this momentum is what Anaar Desai-Stephens (2019) has referred to as 'managing, sustaining, and enhancing face value' (p. 6), which overlaps with the notion of 'exposure' that Fuller and Narasimhan (2014) discuss in relation to improving career prospects (pp. 119–20). Face value, in the sense Desai-Stephens (2019) uses it, 'refers to the recognition that RMTV [reality music television] shows afford their participants – through multiple weeks of performing on camera, being broadcast to millions of households … and meeting and working with the top musicians and directors' (p. 2). In the case of the Tamil dance shows, they are broadcast to Tamil-speaking audiences around the world and contestants have the opportunity to meet and work with top choreographers in the Tamil (and often other languages) film industry. In the first episode of *UYP2*, season one winner Sherif provides this testimonial:

> I was an ordinary dancer before, but today I am a celebrity. Ten people, a hundred people, a thousand people, a lakh people, who did not know me before, now do, since this show finished. Before Prabhu Deva, my signature was just a signature, but after the show, it became an autograph.[3]

While this episode dangles fame and the possibility of a career in dance in front of those who have come to audition, I did not find that the majority of contestants had the big dreams of the *Dance Indian Dance* contestants with whom Chakravorty (2019) spoke (p. 336); instead, dancers talked about proving themselves, having the opportunity to share their love of dance, and meeting their dance heroes.

It is essential to remember that these shows are for dancers, and therefore exhibit some fundamental differences from the reality show singers that Desai-Stephens (2019) writes about, as dancers' experience of interaction with fans can never be disembodied. While her informants were physically present as they sang on television or for their Instagram feeds, most of them dreamed of becoming playback singers, and thus having their voice connected to another body, as an actor or actress became the visual focus and lip-synched and danced to the recorded song. Choreographers are in a similar position, as they orchestrate the movement of other dancers and operate mostly behind the scenes. Dance is inherently visual, as it is precisely the shape and movement of the dancer's body in combination with the emotion and intimacy of their face that forms the core of the dancer's value as a commodity and brand. Chakravorty (2019) complicates this, as she identifies the dancer's body as 'an instrument where movements are mixed through a copy-and-paste technique, producing a particular kind of hybrid disembodied embodiment' (p. 339). While bodies may be seen as instruments, dancers are also interpreters of a choreographer's vision and bring more to the equation than just a skilled, fit body. At any rate, though a performance may be mediated through the screen and a body in a remixed state of hybrid disembodiment (an idea reminiscent of Prabhudeva's 'Mukkala Mukkabla' dance from Kadhalan (1994), in which the visible parts of his body are literally shot off and his clothes continue to dance), the spectators are still always engaging to some degree with the body of the performer.

In addition to face value, middle-class dancers may activate the idea of 'exposure' to their advantage, a term Fuller and Narasimhan (2014) define in relation to maintaining class difference, stating that it mainly 'denotes the process of enhancing social skills and cultural knowledge through new opportunities, challenges, experiences, and sources of information, as well as the improved state that ensues ... Inequalities in social and cultural capital therefore tend to widen' (pp. 119–20).

In addition to the benefits of the reality show brand and connections, these dancers may have studio or family connections that can help them identify and gain access to potential clients, performance opportunities, and spaces. They may also have educational advantages or connections they can leverage to start and run a business, write contracts, or produce content for websites, press releases, advertisements, or social media. Face value and exposure, as well as embodied movement, are central to a strategy of building and broadcasting a dance brand. Face value is a far less stable asset than exposure, which may take the form of an advanced degree, new qualifications, contacts, or world experience. Desai-Stephens (2019) writes that '"face value"... would appear to have a short shelf-life and rapidly diminishing value ... Yet, "face value" is not finite, for it increases as it is circulated and exchanged' (pp. 8–9). In the world of dance, this can be as involved as collaborating on a performance that can be posted on a YouTube channel with another dancer or choreographer or as simple as giving someone a shout out on social media to congratulate them on a new release, saying happy birthday, or re-posting a nostalgic photo.

While television viewers are prone to rapidly move on to the next celebrity, the repetition of being broadcast for multiple weeks helps solidify favourite competitors in their minds and recorded performances can be used to refresh people's memory. Neither of these two shows involves audience voting, so while viewers may be invested in their favourite contestants, their voice is not part of the outcome, and they are not reinforcing the names by texting votes or investing their own time or money on the phone in support. They may, however, take dance classes with these new celebrities, who are far more accessible than film stars, or host a celebrity wedding or party, hiring them to choreograph or perform for a private event. The urgency for dancers to capitalise on their fleeting fame is also greater than for those in other professions, simply because of the short-lived nature of dance as a career. Dancers are mostly finished by around age 30, due to strain on the body as well as director and audience preferences for younger, fitter faces and bodies. Choreographers and singers can work for far longer, using the faces and bodies of dancers and actors as a vehicle.

## Conclusion

Dance used to be a career for hereditary performers, but thanks to television, organised classes and camps, college competitions, and sangeet nights, it has become a viable middle-class profession in terms of both income and level of respect. Class status partially determines the type of career to which a dancer has access, with the streams coalescing only at the level of film dance director. Additionally, reality television is a platform through which dancers can get name and face recognition and transition into either film acting or studio ownership. As people dance more for fitness, fun, and casual competitions and performances, the number of studios in Chennai will continue to grow. The popular film industry has been associated with Indian culture in the diaspora for the last 20 years and that is starting to be true within India as well. Kollywood dance gives the aura of transnational cool, regional pride, and presentability in Gauri Pathak's sense (2014, pp. 317–8). Its music, images, and stars provide inspiration, but television reality shows take it to a new level, where ordinary people remix these things and achieve celebrity in their own right using the wide variety of dance networks and careers now available in Chennai.

## Acknowledgements

Research in Chennai was completed with the support of a Fulbright-Nehru Senior Research Fellowship in 2012. Thank you to the judges, dancers, choreographers, and production staff on both shows, especially Kala Master, Jayanthi Akka, and Vivek as well as to everyone at the L. V. Prasad Institute, especially Uma Vangal, K. Hariharan, and Ananya. And to Vagish Vela, my dance partner, unpaid research assistant, and husband.

## Notes

1 I recently spoke (November 2023) with the producer of *Maanada Mayilada* and he mentioned that there are far fewer dance competition shows now than ten years ago because of the recent changes in copyright law. He said that the shows now need to pay so much in royalties to use the film songs that the format is no longer viable. Shows used to be able to pay a fixed fee to music labels for use of their catalogue, but not only are those fees going up (see Sanyal 2023), but they now have to also pay individual lyricists and composers for each song. In 2012, India enacted the Copyright Amendment Act recognizing creators' (lyricists and composers) rights to works even when the copyright is owned by the film producers. ALMT Legal posted an article on Mondaq.com in June 2023 analysing two rulings that year by the Bombay High Court in favour of the Indian Performing Right Society Limited that interpreted this law to mean that 'the copyrights in original works subsist with its creators, enabling them to claim royalties and enjoy the monetary benefits when their works are used outside the scope of the sound recordings or cinematographic films.' The effect is that 'the recent legal developments has placed the onus on FM radio channels and third-party users [including television shows] to adhere to the new requirement of providing royalties to creators of underlying works.'

2 Malayali Swarna Thomas performed mostly in Malayalam films until she severely injured her back falling off the balcony of her fourth floor flat in July 2013 (see IANS 2013).

3 All translations from Tamil are the author's own.

## References


ALMT Legal, 'India: Analysis and Effect of "IPRS vs. Music Broadcast Limited And Rajasthan Patrika Private Limited",' *Mondaq*, 9 June 2023. https://www.mondaq.com/india/copyright/1327792/analysis-and-effect-of-iprs-vs-music-broadcast-limited-and-rajasthan-patrika-private-limited-

Chakravorty, P 2018, *This is how we dance now!: performance in the age of Bollywood and reality shows*, Oxford University Press, New Delhi.

Chakravorty, P 2019, 'Dance-off or a battle for the future: dance reality shows in India,' in S Dodds (ed.), *The Oxford handbook of dance and competition*, Oxford University Press, New York, pp. 331–45.

Desai-Stephens, AI 2019, '"Face value," reality music TV shows, and speculative logics of celebrity in contemporary India,' paper presented at the 48th Annual Conference on South Asia, Madison, WI.

Fuller, CJ & Narasimhan, H 2014, *Tamil Brahmans: the making of a middle-class caste*, The University of Chicago Press, Chicago, IL.

IANS 2013, 'Malayalam actor Swarna Thomas out of danger, recovering,' *India Today*, 6 July 2013. https://www.indiatoday.in/movies/celebrities/story/malayalam-actress-swarna-thomas-out-of-danger-recovering-169307-2013-07-06

*Kadhalan*, directed by S. Shankar (1994; Chennai: A.R.S. Film International).

Morcom, A 2014, *Illicit worlds of Indian dance: cultures of exclusion*, Oxford University Press, New York.

O'Shea, J 2007, *At home in the world: Bharata Natyam on the global stage*, Wesleyan University Press, Middletown, CT.

Pathak, G 2014, '"Presentable": the body and neoliberal subjecthood in contemporary India,' *Social Identities*, vol. 20, no. 4, pp. 314–29.

Sanyal, D 2023, 'Sour Note: Music Labels Press Pause on Reality TV Song-and-Dance Routine,' *Business Standard*, 26 April 2023. https://www.business-standard.com/companies/news/sour-note-music-labels-press-pause-on-reality-tv-song-and-dance-routine-123042600686_1.html

Shresthova, S 2011, *Is it all about hips? around the world with Bollywood dance*, SAGE Publications, New Delhi.

Shrikumar, A 2015, 'Dance your way to fitness,' *The Hindu*, 29 May 2015. https://www.thehindu.com/features/friday-review/dance/dance-your-way-to-fitness/article7260300.ece

Srinivasan, P 2010, 'The dancing queen of Tamil TV,' Rediff.com, 29 August 2020. https://www.rediff.com/movies/report/south-tv-interview-with-kala-master/20100713.htm

*Ungalil Yaar Adutha Prabhudeva*. Season 2, episode 1, online video, YouTube, 5 February 2012. https://www.youtube.com/watch?v=gy0Fd9CapCY&feature=related, accessed March 12, 2012.

# 18 Surviving Revivals

## Or Why the Work of Resuscitating Indian Crafts Is Never Done

*Clare M. Wilkinson and Alicia O. DeNicola*

### Introduction

If the rhetoric is to be believed, handicrafts in India exist in a constant state of contradiction. They are permanently on the brink of disappearance yet repeated allusions to their demise are only possible because they never disappear altogether. Acknowledging their survival is qualified by pointing to their compromised quality and authenticity, attributes which, as it happens, are never so degraded that they cannot be restored. Tales of decline even 50 years apart are startlingly similar to one another and calls for revival are too. The prescription is invariably to realise India's cultural heritage, elevate consumer tastes, and offer decent livelihoods and dignity to craftspeople. Rarely, however, is the third articulated without the first two taking priority; in short, the path to livelihood and dignity must pass through revival.

Each iteration has served its own economic and political objectives and obeys aesthetic tastes the changeability of which, if acknowledged, would dishonourably submit tradition to fashion. Meanwhile, handicraft producers have continued to interact daily with merchants and tradespeople, exporters, and so forth, none of whom is ever singled out as a reviver or makes any great claims to be. Recurrent revival efforts from the government or the private sector may have ensured handicrafts persist, but none has aimed so low as to claim that it merely 'keeps crafts going.' Instead, each revival not only claims to restore prosperity and distinction but also frames its interventions as though it were the first one to do so. In effect, even as we trace calls to revive crafts back over a century, the apparent need for revival remains just as urgent, and the promised payoff just as elusive.

We contend that revival demands a forgetting of efforts that have been made before, because only forgetting allows new calls to argue for their own, unique effectiveness. The cycles of revival and forgetting then have the effect of planting craft artisans within stagnant historical shallows, never quite fastening on recovery, yet never forfeiting the possibility that it may yet occur. Craftspeople in India are indeed poor, and labour in difficult and stressful conditions; one cannot, therefore, call repeated revivals perseverations that lack cause. At the same time, failure to acknowledge that present revivals only clamber upon the detritus of past ones obscures both the complexities of decline and the structural inadequacies of revival.

DOI: 10.4324/9781351031028-19

### The Idea of Handicraft

What is it that revival latches upon in the Indian context? Soumya Venkatesan (2009) argues that it is an Indian craft 'heterotopia,' an alternate space repeatedly brought into being through social practice, in which the fetishised objects of 'Indian heritage' take centre stage. For Venkatesan, the source for the Indian craft heterotopia is a protean imaginary that can contain critics, development agencies, government bodies, and designers, divergent perhaps in their political affiliations and policies, but united in their romantic idealisation of crafts as 'material symbols of India's cultural ethos' (Rao 1969, p. 15). For us, an equally remarkable facet of the handicrafts imaginary is its invocation of causality while being oblivious of history.

Handicraft in India generally tends to have a very specific and targeted referent: the variety of low-technology techniques and products that are claimed to derive from India's pre-colonial history and whose aesthetic attributes are key to their use and consumption. Talents in improvisation, managing contingency, and fluency in the manipulation of materials are apparent in other labour domains but are not termed handicrafts because they are associated with such contexts as small machine shops, construction, or the recycling of industrial products (Sundaram 2011). The distinction of craft as a matter of morality, identity, and proper consumption depends upon an unrelenting stress upon the artisan as reflexively virtuous and studiously authentic (Greenhalgh 2002; Venkatesan 2009). Connecting a craft to an origin point in the pre-industrial past, and to both pleasurable and moral consumerist drives in the present, is indispensable to the meaning of handicrafts as much as the conditions and capabilities associated with their production.

Entangling craft in India's past has accommodated itself to a variety of political positions. Calls for handicraft revival among British colonialists fell in well with larger arguments about how Indian cultural distinctiveness prevented its population from aspiring towards genuine equality and self-determination. That the ardent imperialist Viceroy Lord Curzon advocated for the 'purification' of Indian tastes to reject what was alien and to re-embrace what was authentically Indian alerts us to the deceptiveness of such colonial encomiums. Solicitous calls to bolster Indian craft typically anticipated a role for the guiding hand of colonial expertise (Metcalf 1989, p. 214). Just as happened with the census and other forms of colonial data gathering (Cohn 1984), the work of connoisseurs and self-described experts to classify crafts shaped the kind of knowledge that was growing up around them (see Gupta's preface to Watt 1903, p. xv). George Birdwood (1884) reminded readers of the literal meaning of 'manufacture' – that which is made by hand – and advocated for bolstering manufacture in India, backed by schools of art and supported by scholarly and critical publication on 'industrial art' (Kipling 1888). Thereafter, the more that India was associated with a distinct form of production compared to Europe, the more the colonial segregation and control of different domains of production could be justified. Carol Breckenridge (1989) makes just this point in her analysis of nineteenth- and twentieth-century World's Fairs in which handicrafts made at the behest of imperial households were adopted as a metonym of India. If India was not industrialised, the argument went, it was because industry was not part of its essential, thus timeless, nature.

The contrast with dominant nationalist thinking could not be starker. United in its hostility towards the economic impact of colonialism, the Independence movement called for rolling back the colonial economic vandalism that subordinated India to British interests and elevated foreign tastes above Indian ones. However, not all Independence activists agreed that the remedy was a resort to handicrafts. Gandhi's charisma was responsible for the perseverance of a utopic vision of the revitalised village economy, but mainstream nationalist ideology, which largely saw industrialisation as the way toward economic success and solvency, advocated for technical training over sustaining dying industries (see Chandra 1966; Dutt 1957, 1960b; Naoroji 1962; Ranade 1982). Unsurprisingly, upon Independence in 1948, industrial development outranked small-scale production and crafts in nationalist policy. But burdened with the Gandhi's politico-economic ideals and Nehru's own 1946 book *Discovery of India*, nationalist discourse discovered the ideological benefits of an alliance with subordinate groups such as craft artisans and peasants (Natrajan 1999). There was, moreover, a benefit to using handicrafts as 'material symbols of India's cultural ethos' to build both a mindset and a market that targeted foreign buyers and affluent Indian consumers alike (Rao 1969, p. 16).

With these considerations in mind, the All India Handicrafts Board (AIHB) was formed in 1952 to advocate for and support handicrafts. By the time of the Central Government's third five-year plan, the AIHB had a wide brief: to research, offer incentives and training, and provide work and marketing support (Rao 1969). The AIHB also presided over a set of high-quality publications describing handicraft achievement, history, and design. Kamaladevi Chattopadhyay, Kamala Dongerkery, R.V. Rao, and later Pupul Jayakar and Jyotindra Jain produced an impressive amount of documentation of crafts (much of it under the AIHB) that echoed the early twentieth-century *swadeshi* movement's call to eliminate imported goods in favour of Indian-made ones (Bayly 1986; Sarkar 1973). 'Indian' did not necessarily entail handicrafts, perhaps, but given the overwhelming industrial character of the 'foreign,' *swadeshi*'s meanings were easily absorbed into an anti-colonial oppositional framing of Western machinofacture versus Indian handicraft. The language of revival in these mid-century texts counterposed a long-lost craft ideal with a wished-for future. Even apparent disagreements over the appropriate level of accommodation to market demands seemed to glide past each other under the protective umbrella of the call for revival.

Within this *swadeshi*-inflected argument, craft and the Indian artisan became quintessential, often gendered, signifiers at odds with modernity, industrialisation, and a capitalist world economy. Reaching back into India's prehistory, the ancient character of crafts was a repeated theme, turning colonial arguments about the engrained traditionalism of Indian culture into a case for the longevity of its highly cultivated ingenuity. Chattopadhyay's (1963, 1980, 1985) work is striking for its elegiac quality, providing copious details of forms and techniques, shifting easily from the past tense ('... used to be done ...') to an eternal present in which the details of production are outlined.

**Design and Taste**

The role of the designer in craft revival has its own compelling history. For three decades, central and state government interventions had centred the collective as its ideal organisation model to compete with already well-established traders, merchants, and middlemen. The emergent designer of the late 1970s and 1980s, more often than not sutured to an NGO, was both of and for the market while being informed by the 'cultural ethos' that handicrafts represented.[1] A Vogue India profile of Ritu Kumar, who came to prominence at this time, noted her four decades of revival of crafts from Bengal to Gujarat (Siganporia 2015). Other fashion initiatives grew out of textile-oriented NGOs within the Delhi retail areas of Hauz Khaz and Dilli Haat, targeting gentrified metropolitan consumers with narratives of decline and revival (Tarlo 1996, p. 293; Wieman 2013, p. 64). Handicraft emporia and *khadi* (homespun cloth) outlets have catered for decades to Western tourists and Indian consumers alike. But the Hauz Khas reconstituted 'village,' as well as subsequent projects and boutiques that borrowed from the Hauz Khas model, swept consumers up in a larger reimagining of a revived and authentic India.

The revival of craft in these endeavours was contingent upon forms of consumerist distinction that went far beyond the occasional, individuated purchase of a given craft item. This was, in fact, the extension of an argument already made in crafts literature for Indian market consumers to compensate for the loss of rural reciprocity and aristocratic patronage. If the decline in craft was yoked to the vulgarisation of the Indian middle and upper class, then refining those tastes should in turn produce a 'revival' of craft (see Greenough 1995; Jain 1986). It was also a dimension along which any given revival could define itself as 'new.' Consider for example, R. V. Rao's 1969 discussion of the rescue of *Nirmal* (a set of painting and model-making practices in Telangana, Andhra Pradesh) from extinction, where he writes approvingly that 'modern paints and varnishes and small machines have also been used without interfering in any way the old motifs [sic])' (p. XX). In contrast, Santhosh (2017) pins revival in *Nirmal* to replacing those self-same modern paints with vegetable dyes (p. 332). Strikingly, Santhosh offers no criticism of the past revival for failing to live up to tradition; instead, it is as though the past revival never happened.

In India's new economy, the designer is a celebrity, far beyond what was conceived in *Hauz Khas* or *Dastkar* in the 1980s and 1990s (Zutshi 2019; Tyabji 2016). Also changed is where the blame is laid for the malaise from which handicraft is to be saved. While industrialisation is still cited as a threat to craft, other culprits now include 'mall culture and aggressive international brand advertising' (Cocoa & Jasmine n.d.).[2] With the full-throated arrival of fashion *qua* fashion, the consumer to be reformed and educated is no longer a middle-class householder choosing table linens, but a sophisticated, cosmopolitan consumer who is invited to bolster this 'first-time' revival. And yet, Sabyasachi Mukherjee's complaint that '[T]he big problem with the consumer is that half are buying things manufactured by foreign brands, from soaps to shampoo to clothing to cars,' has echoes from half a century ago (Mukherjee n.d., para. 16).

With the decisive break between India's socialist, protectionist economic past and its hoped-for, global capitalist future, one might expect craft to be newly vulnerable, bound on one hand to a romantic view of India's anti-capitalist essence, and on the other to staid notions of government-subsidised, modest economic activity having little to with the global economy. Yet far from India's turn to consumerist capitalism dealing a (final) deathblow to crafts, we find instead that it has yielded novel opportunities to conform craft to certain expectations of an Indian essence. The substitution of business-school-inflected rhetoric for the principles of state-subsidised, cooperative activism reveals itself in remarks, like those of designer Tarun Tahiliani, about carrying forward Indian heritage 'away from socialist myths' (Tankha 2017). While NGOs used to advocate for collectives, craftspeople are now exhorted to reinvent themselves as entrepreneurs.

While NGOs foster revival through the introduction of business school models, designers continue to insist on the need for creative interventions. While they profess admiration for what it is the craftspeople can do, there is never a question that designers should concede authorship to artisanal labour. The model of the craftsperson in an atelier, or a fabricator working for an artist, is perhaps at work here, in which proficiency is valued to the extent that it facilitates design, rather than being sufficient in and of itself to generate valuable products. Designer Sabyasachi Mukherjee argues against handicrafts that are not informed by a design sensibility, deploying the language of paternalism to underscore this point:

> Many craftsmen are not educated; they are people who are instinctive about product and have been doing things a certain way for a generation. Because they have little mind of their own as far as external stimulus is concerned, it's very easy to bring a notion to them that they do not understand.
>
> (Mukherjee n.d., para. 9)

In fact, the need for critical aesthetic intervention has long been justified by claiming that artisans are too vulnerable and unsophisticated to know if they are elevating or degrading their own craft. The designer has never been absent from revival rhetoric. Enakshi Bhavnani published a 1969 book of design motifs to inspire craftspeople, but until the 1980s the designer occupied an understated, facultative role. The new designer revivals belong solidly within the domain of high fashion, thoroughly professionalised, bent fully to the demands of the language of the fashion world, and unequivocal about the obligation of the designer to be both creative and recognisable on the global fashion stage. Missing once again from this most recent revival rhetoric is a sense of what exactly it is that craftspeople do outside of the framework constructed for them that is anything other than naivety or sullen opportunism. The erasure of craftspeople themselves calls to mind Ricoeur's (2004) words about 'stripping ... social actors of their original power to recount their actions themselves' (p. 448).

## Assessing Craft Initiatives

Development literature from the 1970s onwards took a rather different approach from crafts literature, conceding little to the overpowering discourse discussed so far. This literature usually had little to say on the topic of heritage, but rather looked critically at the success of handicrafts as livelihood. Official figures point to an increase in exports, production and employment from the 1950s to the 1980s (Jain 1986). However, there were discrepant outcomes for men versus women, failure of wages to keep up with profits, and a crisis of underemployment. Many measures are missing or misleading owing to unreliability and unevenness in translating informal, fluid occupations into quantitative absolutes, making assessment difficult. Still, it is hard to read into these results any imminent death of handicrafts. Rather different is the question of whether artisans have been satisfied with their livelihood; in fact, reluctance to pass along skills to one's children would suggest they are not.

To the extent that handicrafts as 'development' was endorsed by governments and NGOs, it was because its minimal technology, low fixed capital investment, and decentralised production allowed for cheap, easy-to-deliver results. Special appeals were made to the significance and value of craft production for rural dwellers and women, whose work opportunities were otherwise limited. The development studies literature, however, is sceptical of these claims, pointing out that home-based production, the basis for most female handicraft activity, entrenches conditions for more intense exploitation of labour (Boris 2016; Mies 1988; Wilkinson-Weber 1999).

Reconciling the ideological goals of handicraft production with alleviating poverty, exploitation, and underemployment in the informal sector (where handicrafts belong) has remained elusive. Shah and Patel's 2017 study of Gujarat beadwork and hand embroidery notes that the problems associated with handicraft production are too dense, deep-rooted, and complex for any agencies, governmental or non-governmental, to solve. Jahan and Mohan (2015), writing on carpet weavers in UP and Jaipur, stress that an inevitable consequence of productive decentralisation is middlemen, an 'evil' in crafts literature whose structural position seems impossible to erase. In one socio-economic review of handicrafts, Cable (1983) touched on the challenges of fusing the ideological and pragmatic in handicrafts policy, conceding that cooperatives, by themselves, would be insufficient to ensure craft longevity. There was, in other words, no easy way to ensure both excellent products and social and economic justice.

Given the overwhelming dependence on private employers and the market forces of handicrafts producers, it is hard to know to what extent government handicrafts initiatives have contributed to the economic health (or lack of it) of artisans. But what about localised, product-specific schemes that have been implemented? Considering the sheer number of schemes, initiatives, and stimuli for craft production there have been, it is remarkable how little systematic reflection there is upon the gains and losses. Instead, writing tends heavily towards diagnosing problems without determining whether past efforts either contributed to these problems, or simply failed to address them. S. S. Solanki writing on craft for *Economic and Political Weekly* in 2008 concedes that 'not many studies have been conducted to find the causes of the unsatisfactory performance of the government-sponsored schemes' without citing even one (p. 24). Perennial and entrenched problems of poor documentation and recording have stalled competent assessment of craft initiatives, inadvertently allowing for the kinds of 'revivals' that can omit mention of those that went before. A few studies pinpoint areas of structural weakness and dislocation that continually beset handicraft schemes. Koczberski (1998) critiques the notion that more organisation and control of schemes will generate positive outcomes. Particularly incisive is Mayoux's 1998 study of craft training schemes in West Bengal, where most beneficiaries of aid are upper-class and upper-caste individuals rather than the most disadvantaged. That the 'forgetting' and revivals we write about here serve caste interests is an argument for an entire paper by itself; suffice to say here that differentiation among craftspeople and the uneven distribution of craft aid is precisely the kind of problem that crafts rhetoric erases.

Without any kind of accountability for craft revival efforts, there can be no thorough appreciation of what works or what does not, as each successive wave of revivalists pretend that no one came before them. In turn, the collapsing of history that repeated cycles of crisis and revival engender means that the social and political contradictions inherent in these efforts remain undefined. It is important, then, to push back against the ideologically inflected discourses that dominate craft, if for no other reason than to insist that we place craft within, and not outside, India's broader labour and employment structure.

If there are relatively few assessments of the success (or lack of it) of particular crafts revival efforts, there are now more critical voices on handicrafts as ideology. These range from Greenough's 1995 analysis of the performativity of craft at the Crafts Museum to 2015 Da Costa's demolition of 'heritage as ideology' in Ahmedabad. Da Costa brilliantly pinpoints the erasures of 'sentimental capitalism' that premises revival upon the sparking of an entrepreneurial spirit among workers who are routinely marginalised and exploited. In response to writers that reflect, without irony, upon crafts that have been apparently 'dying' for nearly 100 years, Da Costa's bracing analysis makes plain that the appearance of 'dying' is in fact precisely what one would expect among producers who have culled a living for so long from so little.

## Revival and Forgetting

Crafts revival is a 'charter myth' (in Malinowskian terms) of the irrecoverable loss of a better past, and the present hope of a revitalised future.[3] At each point of revival, the possibility of resolution beckons, but what is to be done, and who is to do it, perceptively shifts. Given the confidence with which revivals are justified, perhaps it would be to the revivalists' advantage to allude explicitly to inadequate predecessors, allowing the new revival to flaunt its comparative strengths. That this does not happen suggests that it is either easier to simply pretend no revivals happened before, freeing the new revival from having to explain itself in more rigorous terms; or that there is a *tabula rasa* where the memory of past revivals should exist; or that the condition of needing revival is itself seen as, to some extent, essential and unchanging, meaning that revival too is a never-ending obligation, with indeterminate outcomes.

Battaglia's (1993) work on social practices of forgetting in funerary ritual is particularly useful in this case, for all that mourned handicrafts are not persons, and revivers are not survivors. What is instructive in the foregrounding of forgetting as not simply 'not remembering' is that it draws our attention to what is gained by these repeated acts of neglect. As Battaglia puts it, 'social forgetting is a breeding ground for ideological inscription, rather than merely its effect' (p. 439). For one thing, forgetting shrinks the expanse of time over which the remaking of handicrafts has struggled to encompass both the ideological and pragmatic goals with which it has been encumbered for over a century. While industrial manufacturing and resource extraction are almost always seen as subject to history, craft, because of the mythos surrounding it, can be allowed to escape in order to comply with the ideals with which it is associated. This remains true even when we realise that not all handicrafts are extremely old, or at least the evidence for suggesting they are extremely old is flimsy to say the least. Instead, handicraft's supposed antiquity allows us to ignore other contemporary industrial practices to which craft is related. The burden then of collective, repeated and, critically, unacknowledged acts of forgetting is that forgetting itself is forgotten, so the rupture of India's unproblematic craft past from its unsatisfying present endlessly invites intervention.

The creation of tradition and the effects of the global market on everyday lives is a story about the way that the 'global world' transforms the ways that we think about ourselves and our work. Ideas of 'revival' also point to the unresolved distinctions that it seeks to erase by its very existence as a discourse. If we understand discourses, and the consistency of revival in India, to represent places in which culture has become visible through its ruptures, then the discursive project of selling tradition – of 'revival' – may very well tell us something about the ways in which the local and the global, the old and the new are negotiated and 'sutured' through their various narrations (Hall 1996). In other words, it is important to see the ways in which this discourse of old and new – and that of consistent revival – points to actual bodies, places, and time elements that are marked as either traditional or innovative, but are seldom *marked* as both, despite the 'mixture' of the end product.

POSTSCRIPT: In the final drafting phase of this paper, news came from India of the government's abolition of the AIHB and the All India Handlooms Board. This striking decision was handed down in the midst of the Covid outbreak and came with no proposals for a replacement. As legitimate as the stated reasons for abolishing the AIHB may be, the move appears to conform to a larger abolition programme directed at the symbols and institutions of the immediate post-colonial government. Not only that, but writing in First Post, Macherla Mohan Rao (2020) argues that the ultimate reason for withdrawing from support of craftspeople is to facilitate the appropriation of labour and resources from the sector into large capitalist enterprises. The full implications for craftspeople will become apparent in time; however, the removal of the AIHB from the scene by no means implies that the language of revival that it spearheaded for so long has vanished. Revival, as we argue in the chapter, had already implanted itself in corporate rather than public institutions. If Rao is correct, then the contortions of 'revival' will become more, rather than less exaggerated.

## Notes

1 A history of the designer as mediator between tradition and innovation, rural and urban, and printer and consumer merits its own essay. Such distinctions work to manifest power among those who can distinguish themselves as creative elites and experts. Designers, especially in North India, have a reflexive and well-articulated narrative of innovation and tradition, that at once embraces and refutes traditional India, carving out spaces for those who are to 'be' traditional and those who are to protect and maintain that tradition. Today, then, the designer's very occupation is at least partially dependent upon the ability to create something that the artisan cannot. In this discourse, innovation is the realm of the designer, while tradition is the realm of the printer, a division of cultural labour that ensures that high-end designers or entrepreneurs who consider themselves artisans never need 'revival.' What is implicitly at stake in this narrative is a class distinction: one that borrows from local caste understandings of patronage and responsibility at the same time that it manages to negotiate the global market system.

2 This wording came originally from a speech given by Tyabji on the occasion of the thirtieth anniversary of DASTKAR. This material has now disappeared from the internet; the precise phrasing however recurs in the blog post cited, which is an interview with Tyabji herself.

3 Bronislaw Malinowski (2013[1926]), in a now classic contribution to the literature, noted that change in Trobriand origin narratives shifted depending upon the current political realities they helped explain.

## References


Battaglia, D 1993, At Play in the Fields (And Borders) of the Imaginary: Melanesian Transformations of Forgetting' *Cultural Anthropology*, vol. 8, no. 4, pp. 430–442, http://www.jstor.org/stable/656476.

Bayly, C A and Arjun Appadurai 1986, 'The Origins of Swadeshi (Home Industry): Cloth and Indian Society, 1700–1930.' *The Social Life of Things: Commodities in Cultural Perspective*, New York: Cambridge University Press, pp. 285–322, https://doi.org/10.1017/CBO9780511819582.012.

Bhavnani, E 1969, *Decorative designs and craftmanship of India*, D. B. Taraporevala Sons, Bombay.

Birdwood, GCM 1884, *The industrial arts of India*, Chapman and Hall, London.

Boris, E 2016, 'Difference's other: the ILO and "women in developing countries",' in N Lichtenstein & JM Jensen (eds.), *The ILO from Geneva to the Pacific Rim: West meets East,* Palgrave Macmillan, London, pp. 134–55.

Breckenridge, CA 1989, 'The aesthetics and politics of colonial collecting: India at world fairs,' *Comparative Studies in Society and History*, vol. 31, no. 2, pp. 195–216.

Cable, V 1983, *Indian handicrafts and handlooms: production for the world market*, Indian Council for Research on International Economic Relations, New Delhi.

Chandra, B 1966, *The rise and growth of economic nationalism in India: economic policies of Indian national leadership, 1880–1905*, People's Publishing House, New Delhi.

Chattopadhyay, K 1963, *Indian handicrafts*, Indian Crafts Council, New Delhi.

Chattopadhyay, K 1980, *India's craft tradition*, Publications Division, Ministry of Information and Broadcasting, Government of India, New Delhi.

Chattopadhyay, K 1985, *Handicrafts of India*, Indian Council for Cultural Relations, New Delhi.

Cocoa & Jasmine n.d., 'Exploring the mela model with Laila Tyabji of Dastkar,' blog post, 23 August 2019. https://www.cocoaandjasmine.com/the-craft-project/exploring-the-mela-model-with-laila-tyabji-of-dastkar

Cohn, BS 1984, 'The census, social structure and objectification in South Asia in culture and history of India,' *Folk*, vol. 26, pp. 25–49.
Da Costa, D 2015, 'Sentimental capitalism in contemporary India: art, heritage, and development in Ahmedabad, Gujarat,' *Antipode*, vol. 47, no. 1, pp. 74–97.
Dongerkery, K & Kulkarni, S 1951, *The romance of Indian embroidery*, Thacker & Co Ltd, Bombay.
Dutt, RC 1957, *The economic history of India in the Victorian age from the accession of Queen Victoria in 1837 to the commencement of the twentieth century.* Routledge and Kegan Paul, London.
Dutt, RC 1960, *The economic history of India - Vols I and II*, Publications Division Ministry of Information & Broadcasting, New Delhi.
Greenough, P 1995, 'Nation, economy, and tradition displayed: the Indian Crafts Museum, New Delhi,' in CA Breckenridge (ed.), *Consuming modernity: public culture in a South Asian world*, University of Minnesota Press, Minneapolis, pp. 216–48.
Greenhalgh, P 2002, *The persistence of craft*, A&C Black, London.
Jahan, M and Mohan, M 2015, 'Indian carpet industry: a study of handknotted carpets,' *International Journal of Current Research*, vol.7, no. 04, pp 15436-15441. [online] Available at: https://www.journalcra.com/sites/default/files/issue-pdf/8662.pdf. [Accessed 20 Apr. 2024].
Hall, S, and du Gay, P (Eds.) 2011, *Questions of cultural identity*. SAGE Publications Ltd, https://doi.org/10.4135/9781446221907.
Jain, LC 1986, 'A heritage to keep: the handicrafts industry, 1955–85,' *Economic and Political Weekly*, vol. 21, no. 20, pp. 873–87.
Kipling, JL 1888, 'The industries of the Punjab,' *The Journal of Indian Art, 1886–1916,* vol. 2(17–24), pp. 37–80.
Koczberski, G 1998, 'Women in development: a critical analysis,' *Third World Quarterly*, vol. 19, no. 3, pp. 395–410.
Malinowski, B 2013[1926], *Myth in primitive psychology*, Angell Press, London.
Mayoux, L 1998, 'Gender accountability and NGOs: avoiding the black hole,' in C Millar, & S Razavi (eds.), *Missionaries and Mandarins: feminist engagement with development institutions*. Practical Action Publishing, Rugby, pp. 172–93.
Metcalf, TR 1989, 'An imperial vision,' *Indian Architecture and Britain's Raj*. Oxford University Press, New Delhi, pp. 161–3.
Mies, M 1988, *The lace makers of Naraspur*, Zed Press, London.
Mukherjee, S n.d., 'Designer Sabyasachi Mukherjee discusses craft & sustainability,' *Border&Fall*, blog, accessed 21 August 2019. https://www.borderandfall.com/karigar/designer-sabyasachi-mukherjee-craft/
Naoroji, D 1962, *Poverty and un-British rule in India*, Publications Division, Ministry of Information and Broadcasting, Government of India, New Delhi.
Natrajan, B 1999, *Ailing artisans, dubious development: potters in Central India*, University of Iowa, Ann Arbour. https://www.proquest.com/openview/3844ff41640389eb6eee781e640f3555/1?cbl=18750&diss=y&pq-origsite=gscholar&parentSessionId=fMyJP2KZYCDx1mNvalyG0ze6QXYxRguZfU%2BzSl29DoA%3D.
Nehru, J 2004[1946], *The discovery of India*, Penguin Books, New Delhi.
Ranade, MG 1982, *Essays on Indian economics: a collection of essays and speeches*, Publications Division, Ministry of Information and Broadcasting, Government of India, New Delhi.
Rao, BG 2016, 'Reviving traditional fabrics,' *Apparel India* in Focus-An India-Inspired Revival (July).
Rao, MM 2020, 'Abolishing handloom, handicraft boards during COVID-19 crisis is hasty move, reflecting govt's neglect of sectors,' *Firstpost*, 8 August 2020, viewed 13 October

2020. https://www.firstpost.com/art-and-culture/abolishing-handloom-handicraft-boards-during-covid-19-crisis-is-unfortunate-hasty-move-reflecting-govts-neglect-of-sectors-8686021.html
Rao, RV 1969, *Indian handicrafts*, Booklovers, Hyderabad.
Ricoeur, P 2004, *Memory, history, forgetting*, University of Chicago Press, Chicago, IL.
Santhosh, D 2017, 'Nirmal a historical cultural craft centre in Telangana: a study,' *International Journal of Advanced Educational Research*, vol. 2, no. 6, pp. 328–32.
Sarkar, S 1973, 'The swadeshi movement in Bengal 1903-1908. People's Publishing House, New Delhi.
Shah, A & Patel, R 2017, 'Problems and challenges faced by handicraft artisans,' *Voice of Research*, vol. 6, no. 1, pp. 57–61.
Siganporia, S 2015, 'How Ritu Kumar is keeping traditional crafts relevant in the modern age,' *VOGUE India*, 17 December, https://www.vogue.in/content/how-ritu-kumar-is-keeping-traditional-crafts-relevant-in-the-modern-age/
Solanki, SS 2008, 'Sustainability of rural artisans,' *Economic and Political Weekly*, vol. 43, no. 19, pp. 24–7.
Sundaram, R 2011, *Pirate modernity: Delhi's media urbanism*, Routledge, New York.
Tankha, M 2017, 'On revival mode,' *The Hindu*, 20 April, sec. Fashion. https://www.thehindu.com/life-and-style/fashion/on-revival-mode/article18152333.ece
Tarlo, E 1996, *Clothing matters: dress and identity in India*, University of Chicago Press, Chicago, IL.
Tyabji, L 2016, 'Revivalism and revivalists,' *Marg*, vol. 67, no. 4, pp. 32–41.
Venkatesan, S 2009, 'Rethinking agency: persons and things in the heterotopia of "traditional Indian craft,"' *Journal of the Royal Anthropological Institute*, vol. 15, no. 1, pp. 78–95.
Watt, G 1903, *Indian art at Delhi 1903: being the official catalogue of the Delhi Exhibition 1902-1903*, Motilal Banarsidass Publications, New Delhi.
Wiemann, D. 2013, Cities of the mind – villages of the mind: Imagining urbanity in contemporary India. *Zeitschrift Für Anglistik Und Amerikanistik*, 61(1). pp 59-72 https://doi.org/10.1515/zaa.2013.61.1.59.
Wilkinson-Weber, CM 1999, *Embroidering lives: women's work and skill in the Lucknow embroidery industry*, State University of New York Press, New York.
Zutshi, C 2019, Kashmir, Oxford University Press, New Delhi.

# Index

Note: **Bold** page numbers refer to tables; *italic* page numbers refer to figures and page numbers followed by "n" denote endnotes.

For Product Safety Concerns and Information please contact our EU representative GPSR@taylorandfrancis.com
Taylor & Francis Verlag GmbH, Kaufingerstraße 24, 80331 München, Germany

www.ingramcontent.com/pod-product-compliance
Ingram Content Group UK Ltd.
Pitfield, Milton Keynes, MK11 3LW, UK
UKHW020009200926
475702UK00015B/2566

* 9 7 8 1 0 3 2 8 8 7 9 8 2 *